ANXIOUS YOUTH:
Dynamics of Delinquency

WILLIAM C. KVARACEUS

PROFESSOR OF EDUCATION AND DIRECTOR OF YOUTH STUDIES

The Lincoln Filene Center for Citizenship and Public Affairs
Tufts University, Medford, Massachusetts

Charles E. Merrill Publishing Co., Columbus, Ohio
A Bell and Howell Company

Library of Congress Catalog Card Number: 66-14403

2 3 4 5 6 7 8 9 10 11 12 13 14 15-76 75 74 73 72 71 70 69 68

Printed in the United States of America

Preface

This book has been prepared for those with a deep concern for juveniles who persist in seriously violating the community's norms of acceptable and approved behavior. It incorporates many observations and research efforts carried out on the local, national, and international levels.

More specifically, this study has been prepared for those with professional interests in education, psychology, or sociology; for the parent who is concerned with the behavior of his own and other children; and for the layman who is elected to serve as a trustee, school board member, PTA officer, or who volunteers his services in working with youth and their families. Delinquency prevention is everyone's business; hence, the study of delinquency should be of concern to everyone.

A work of this kind stems partly from the conviction that the professionals working by themselves will make very little headway against the strong and steady tide of serious and persisting norm-violating youth—as seen particularly in the large cities—without the active participation of parents, laymen, and youth themselves. The professional "outsider" can help, but only parents and youth can solve what is essentially a family-school-youth-peer group problem.

The question is raised here, "Can there be any effective prevention and control in countries lacking psychiatric, psychological, and casework services?" An answer may be found through more basic or primary approaches that attempt to increase parent and lay understanding of the true meaning and nature of delinquent behavior, with a change in attitude and posture in helping all youth, including delinquent youth, grow and mature.

This book also stems from my conviction of the increasing opportunity and responsibility that is ever present in the school agency for

v

changing and improving the personal-social behavior of children and youth. In consideration of my own perspective and predilections as an educator-psychologist and the orientation of much of my research and writing on the school's role in delinquency prevention and control, much of the study centers around the functions of the teacher, principal, and guidance counselor as they may affect the behavior of individuals and groups of students. The school represents a central force for prevention and control in every community for a number of reasons. The schools receive all the children early and maintain close and continued contact with them for many years; no other agency, outside of the home, can play a more important role in developing well-integrated and socially effective youths.

With the publication of *Juvenile Delinquency—A Problem in a Modern World* by UNESCO in 1964, I was able to report on delinquency problems and program needs on an international level. Following a year, 1961-62, with UNESCO as program specialist on the psychology of the adolescent with special reference to the socially inadapted, I studied the research trends, methods, and problems relating to the delinquent on an international scale. This study culminated in a meeting of experts from twelve countries at UNESCO House in Paris, June 4-8, 1962. More recently, I have worked with the International Union for Child Welfare (Vaucresson, France, 1965) and the International Organizations for the Safeguard of Children and Youth (Evian, France, 1966) in continuous research and study of the same problem. Hence this volume also includes some international aspects of both the problems of youth and the opportunities for youth. Delinquency is a problem confronting all nations—developing and developed.

In preparation of this manuscript I have been fortunate to have the advice and assistance of a number of colleagues. Dr. John S. Gibson, Acting Director of the Lincoln Filene Center for Citizenship and Public Affairs, and Dr. Daniel W. Marshall, Chairman of the Department of Education, have been a steady source of encouragement; Dr. Helen J. Kenney, Research Associate in Psychology, Harvard Medical School, has served me as a critical reader; Marie Johnson has assisted me in various writing and editorial chores; and Isabelle Staff served well as my typist.

WILLIAM C. KVARACEUS

Tufts University
June 1, 1966

Acknowledgments

In the preparation of this volume I have drawn heavily from my publications that have appeared in recent years in various journals, yearbooks, and texts. The following publishers and periodicals have generously permitted me to reprint my work and the work of my collaborators, in whole or in part, from their original sources:

Alabama Correctional Research, 2 (October, 1955), 11-15.

Alabama Correctional Research Association, University of Alabama, "The Police: An Active or Passive Defense Against Delinquency?"

Arthur C. Croft Publications, "The Pupil Who Makes Trouble," *Professional Growth Guide,* 1959.

The Bobbs-Merrill Company, Inc., "The Status and Function of Personnel Services," Reprinted from the December, 1960, issue of *Education.* Copyright 1960 by the Bobbs-Merrill Co., Inc., Indianapolis, Indiana.

Educational Leadership, "School and Home Cooperate to Meet Juvenile Delinquency," 10 (January, 1953), 223-228; "Future Classroom: An Educational Automat?," 18 (February, 1961), 288-292.

Educational Testing Service, "Prediction of Maladjustive Behavior," *Invitation Conference on Testing Problems: Proceedings,* 1958, pp. 26-34.

Exceptional Children, "Forecasting Juvenile Delinquency: A Three-Year Experiment," 27 (April, 1961), 429-435; "Helping the Socially Inadapted Pupil in the Large City Schools," 28 (April, 1962), 399-404.

Federal Probation, "Some Cultural Aspects of Delinquency," 23 (March, 1959), 8-13.

The High School Journal, "Social Stresses and Strains on Children and Youth: Some Implications for Schools," 47 (January, 1964), 140-145.

International Child Welfare Review, "Prevention of Juvenile Delinquency—Evaluation of Different Types of Action," 19 (Spring, 1965), 7-39.

Journal of Education, "Forecasting Juvenile Delinquency," 138 (April, 1956), 1-42.

Journal of Educational Sociology, "Juvenile Delinquency and Sociology," "Juvenile Delinquency and Social Class," 18 (September, 1944), 51-54.

Journal of the National Education Association, "Teachers and Delinquency," 47 (November, 1958), 535; "Culture and the Delinquent," 47 (September, 1959), 14-16; "Danger: Handle with Care!" 48 (December, 1959), 27-28; "What Kind of Help for the Delinquent?" 48 (February, 1959), 12-15; "Delinquency International—Ambivalent Obsession," 51 (September, 1962), 22-24.

National Association of Secondary-School Principals. "Meeting the Serious Behavioral Problems of Junior High Schools, *Bulletin of the National Association of Secondary-School Principals,*" April, 1959, Copyright: Washington, D. C.

National Council for Social Studies, "Tomorrow's Youth and Tomorrow's Citizens," *Citizenship and a Free Society: Education for the Future,* Chapter II, pp. 16-32.

National Education Association, *Delinquent Behavior: Culture and the Individual,* Chapters 6, 7, 8, and 11, 1959.

Overseas, "Crusade and Crucible," 2 (January, 1963), 2-7.

Personnel and Guidance Journal, "Prediction Studies of Delinquent Behavior," 34 (November, 1955), 147-149; "The Counselor's Role in Combating Juvenile Delinquency," 36 (October, 1957), 99-103.

Phi Delta Kappan, "Behavioral Deviate in the Secondary School Culture," 40 (November, 1958), 102-104; "Alienated Youth: Here and Abroad," 45 (November, 1963), 87-90; "Teacher and Pupil in the Technological Culture of the School," 46 (February, 1965), 269-272.

Syracuse University Press, "The Behavioral Deviate in the Culture of the Secondary School," *Frontiers of Secondary Education,* III, Paul M. Halverson (ed.) 1958, pp. 18-27.

Trustees of Tufts College, "The State's Responsibility for its Youth," *State Government and Public Responsibility,* Vol. II, 1960, pp. 81-93.

University of Chicago Press, "Selected References from the Literature on Exceptional Children," *Elementary School Journal,* 1954-65.

University of Pennsylvania Press, "The Delinquent in School and Court," *Education and the State* (Brumbaugh Lecture), Frederick Gruber, (ed.), Philadelphia, 1959, pp. 63-81.

Way Forum, "Return from Exile," Summer, 1963, 2-5.

Contents

"Here by the labouring highway
With empty hands I stroll . . ."

A Shropshire Lad

A. E. Housman

PART ONE

Youth in Ferment

1 Youth—A Surplus Commodity

The capacity of young people for idealistic, energetic, and enthusiastic action, if not focused in a positive direction, can burst out into undisciplined, aggressive, even destructive behavior. What is being done to channel youth's powerful potentialities into significant and useful behavior? How can adults offer worthwhile, mature projects that will challenge the adolescent mind to mature, responsible action?

One of the most hazardous occupations in developed and developing countries today is to be a youth. With the steady and conclusive shift from farm and rural culture to organized and technological society, the importance and function of youth have diminished to the point where youth now represent a surplus commodity on a glutted market. Lacking any important role or function, youth face the problems of growing up in exile or, worse, *in nihilo*.

An ancient psalm advises us: "As arrows in the hand of the mighty man; so are children of the youth. Happy is the man that hath his quiver full of them. . . ." In the predominantly rural-agricultural way of life of earlier times, children and youth were indispensable. They had important roles and functions in the production of food and clothing and in the building, maintenance, and protection of home and property. Youth helped in planting and reaping, in spinning and sewing, and in gathering and storing of fuel and fodder for both humans and livestock. Life itself depended upon the responsible execution of these all-important and essential functions. Indeed, happy was the man who had his farmhouse filled with strong young hands. As the family status

3

has turned from that of producer to consumer, the contemporary singer of psalms must change his tune and his lyric, for the arrows in the hands of the mighty man are turning to millstones around the neck of the parent.

Automation with its elimination of routine chores that once depended upon youthful hands, labor laws written in the spirit of safeguarding children and youth, and labor unions organized to protect the adult worker, have all combined to diminish the need for strong young hands. Even the compulsory classroom, now extending through the teen-age years, has tended to shunt the young learners from the main stream of social, civic, and economic life activity of family and community, thereby retarding the process whereby youth join the adult world. In a sense, the young now experience an organized isolation from the regular community. The results can be seen in a youth stigmatized, infantalized, down-graded, and disengaged. Today's major youth problem centers around the need to regain a sense of self-respect and self-worth. The modern young refuse to be shut out or to be shelved for deferred purposes; they refuse to accept the status of second-class citizenship.

Just as nature abhors a vacuum, so do the young loath their *in nihilo* status. To be a nothing and a nobody, to be excluded from significant roles and tasks, to have little or no *raison d'être*, to feel unneeded and unnecessary, to lack any voice or vote in important decisions concerning one's self, to be exiled for the life space of one's adolescence—all of this is hard to take, especially when youth see how badly adults around them are managing the business of the world.

It is doubly hard for a youth when he is contrasted, for example, with the somewhat similar status of the aged and retired citizen who still retains the memory—if not the fire—of his younger days, as well as the right to cast his ballot. For youth, more than any other age group, has unbounded energy, wondrous imagination, unfolding intelligence, and a strong spirit of courage and self-determination. Other ages have witnessed the remarkable results of this idealism and energy which charge through young people and inspire them to historic action. The tragic, yet awesome story of the Children's Crusade in the early thirteenth century is just one example of this type of vigorously enacted, forcefully channeled activity. The first Crusade originated in France and was organized by Steven, a twelve-year-old shepherd. Steven carried a "letter from Christ" commissioning him to lead a young army against the infidels and to conquer with force where the adults had failed. Even though King Philip of France judged the commission from Christ to be a forgery, young Steven, who was a persuasive orator, gathered about 20,000 to 30,000 youngsters, most of whom were under the age of twelve, and led his crusade southward to Marseilles. When the Mediterranean failed to divide before him, the "minor prophet" lost face. However, the situation seemed to be saved when two merchants offered the young crusader free passage on seven vessels. Two of these ships went down in a storm, and the rest of the fleet was never heard from again. Some years later, travellers from North Africa reported the children had been sold as slaves.

The second Crusade gathered in the Rhineland, not long after Steven's ill-fated expedition. It was led by a lad named Nicholas. He preached conversion, and he promised that boys would do better than grown men in the holy wars, and that the sea would open up a path so as to assure the redemption of the infidel. This second large gathering of German youth split enroute, with Nicholas leading on land over the Alps and ultimately to Genoa, and the other group making its hard, mountainous way to Brindisi. When the oceans failed to roll back before them, most of the survivors of the long trek decided to settle permanently in the vicinity, although a few finally did work their way back to the Rhineland. The furious parents of children who did not return seized and hanged Nicholas's father for his alleged complicity and his encouragement of this second Crusade.

Should Steve or Nick attempt a similar youth enterprise in the United States today—say a mass march on Washington to press Congress on the passage of an Aid to Education Bill in an effort to obtain adequate classroom space and to improve their teachers' salaries— they would surely be picked up by the Child Welfare authorities, aided by the Juvenile Police details. The parents would not be hanged, but they would be summoned before the Juvenile Court and perhaps subpoenaed by one of the many congressional committees concerned with juvenile delinquency, Youth Conservation Corps, or subversion.

The Children's Crusades embodied tremendous initiative and energy investment for a social-spiritual purpose. What is their relation, if any, to the youth groups of the twentieth century?

Juvenile delinquency in all countries today reflects a heavy investment of initiative and youthful energies but not for social-spiritual purposes. The overflow of energy hints strongly of the vast reservoir of unused power that is available. This source of youthful power and initiative could be readily tapped for social, civic, cultural, and economic betterment, and youth, aware of this potential for energetic participation in challenging activities, are bursting out against the frustration and repression stemming from so many social and economic forces. To prove themselves and to be heard, they have frequently followed the delinquency routes in various parts of the world. Students on college campuses in India have rioted and have created widespread problems of "school indiscipline." In West Germany, the excesses of the *Halbstarken,* after the noisy years 1955-57, gradually disappeared, but only after interaction with youth showed that many of them were willing and anxious to cooperate with adults in a search for preventive methods. Given an outlet for their technical interests and competitive instincts, together with widened scope in freedom of movement, West German youth were not long in finding more positive outlets for their energies and interests. Similarly, the antics of the Blousons Noirs and the Blouson Doreés in Paris or of the organized gangs in New York City testify to the boundless energy of youth who intend to be seen and heard—even though this means the violation of legal norms and the risk of court trial and jail.

All these youth movements reflect powerful adolescent forces which lack legitimate goals and direction. In common they represent a deep-seated movement among youth to be noticed and to be recognized. Here is where skillful adult leadership (not manipulation) can help by identifying more constructive and meaningful goals, by providing opportunities for worthwhile activities, and by giving direction when needed. Youth can never attain self-realization and maturity if forced to live in a vacuum. In seeking out answers to the questions "Who am I?" "Who am I going to be?" and "Where am I going?" the young must be released from their empty tomb. They can find the answers for themselves only through meaningful and important activities which carry personal and social significance.

Adults who are aware of the pressing needs of youth are now asking themselves some questions also. The phrase that is heard more than any other in different countries and at various international conferences on youth stresses "initiative groups with social-civic purposes," and thoughtful people are considering how to involve youth in challenging activities that will draw off much of their energy and focus their interests on positive, worthwhile projects. Eastern European countries are involving youth in many activities which are adult enough to make them feel mature and inspiring enough to appeal to their idealism. In Yugoslavia, Poland, and the USSR, the people take pride in revealing the many examples of youth participation in important and productive activities on the political and labor fronts. For example, the voluntary labor contribution of young Yugoslavs to road building has resulted in a monument built by Yugoslav youth and dedicated to national development—significant evidence of youth involvement and importance.

What can be done in working with youth when the adult approach is informed and trusting has been amply demonstrated in many parts of the world through the system of Associated Youth Enterprises. The Youth Enterprises involve a mutual collaboration of the UNESCO apparatus with many international youth organizations and/or governments. Since the inception of the program in 1955, more than one hundred youth projects involving initiative and international understanding have been undertaken in all parts of the world.

The International Youth Hostel Federation, for another example, joined with UNESCO to sponsor a youth hostel expedition that spent six months touring India and Pakistan via Yugoslavia, Greece, Turkey, Lebanon, Syria, Iraq, and Iran. This small band of young people, moving from London slowly and at times tortuously in a motorized caravan, brought films, sound recordings, and photographs on Western culture to various hostels and collected similar materials for use and demonstration in Western countries. En route the group met with representatives of youth organizations, visited hostels and discussed programs and problems with wardens, showed films and slides, and conducted interviews with the press and radio.

In Turkey—the scene of the crimes of earlier crusaders—members of the UNESCO-International Youth Hostel expedition participated in a press conference, took part in a radio broadcast, met with representatives of the National Organization of Turkish Youth which had recently published a brochure, *Genclik Hosteli,* introducing the youth hostel idea to Turkish young people. In Ankara's public squares, they showed films of youth hostelling to large audiences.

Lately, attention has been focused on assistance to emerging nations in Africa. Many youth enterprises in the past years have been diverted to this area of need. An early cooperative youth endeavor linked UNESCO support to the Overseas Work Camp Program of the American Friends Service Committee on a Kenya Work Camp Project operated by a number of Quaker organizations. A group of six young men from different countries and a larger group of young workers from inside Kenya labored side by side for two years on this project. These young pioneers built huts for convalescents and constructed a part of a ward for tuberculosis patients under the Tuberculosis Rehabilitation Scheme organized by the Friends Hospital in Kaimosi. They also helped maintain a vegetable garden, which provided light work for the patients and supplied them with food. Simultaneously, the projects increased understanding by encouraging Africans and Europeans to live and work together in an atmosphere of harmony, self-help, and self-government.

In another part of the world, student groups focused on the problems of illiteracy. Participation of university students in combatting illiteracy had been given high priority in the goals of the Cooperating Secretariat of National Unions of Students. A pilot project sponsored by the Secretariat, the Confederation Universitaria Boliviana, and UNESCO brought together 50 Bolivian students from eight universities. The experiment included a three-week seminar, followed by an extended field operation high up in Oruro, 200 kilometers from La Paz, a mountain city of 185,000 inhabitants with an estimated illiteracy rate of 65 to 70 per cent of the total population. In a short space of time, these young students equipped themselves through a concentrated course of study and went into the field to try to apply what they had learned. A thousand illiterate workers from the mines and factories were contacted. Study groups of ten to fifteen were scheduled to meet twice daily, and each student-teacher worked with one group. In addition to teaching reading and writing, they also participated in a careful survey and diagnosis of the social, economic, and cultural factors associated with illiteracy and with the possible aftereffects of reading instruction on a big city.

The lessons learned in the pilot student-project will go beyond the Bolivian borders. They can have a broadside effect on world illiteracy as the memberships of affiliate groups of the Secretariat of National Unions of Students marshal their power and talent for basic instruction in different countries.

But youth do not need to undertake a long, dangerous trek from London to New Delhi, or move to a remote African village, or climb to a high mountain in South America to use their potential in important and exciting tasks. A frontier can always be found in the backyards and depths of any metropolitan area or even in any new housing development. The "City Frontier" program of urban renewal, sponsored over a period of years by the Philadelphia Friends Society, through hundreds of week-end camps has called upon thousands of families, white and black, young and old, in order to meet the challenging task of improving living conditions by stemming the tide of rot and rats that infest the decaying urban neighborhoods. Cleaning, painting, plastering, and decorating demand hard work, but these activities can also provide a deep-rooted satisfaction that is close to the basic needs of food, shelter, and human rapport.

A number of Presidential messages to Congress in recent years have aimed to assist youth via a Youth Conservation Corps, a National Service Corps, or a Domestic Peace Corps. These messages have directed the spotlight on legislative action in this country that would enable all youth in the United States to achieve self-realization and self-determination through creative activities that have social and personal significance. The result has been a profusion of opportunities, especially for the deprived and disadvantaged youngsters and their families. Currently in Massachusetts and most other states, one can find six different categories of social, educational, or welfare programs including: (1) the Job Corps under Title 1-A of the Federal Poverty Program; (2) the Neighborhood Youth Corps under Title 1-B of the same program; (3) the work-study program for college students under the same program; (4) the VISTA Volunteers of the Domestic Peace Corps; (5) the Commonwealth Service Corps Volunteers; and (6) the CAUSE employees under the Federal Manpower Development Training Act.

The signing of the Elementary and Secondary Education Act of 1965 provided more than one billion dollars—$1,307,582,973—to help children and youth through five major programs: (1) aid to schools with a large percentage of low-income families; (2) provision of texts and library material; (3) establishment of supplemental educational centers; (4) development of regional centers for cooperative research; and (5) strengthening of state departments of education. Such widespread financial support for school-community programs can do much to uplift youth and to raise levels of aspiration and achievement, if local and state school authorities can respond with the equivalent in imagination and creativity.

The continuation of funds extending the Juvenile Delinquency and Youth Offenses Control Act of 1961 to June of 1966 reflects the national concern for the study of delinquency, the training of personnel to work within delinquency prevention and treatment programs, and the coordination of community resources in helping young offenders. More specifically, the authorization of the special study of compulsory school attendance and child labor laws together with a special anti-juvenile delinquency demonstration project in the Washington, D.C., area illustrate the resources as well as the commitment that can be found in many parts of the United States to assist youth. The problem is no longer one of funding; it is now a problem of ideas, program planning, and personnel.

At the local level, many communities in the United States have already moved to help youth help themselves. Some examples taken from one state, Massachusetts, illustrate how schools and communities have included young people as worthy partners and citizens in their own right.

In the city of Newton, under the direction of Dr. Franklin Patterson, past Director, Lincoln Filene Center for Citizenship and Public Affairs (Tufts University), new educational and action approaches to modern youth have been tried out in a pilot program[1] aimed to help youth re-engage themselves in shaping the destiny of a free society. A summer program in public affairs, aimed to relate youth to their school, their community, and the issues of the larger world, has been carried out with a small group of eleventh graders.

The general design of this experiment called for (1) intensive study of selected problems drawn from crucial socio-civic areas of modern life; (2) parallel study of representative problems of the community, using problem-solving approaches with data collected by the students themselves; (3) performance of needed work service in school and community; (4) self-government participation in the planning and management of the summer program; (5) participation in a rich and varied schedule, with enough time for learning in depth.

Through study, discussion, and planning, these students considered crises in race relations, crises in culture, crises in the community, and crises of war and peace, working out through these processes the responsibilities of the educated citizen.

Field surveys of activities and facilities, both formal and informal, available to community youth in evening hours were carried out. Several major work-service projects much needed by the community were undertaken, e.g., cleaning and repainting the Newton Community Center. Other valuable opportunities for study, work service, and possible civic action centered on cleaning up and improving a thirty-three acre park in the center of the city. The boys and girls studied the physical resources and plans for the further improvement and development of them. They examined alternative policies and plans for the park and decided upon recommendations to be placed before the city government. For direct action the youths went to work to clean out and improve the abandoned trails which had been allowed to deteriorate for many years.

Through this summer experience, boys and girls of high-school age were engaged in the study and solution of important community problems. Together they studied, planned, engaged in work-service, and participated in decision making and self-government.

In two other Massachusetts communities, Arlington and Andover, high school students every Tuesday and Wednesday assist professional workers to care for the mentally maimed in a nearby Veterans Adminis-

---

[1] Franklin Patterson, *Public Affairs and the High School* (Medford, Massachusetts: The Lincoln Filene Center for Citizenship and Public Affairs, 1962), p. 43.

tration Hospital. These boys and girls perform many different kinds of duties. Some work with nurses and technicians in social service, manual arts therapy, occupational therapy, and in the library and pharmacy. Others perform important tasks in dental laboratories and in the hospital's general offices. Through such service, youth not only help out in the important task of aiding sick patients, but they themselves profit by gaining insights into their own career development; they also acquaint themselves with the problems of those who are mentally afflicted and who may someday return to the community to live a normal life.

Citizenship in Action programs engage young people in many communities under the supervision of Dr. Thomas J. Curtin, formerly Director of Civic Education, Massachusetts Department of Education.

Wareham High School girls organized a Future Nurses Club to stimulate interest in nursing and to render community service through volunteer work in local hospitals. Students from Wachusett Regional High School, working through their Student Council and Future Teachers of America, participated in the American Field Service Exchange Student Program. As a result, two exchange students from Indonesia and New Zealand visited the community and three local students presented their candidacy for the *Americans Abroad* phase of the program. Funds for these activities were raised by group action through various school events and a Bonds for Democracy Drive. These youths plan to continue participation in projects for better international understanding.

Other students in North Andover produced a sound and color film describing for the citizens of the community and for the members of each new entering class their high school's organization, procedures, and curriculum. The entire production, depicting school life and the overall program, was produced, directed, and financed by the students, assisted by faculty members. The amount necessary for production ($550) was raised through various activities, and work on the production itself took a year and a half. Since its completion, the film has been shown to more than twenty organizations in the local area.

It seems clear from these few examples of youth initiative and involvement for social purposes that adults have only to look around, to encourage, to trust, and to support. Youth will supply the imagination, energy, and enthusiasm. Unfortunately, the very special qualities of adult faith in, and hope for, youth are rare commodities in the modern world. The old cry, "Youth is our most precious resource" is now regarded as a time-worn cliché. Too few of us believe that there is still a great deal of solid wisdom in this statement.

A study of the patterns and forms that delinquency has taken in different countries reveals a definite lack of originality in juvenile misbehavior. This standardization is attributable to the powerful and persuasive effects of mass media—not as a direct cause of delinquency but more as a transmitter of forms and styles of delinquent behavior The patterns reflected in the Presley gyrations, the Beatles' costume and coiffure, the warring gang, the beatnik, and the argot of the in-group, all display a monotonous sameness derived heavily from American sources and popularized by the mass media.

In this age of conformity the average adult is likely to damn out of hand the non-contributive, non-constructive indifference of present day youth, making no allowance for their often forward intentions and actions. But it is far more frequently the adult who should be, and is, excoriated by the adolescents he has so roundly denounced and flagrantly failed.

Youthful energy, intelligence, and initiative can be turned by adults either in the direction of destruction and delinquency or in the direction of constructive activity and creativity. These powers of youth cannot be contained for long in a vacuum. Youth must be released from their exiled status and from their enforced immaturity. Given a responsible role, the young have shown that they can and will find their identity, their independence, and their destiny.

2 Some Cultural Aspects of Delinquency

The universal anxieties and fears raised by the overhanging threat of war, unemployment, automation, adult domination, and exploitation can do much to unsettle today's youth; but what of other pressing forces that stem from differing and shifting standards? How does the urgency to achievement and self-realization affect the behavior of youth in home, school, and community? What general cultural patterns appear to act as strong determinants of norm-violating and norm-conforming behavior? Are there any dominant cultural forces that are to be found in all American communities?

Every delinquent is the product of the interaction of many inner forces such as ego strength, self-concept, and I.Q. with many environmental ones like peer group pressures, poverty, exploitation, and unemployment. In most causative studies of delinquent behavior one finds a strong preoccupation with variables within the personal makeup of the nonconforming youngster and underemphasis of the cultural aspects of the environment. Yet these cultural forces act to set up patterns of behavior and modes of adjustment. Since they provide a normative structure of how to act and how not to act, they can be strong determinants of desirable or undesirable behavior.

Cultural forces that play on the growing boy and girl tend to be more amorphous than factors in personality or in the home-family-neighborhood environment. Hence, they are less amenable to treatment. Nevertheless, we must keep in mind that delinquency does not take place in a vacuum; it thrives in a culture which it reflects and reinforces. Because of the pervasive nature of the cultural imprint on all behavior and because of the difficulties presented in coming to grips with these impelling forces, there should be more, rather than less, concern for these roots of delinquent behavior.

There is no such thing as "the American culture" in which we rear all children. Rather, there are many cultures and subcultures in American society. In fact, the variance between the value systems found in different cultures and subcultures in itself presents a confusing and conflicting problem to many children which often constitutes a causative aspect in the genesis of delinquent behavior, as Cohen[1] has illustrated in his analysis of the dynamics in the boy gang. All children acquire behavior patterns and modes of adjustment through the natural process of cultural osmosis. The purpose here is to isolate some of the more common and, hence, more permeating cultural and social determinants and to indicate how delinquent behavior often reflects these forces. Seven cultural influences that provide strong currents for delinquent behavior in our everyday living will be discussed.

Solving Personal-Social Problems Through Violence

With two world wars behind us and another threatening, all parents, as well as many youngsters, have witnessed the futile attempts of man to solve his problems through force, only to discover after each conflict more insurmountable problems than were at hand originally. Living in the fear-and-force climate of the atomic and hydrogen bomb and supporting a heavy national defense budget geared to maintenance of armed might readied for immediate action, a citizen should not awake surprised to find the young delinquent utilizing knives, guns, and fisticuffs to win a point or to solve his problems. Personal assault has become a more common complaint against the delinquent, as the juvenile (and adult) court records in any large city will reveal.

If the warring imprint appears remote from the everyday life of the adolescent, he can still find the violence theme in the steady stream of murder and mayhem that flashes across the TV screen in every home. The extraordinary popularity of the westerns (adult and juvenile) is noteworthy in that they drive home the solution-through-violence theme with each performance. Here the forces of virtue (the good men) and the forces of evil (the bad men) oppose each other and engage in conflict to achieve a goal: to save or steal a mine; to rescue or abduct an innocent female; to pay up or foreclose a mortgage; to hold up a stagecoach; or to get a herd of cattle through. But the

---

[1] Albert K. Cohen, *Delinquent Boys: The Culture of the Gang* (Glencoe, Illinois: The Free Press of Glencoe, Inc., 1955).

rest of the story seldom varies from the standard script. The good man (virtue) wins out, but the conflict can be resolved only via fisticuffs, shooting, and destroying a roomful of furniture. Right conquers wrong but not through any rational process of the conference table or the courts. Right prevails but only through superior might.

Currently, the violence and defiance exemplified from Little Rock to Selma as a part of the integration crisis, in which the law of the land is side-stepped, present to the youth of these communities and of the nation as a whole a pattern than can only stimulate a similar response in juvenile misconduct.

The Cult of Pleasure and Self-Indulgence

American living has been moving rapidly from a work-oriented to a play-oriented culture. This can be seen in the shrinking of the work week, in the heavy recreation spending, in the switch in respect for the traditionally hard-working craftsman who would perseveringly stick to his bench with his lunchbox by his side, to the "worker" who is free to leave the office at will. We now admire the man who comes to the office late and leaves early, carrying his golf bag as a symbol of his freedom from the discipline of hard work.

If the delinquent is sometimes viewed as pleasure-bent, riding heavily on a want-it-now track, it is because he is surrounded by elders who set the pattern. When the adult wants something (which he cannot afford and perhaps does not need), he need not indulge in any childish temper tantrum. Inventively, he has devised the ubiquitous installment plan which enables him to procure an automobile, a TV set, a vacuum cleaner, a suit of clothes—in fact, any item—even a vacation. Any citizen today, through the indulgence of installment buying, can even make his contribution to charity or to his alma mater on the pay-as-you-go basis.

It is rumored that the hardy New Englander once was wont to discipline himself through self-denial for some future good, that small sums would be deposited regularly, and that the accumulated savings would then be used to make a cash purchase. But, alas, even in New England communities the *cash only* signs have been replaced by the credit card mode of living.

This adult lesson of self-indulgence is not lost on youth. Our technological culture is inventive and produces many gimmicks and gadgets that youth really do not need, but which they feel they must have after the hucksters get through and one member of the peer group has succumbed. What parent has not tried to withstand the "gimmee" pressures for coonskin caps, blue jeans, Batman outfits, or space gear! Some youngsters, who cannot withstand the advertising pressures and the pressures of the peer group, may steal to procure whatever it is they think they must have.

The pattern of the easy way of life is most evidenced in the trends visible in leisure-time pursuits. Only a few years ago, if you went to the movies you would dress, shave, and put your shoes on. Today it is possible to jump into your car with your bathrobe on and motor to the nearest drive-in theater without the old rituals that demanded so much effort and discipline. Better still, it is no longer necessary to leave the house ever. It is possible to enjoy continuous entertainment merely by absorbing sound and light. Even the eyeballs need not move. You can sit unclothed and unshaven and enjoy, with a minimum of effort, any number of shows. The only danger comes from consuming too rapidly one bad show after another, which may result in a mild case of intellectual constipation. The only easy remedy is to turn the TV set off and to read something (preferably no stronger than the local newspaper).

Serious reading, in contrast to TV viewing, calls for more effort and discipline. The eyeballs must move, and the pages need to be turned. But even with this more demanding form of entertainment (sometimes it gets too close to work and effort, if thought processes become involved), the easy way of life has made its inroads. Witness the popularity of the graphically-supported magazines which invite effortless and painless reading. Research studies on comic book reading indicate that this is as much an adult form of literature as it is children's fare. This can be gleaned by a careful look at the advertisement sections which are geared to adult needs as much as to children's wants.

Researchers in the delinquency field have pointed out the indulging nature of the personalities of some delinquents who live out their infantile pleasure roles. This style of living finds strong reinforcement in the adult way of life in many homes.

Anonymity of Modern Living

Many aspects of today's living combine to hide the personal identity of adults and children. Rebelling against the ego-disintegration that comes from being a nothing, a nobody, many youngsters are striving to be heard or "to be something" even if it draws them to delinquency. At the same time, the cloak of anonymity may also serve as a protective mantle for the youngster who may get into trouble. Anonymity stems from a number of factors in our society.

The mobile family represents a necessary prerequisite to our economic structure. One family in five moves every year. The rootlessness that may result from the lack of any permanent address (or the censorship of permanent neighbors) may leave the youngster detached. Unanchored in the neighborhood, and with the anticipation of another move, the young individual may tend to have fewer restraints and to be less concerned about the personal and property rights of those around him.

At the same time, the automobile today enables any young person to become anonymous by driving an hour's distance from his home and his neighborhood. The lessening of controls because no one knows who you are can be found frequently in the case histories of delinquents.

Many delinquents reside in large multi-family housing projects in large cities where living is impersonal, if not anonymous. They attend large factory-like schools with crowded classes. Over-burdened teachers who see, at the junior and senior high school levels, 150 or more students daily are seldom able to establish any close personal relationships with any of them. Bigness has been shown to be closely related to misbehavior and delinquency: teachers who have the largest classes and who work in the largest schools have reported a sharp increase in misbehavior in contrast to teachers who work in smaller schools and who have smaller classes. Bigness becomes synonymous with anonymity and impersonality. One way to help a growing boy or girl is through human relationships. Many facets of our modern living prevent rather than foster such relationships.

One last comment is in order concerning the youngster who is striving to establish his identity and his individuality. For him, the status of anonymity may push too close to personality disintegration, if not annihilation. There are some delinquents who have tried to find some measure of identification, if not fulfillment, through the notoriety of anti-social and bizarre behavior. These youngsters need help in order to discover and realize themselves through more positive and constructive channels.

Adult Attitudes Toward Youth—A Romantic but Surplus Commodity

Youth will always reflect and react to the esteem in which they are held by their elders and especially to the concept of the youth role which their parents and parent surrogates display. Youth in American society are subject to a strange mixture of adult attitudes. On the one hand, youth are regarded in a sentimental and romantic glow. To be old is to be slurred, but to be young is to be attractive, healthy, and envied. Witness the use of the young and the pretty faces in the not-so-subliminal ads that sell cigarettes, beer, stockings, refrigerators, and cars. This is in sharp contrast with other cultures where old age is revered and where the hoary crown of the elder would do a better sales job. On the other hand, adult attitudes toward youth tend to immobilize and to retard through overprotection and separation of youth from the stream of real-life activities and problems.

Youth suffer today from outmoded child-labor legislation which denies them the maturing life experience that can come only from work. Many adults who come in close contact with youth will readily agree that labor laws need to be revised in the light of the new job opportunities, the improved plant and working conditions, the strong potential for growth and education that can come from cooperative schoolwork programs, and the physical and mental maturity of youth themselves. Adult society denies youth the opportunity to mature into adulthood by setting undue restrictions for employment, which hang over from abuses and conditions of the last century. Many delinquent youth today find themselves in exile between the time they leave school and the time they can take up adult employment. Frustrations suffered during this deep-freeze period can eventuate in overt and aggressive attacks against the community.

The reluctance of most states to reduce the voting age to eighteen also indicates a lack of faith and a strong distrust of youth. Yet, the nation has been willing to draft eighteen-year-olds to carry arms in the defense of the nation. Youth have been sensitive to this lack of faith and this willingness to exploit.

This paradoxical adult attitude of romantic glow and lack of trust impedes youth in the establishment of a positive self-concept. Many youth regard themselves at the high school and post high school level as alienated and of little worth. There is little for them to do that represents real, honest, and important work in the home or the community. This situation has tended to foster a *sui generis* culture of adolescent inferiority which is trying in many ways to prove itself. Unfortunately, delinquent behavior represents one of the more popular techniques for a large segment of American youth. This self-concept of youth inferiority is so pronounced in the later teen-age groups that they have come to represent the outraged personality of the mid-twentieth century. Delinquency and crime statistics on this age group will tend to confirm this harsh self-concept.

Of particular interest here might be the observation that American youth, except for sports and sex, have made few significant contributions to the stream of important life activities. In contrast to their foreign counterparts, American youth until recently have shown no real or universal interest in the political arena. Instead of political revolt and rebellion that is standard behavior in European and South American universities, the American campus denizen carries on with his annual pantie raids. College youth's participation in Free Speech and integration movements and "teach-ins" represents a better investment of energy and interest. Also it must be pointed out that American youth's contribution to the arts, literature, and science has been negligible. Youthful poets, novelists, composers, and artists do not abound, and, if they emerge, there is a limited press (always adult-controlled) that will risk publication of their efforts. Youth, however, are good consumers. The record business would fold without their support. This may be good for American economy, but it does not reinforce creativity in youth. One is forced to inquire whether the overt and aggressive behavioral expression, visible in the steadily rising delinquency trends, does not represent the main stream of expression and creativity of American youth.

Nature of the Adult Imitative Example to Which Youth are Exposed

Youth will and do reflect what adults think of them and the esteem in which they are held. Adults must move first to lift and improve their own expectations of youth. They must show greater trust and belief in their abilities, in their maturity, and in their potential. The adult must be willing and ready to attribute a higher self-concept to youth; youth in many areas have indicated that they are ready to attain it.

One of the most difficult tasks for any youth who has fallen into the delinquent pattern is to find someone respectable to emulate, or someone with whom to identify. Children and youth are much affected by the quality of the model behavior presented to them by prestigious adults whom they admire in the person of the parent or parent surrogate. Yet most boys and girls will indicate, when confronted by a serious personal or social problem, that they cannot discuss their problems openly or easily with their own parents. Either they have no easy communication or they cannot relate to them with any effectiveness. Too often parents appear dull, unromantic, and unsympathetic.

Youth find it easier to identify with a currently popular starlet or with a Beatle or a member of a popular band. Note the dress, the coiffure, the mannerisms in speech, and the dancing styles of young people. The tragedy centers around the fact that youth cannot find anyone more glamorous, more exciting, or more appealing among the teachers, the statesmen and politicians, the clergy, or the scientists that inhabit their world. We have a serious situation in a society when the work of a Salk appears listless, dull, and uninspiring when pitted against the hip swinging and guitar strumming of a male song stylist. Surely the homes and the schools, not to mention the press, radio, and TV, can present in their true light and importance the adventure, excitement, and romance to be found in the work of the teacher, the scientist, the statesman, and the clergy. If worthwhile and inspiring adults can capture the imagination and the interests of young people, they may be able to turn the course of youth's actions to more constructive and promising pursuits.

Accent on Sociability and Popularity

Most juvenile delinquency represents a popular form of overt and aggressive socialization. The solitary delinquent is somewhat of a rarity. Being popular and right with the group may end up in being wrong with the adults. To have no dates and no friends is the greatest misfortune that can befall high school students. The nature of the adolescent is essentially gregarious; his peer group values are paramount in determining his tastes and his behavior.

Most school, church, and club programs foster exclusively large group social activities in the form of dances, athletic events, and parties. There is, in most institutions, with the exception of some forms of church and library activity, little attempt to develop worthwhile solitary activities that render the individual independent and resourceful, especially when he is alone and away from the crowd.

The overemphasis on socialization and being popular that is so much in the air in every family, neighborhood, and school fits too closely the pattern of socialization that can be found in group delinquency.

The Urgency to Succeed

Our American culture abounds in success stories in the tradition of Horatio Alger, or in the fast success story found in hitting the right combination in some lucky jackpot. The number of contests that are conducted in America is astronomical. They may range from the simple honor role in the classroom to the pulchritude pageant conducted annually at Atlantic City to select the American Beauty Queen (possessing at least enough intelligence to answer three questions orally). These contests enable many persons to achieve "success."

There is no doubt that the security that comes through success fulfills a basic need in strengthening feelings of personal worth. For the adolescent, one major source—sometimes the only source—of success is through his performance in school studies, in sports, or in other extracurricular activities. The typical teenager can find approval and meet smiling faces at home and in school only if he is a scholastic success via the report card route. But most delinquents show a bankruptcy status when their school records are examined. They seem to make a success of failure. This may be due to subculture and peer group values where it is considered smart to fail, albeit this may bring the pupil into sharp conflict with his teachers, principal, and parents. Many delinquents, and this perhaps includes the majority, whose abilities and interests are nonacademic, whose home problems are overwhelming, or whose classroom setting is unpromising, seldom feel the benign effects and the rewards that come through successful achievement. Failures in school, they must prove their worth some other way—perhaps by vandalism or truancy. Thus, proof is rendered of their ability and respectability in the eyes of their peers.

Many delinquents, as well as nondelinquents, who have the bad fortune to be surrounded by predatory parents who are attacking, rejecting, or exploiting, find in school failure and misbehavior an effective weapon with which to combat the old folks. This is especially true in the more respectable middle class homes where success in school and admission to college are always major issues. Consciously or unconsciously, the growing child learns that he can use the failure-ridden report card like a knife. Teachers, for whom the academic success of their charges becomes a paramount concern, can be dealt with in similar fashion.

In summary, delinquency does not exist in a vacuum; it exists in a culture. There are many cultural forces that are reflected in the delinquent act. These include violence in solving personal and social problems, the principle of pleasure and self-indulgence, anonymity in modern living, the low self-concept that adults pass on to youth, the nature of the adult imitative example to which youth are exposed, the over-emphasis on sociability and popularity and the urgency to succeed.

Can the community do anything about changing the culture? The response to this question can only be given in a pessimistic vein. However, there may be some hope in the reconstructionist movement that aims to use agencies, institutions, and the mass media to bring about desired changes in the behavior of large masses of people. *If the behavior of large numbers of adults and future adults can be changed,* the culture can be changed to the advantage of present and future generations. Failing in this, delinquency will long be with us, and many of the procedures used to prevent and control juvenile delinquency today will prove even more ineffective and irrelevant tomorrow.

3   Where Begot, Where Nourished?

Ambivalent obsession on the sociological level: Eastern European countries see little delinquency among their youth; America finds it, scrutinizes it on every level of its society. Is America's culture and philosophy the source from which it sprang fully armed? Is the U.S.S.R. untouched by hoodlumism and gangs? What does the West's self-conscious, scrupulous examination of delinquency mean?

Whether you work in the Orient or the Occident, assisting the unadjusted youth of developing or developed countries, you invariably come up against either a neurotic denial of any delinquency problem or a neurotic preoccupation with it. It is difficult to say which of these obsessions is worse; you can almost take your pick. Every American conference on youth includes a generous reference to the problems of delinquent juveniles. In contrast, there is a steady and strong denial of the hooliganism phenomenon at international conferences.

Dr. H. Cybulska-Veillard, speaking at a meeting of the International Union for Child Welfare at Freiburg-en-Breisgau, August 1961, described the mythology and denial that have characterized the eastern European orientation to delinquency:

> Hooliganism is merely a marginal and atypical phenomenon. It is even foreign to the structure of socialistic society. The fact that hooliganism is increasing now can only be attributed to the activity of the enemy of the working class. It is the old game of capitalism rearing its head in bourgeois milieux. This anachronism will disappear inexorably, as communism develops.

As suggested here, delinquency is viewed as the waste by-product of the psycho-socio-economic influence of capitalism.

Although there has been a perceptible shift from this point of view, particularly in Poland, Czechoslovakia and Yugoslavia since 1956—the year of the "Fall Revolution"—the tendency to slough off any youth problem and to point to delinquency and hooliganism as an exclusively western commodity still prevails and presents a serious barrier to helping socially inadapted youth in the closed Soviet circle.

At the other extreme, many public officials in the United States have developed the open habit of attacking and advertising the youthful offenders as a national scourge and a major educational problem. Typical is the following statement of a distinguished superintendent of schools in a large midwestern city:

> The bad boy of America has no counterpart in any other part of the world. In Europe, youth is docile and respectful; in Asia and Africa, childhood is at least in keeping with its surroundings; but the bad boy of America is an anachronism, he is savagery growing up in the midst of civilization, impiety mocking at religion, lawlessness whistling defiance at law and order, and license masquerading in the costume of liberty. His language is slang and profanity. His amusement is violence, his education a blank, and his name a terror to society.

This kind of verbal flagellation is peculiar to the United States. This brand of irrational, self-incriminating, and emotionalized rubbish—the scrap and waste product of fear, anxiety, and ignorance—is not generally found in other countries.

Most western European countries, although acknowledging their youth problem, deftly deflect attention away from their own delinquency rates by pointing to other countries where the problem appears to be more pressing. Frequently, they will point the finger at the United States as the habitat of the juvenile delinquent. For example, Aimée Racine, reporting on the Belgian situation—roughly about two delinquents per thousand youngsters among the eight- to eighteen-year-olds—has said: "On the whole, juvenile delinquency in Belgium does not present the spectacular aspects that it does in certain other countries."[1] Although she states that Belgian delinquency has not taken on the spectacular proportions that recur and haunt other countries, her own data on Belgium report a 216 per cent increase by 1959 of referrals and complaints to the juvenile courts with a corresponding increase of only 129 per cent from cases actually adjudicated since the war years.

---

[1] Aimée Racine, *La Délinquance Juvénile en Belgique de 1939 à 1957* (Brussels, Belgium: Centre Etude de la Délinquance Juvénile, 1959).

This dramatic imbalance in the number of cases referred for delinquency hearing and the actual number of cases finally adjudicated as delinquent in Belgium is typical of what is happening in many countries. Adults—especially the city-dwelling species—are much faster on the draw today. Any malbehavior, no matter how trivial, can be enough to draw the attention and the wrath of super-sensitive adults and thus bring an offending youngster before the courts. It no longer requires a major offense to get transgressing youth before official adult authority. Consequently, it is hard, even dangerous, to be a non-adult today—whether you live in Brussels, Bombay, or Boston. Whether the youth of the world are more delinquent is still debatable, but there is no questioning the fact that the adults themselves are universally more concerned with and sensitized to youth's infractions and maladaptations.

Of late there has been much interest expressed in the problems of the emerging nations of Africa. In this connection, the African delinquents, real and imaginary, have not escaped the ubiquitous technical assistants. A Workshop on Extension of Family and Child Welfare Services within the Community Development Programs (United Nations Economic and Social Council, Economic Commission for Africa, Third Session meeting in Accra, November 21 to December 3, 1960) reported:

> The problem of juvenile delinquency, though not particularly serious in African countries, has been tending to claim increasing attention from most governments in Africa in recent years; and, since with the present general trend towards rapid economic and social change the problem is likely to become more acute, particularly in the main centers of population, the opportunity afforded to participants in this Workshop to examine various policies and methods for prevention or solution was most welcome.

The workshop members were probably rolling up their sleeves, rubbing their hands, and saying: "Quick, now, bring on those African delinquents-to-be!" when we are not sure exactly what to do with the activist American, Belgian, and Polish delinquents who have been legally labelled and classified. People in all countries today like to think delinquency and talk delinquency. Of course, there is wisdom in being forewarned and prepared, but there is also the danger of overenthusiastic adult intervention that can reap a premature harvest.

Sensing this artificial acceleration of delinquency, the second United Nations Congress on the Prevention of Crime and Treatment of Offenders (London, August, 1960) cautioned, and for good reason, that the scope of the problem should not be unnecessarily inflated. This congress did not attempt to formulate a standard definition of what should be considered juvenile delinquency in each country but recommended that the term juvenile delinquency should be restricted, as far as possible, to violations of the criminal law. The congress also recommended that specific offenses for which adults would not be prosecuted should not be created in order to penalize small irregularities or maladjusted behavior of minors.

In a sense, this recommendation reduces delinquency by redefinition and narrowed focus on the legally labeled. It ignores all those unofficially delinquent youngsters who are behaving like the legally labeled but who have not been passed through the stamping machine of the court. Hence, those countries, particularly in the underdeveloped category, that are slow or lackadaisical in apprehending, adjudicating, classifying, recording, and reporting, often tend "to look better" than the more developed and affluent nations when official delinquency rates are studied. The result is that affluence is now being associated with delinquency.

A good example of how an expansion of probation and court services can produce a rapid "increase" of official delinquency can be found in a study of delinquency trends in Israel. A steep jump from 3.59 to 5.30 cases per thousand in the general population was visible between 1953 and 1954. However, these figures must be evaluated in light of the fact that until 1954 the juvenile probation service did not cover all areas of the country. Most cases in these unserviced areas "were closed by the police" or "adjourned indefinitely" and therefore were not registered at the probation service. With the addition of more probation personnel, more juveniles were arrested and referred to the appropriate officials resulting in a "marked increase" in official records. Fortunately, Israeli officials were alert to the fact that "additional probation service means more delinquency."

Still another reason why the United States appears to have more delinquency can be found in the fact that we engage in more investigations, surveys, and research studies, and we publish more than any other country. All these reports on delinquency are read widely, and many of them appear in translation.

All foreign bibliographies are rich in up-to-date American references. For example, the Polish study *Mebecpjeczne Ulice* [*Dangerous Streets*], (1960) by Cz. Scapow and St. Manturzewski, cites more than two hundred American references; the French report on gangs, *Le Phenomene des Bandes* (1961) by M. Ceccaldi, shows 31 American sources out of a total of 90 citations: a similar study *Jugend Gangs* (1959) by Otto Wilfert in Austria, offers a brief bibliography in which half the sources come from American literature.

As a strong contrast, it is the exceptional author in the United States who would or could cite a single reference from the Polish, French, or Austrian sources. The obvious result is a steady flow of research findings on a one-way route—from West to East. This cross-fertilization promises much for improving the theoretical conceptualization of the delinquency phenomenon and the planning of action programs for prevention and treatment of delinquents in foreign countries. But the very insular orientation of much of the American research effort now risks inbreeding and the danger of running to seed.

Delinquent behavior has taken on a very familiar—even monotonous—look in most countries. Indeed, it is difficult to identify many "new forms" of delinquency although Judge Wolf Middendorff of West Germany attempted to delineate the forms in his report to the United Nations.[2]

The rapid standardization of the forms and styles of delinquent behavior can be attributed in large measure to the effectiveness of our mass media—cinema, radio, TV, records, and the journals—all of which have tended to give the delinquent act in all parts of the world an American Look. There is no doubt that the style center for delinquency has been localized in our part of the world with New York City à la *West Side Story, Blackboard Jungle,* etc., having the foremost showing. The result is that many persons in other countries are prone to place blame on the United States for the norm violations of their own youth—so much of it reflects the American mode of dress, coiffure, stance, and patois. Whenever originality in delinquency becomes visible, it is usually attributable to adult inspiration. The juvenile, no matter what his national origin, tends to be a poor innovator; nonetheless, he remains always a good consumer and imitator.

After surveying the world social situation, the United Nations in a Report of the Social Committee (32nd session, July, 1961) asserted: "The Economic and Social Council stresses the particular seriousness of the problem of juvenile delinquency and of prevention of crime in all countries."

What the Social Committee publicly and bluntly said was: "Every nation has it." The Committee made no exceptions. Without a doubt, some countries do have more than others. But at the present stage of definition, data gathering, reporting, and, of course, political mind and attitude, it is not possible to make any direct and meaningful comparison across national borders.

---

[2] Wolf Middendorff, *New Forms of Juvenile Delinquency: Their Origin, Prevention and Treatment* (New York: United Nations, Department of Economic and Social Affairs, 1960).

In East or West, in countries economically developed or developing, the first and essential step in helping the delinquent will require a more realistic testing of the true nature and scope of the nation's juvenile problem. Extreme care will need to be exercised lest the inadaptations of youth be unduly magnified or minimized. This means breaking through the tight and elaborate system of defenses that exists in all countries. Taking this first step will demand that each nation stop emotionalizing the juvenile delinquent. As always, the first step is the hardest.

PART TWO

Definition and Dynamics

4   What Is a Delinquent?

On the legal and psychological levels, what kind of person and behavior can be defined as clearly delinquent? What are the modalities of delinquency? How does "hidden delinquency" distort statistics so that available figures are not reliable? What are the limitations of definition and segregation by types according to modalities? How effective are juvenile courts? What are the inherent drawbacks in the state institutions? Can we look for institutions whose philosophy and practices will be positive aids to the young norm-violator? What special type of training must personnel have in order to develop maximum competence in working with delinquents?

Few terms in the educator's professional vocabulary have been used more loosely or freely than the term *juvenile delinquent*. It is a handy label to pin on any youngster displaying some degree of norm-violating behavior; but, in the legal sense, when is the youngster considered *delinquent?*

Most statutes point out that delinquent behavior constitutes a violation of the law or municipal ordinance by a young person under a certain age. Even this age is not consistently set, however; in many states it is eighteen, but this limit varies widely from state to state and even within a state. Also included within the legal concept of delinquency are neglected, wayward, and habitually disobedient children, the habitually truant, and the child who usually deports himself so as to impair or endanger the morals or health of others. And technically, a child is not a delinquent until he has been adjudged so in court.

In recent years, there have been a number of promising trends in the definition and treatment of delinquency. Many states have raised the age limits; the juvenile courts have been given broader jurisdiction over all cases where the child may be in need of protective custody, and treatment by professionally trained personnel in a special juvenile court rather than punishment has become more common.

However, there still remain many sharp differences among various state laws relating to the delinquent, and there is also a serious and obvious lag between the laws that have been enacted and current local juvenile court protection. Little improvement can be expected in helping the delinquent child without first redrafting state and local legislation to fit within the spirit and working of the Standard Juvenile Court Act and then implementing the legislation at the local level.

Psycho-Social Definition

Behaviorally, the delinquent child is expressing himself by aggressive, overt action which does not coincide with the demands and expectations of society. To those who observe him, his offensive behavior is troublesome to a greater or lesser degree, depending on the tolerance and irritability level of the community. For the delinquent himself, however, his behavior is generally purposeful and adjustive; hence his act can be considered to be more symptomatic than significant in and of itself.

Modalities of Delinquency

Because delinquency is such a vague, omnibus term, many researchers have attempted to identify modalities or grouping of misbehavior according to common causative characteristics. In this way, delinquents can be differentiated according to patterns of behavior traits. While it is very nearly impossible to work out neat and clearly-defined categories and typologies in such an amorphous area, many promising approaches have been made by a number of investigators. Modalities ranging from the identification of the "socialized delinquent" to the "emotionally disturbed," to the "group-intoxicated," and many subtypes, have been recognized and categorized. Yet, many of the modalities are overlapping, and some of the investigators are using different typological terminology to describe the same traits. Much needed is a further refinement to identify the mutually exclusive modalities in the broad spectrum of delinquent conduct. Without better classification and more precise definition or reference as to the kind of delinquent being investigated, it is doubtful whether the present or future investigator can add significant data to the existing store of information on this topic.

Hidden Delinquency

One of the problems in estimating the incidence of delinquency in a given area is the type of statistics that are kept and the number of cases that are actually referred to court, as contrasted with those that never reach official recognition. A kind of screening which tends to shelter or protect the offender against becoming a court statistic often takes place in an average community; this accounts for a so-called hidden delinquency which is never recorded but which, nevertheless, is very real.

Two studies of hidden delinquency are noteworthy and ominous in their implications as to the widespread nature of delinquent-like conduct in our culture. The Cambridge-Somerville (Massachusetts) eight-year study[1] uncovered in a control group the fact that of 6,416 known infractions of the law, conservatively estimated to have been committed by 114 boys over a five-year period, only 95 or less than 1.5 per cent of these infractions eventually became a matter of official complaint. Of all these infractions, 616 were labeled "serious," yet only 68 eventuated legal action. Similarly, Austin L. Porterfield, using a check list based upon offenses committed by a large sample of delinquents, reported that college students, male and female, all reported committing one or more offenses, with an average of more than 11 offenses per youth.

These studies suggest: (1) a very wide prevalence of antisocial and illegal behavior among youth which may be considered tantamount to a cultural pattern, and (2) the operation of a high degree of selectivity within the community as to who will be officially recorded as delinquent. Two corollaries are now indicated: (1) there are a large number of cultural pseudo-delinquents who appear to solve their problems without the help of a vast network of social agencies and whose delinquencies may be considered as a "normal" aspect of the growth process; and (2) the sample of delinquents who eventually come to inhabit the courts and state institutions represents, without question, a special brand or breed of delinquents. This latter consideration raises

[1] Edwin Powers and Helen Witmer, *An Experiment in the Prevention of Delinquency: The Cambridge-Somerville Youth Study* (New York: Columbia University Press, 1951).

a serious question concerning the degree of bias present in most studies of delinquents and their home and family backgrounds which are made at the official court and institutional levels. A delinquent, technically, can be identified as a person who has been adjudicated as such by the court.

The Juvenile Court Idea

Studies of organization, structure and functioning of the juvenile courts have shown that, with a few notable exceptions, most juvenile courts fall far short of the recommendations set forth in the Standard Juvenile Court Act. New issues faced by the juvenile courts today have been considered jointly by the National Probation and Parole Association and the National Council of Juvenile Court Judges. Their recommendations only tend to accentuate how far most juvenile courts must go if they are to approximate minimal standards as specialized courts dealing with children under the happy union of child welfare and the behavioral sciences. Several states including Utah, Rhode Island, and Connecticut have established state-wide, full-time juvenile courts.[2]

Institutions for Delinquents

The detention facilities for delinquents throughout the country are still the shame of the nation, as reported several years ago by the U.S. Senate Subcommittee Investigating Juvenile Delinquency. Detention of young people in jails and lockups continues to be a widespread and damaging practice.

State institutions continue to be overcrowded, understaffed, financially neglected, and hidden away in the less populated sections of the state. The result can be seen in programs that are more custodial than therapeutic; these training centers have often been described as "schools for crime and depravity." An attempt to upgrade the programs in the institutions can be seen in the combined statements of the U.S. Children's Bureau and the National Association of Training Schools and Juvenile Agencies published as guides and goals for institutions serving delinquents.[3]

---

[2] For further discussion, see Sol Rubin, "State Juvenile Courts: A New Standard," *Focus*, xxx (1951), 103-107.

[3] *Institutions Serving Delinquent Children: Guides and Goals,* prepared by U.S. Department of Health, Education, and Child Welfare, Children's Bureau, in cooperation with the National Association of Training Schools and Juvenile Agencies (Washington, D.C.: Children's Bureau Publication No. 360, 1957).

Perhaps the most promising development along the lines of treatment, especially for the more severe cases, has been forthcoming from the small and expensive residential treatment centers, more adequately staffed as to both number and quality of personnel. These programs usually offer milieu therapy and include such diverse methods as individual psychiatric interviews, play therapy, and group therapy, together with all the skills of the various disciplines. Notable along these lines are the pioneering efforts of Bettelheim in therapeutic living at the Sonia Shankman Orthogenic School of the University of Chicago; of Redl and Wineman in Detroit, Michigan; in the reported research of McCorkle, Elias, and Bixby in the Highfields, New Jersey, experimental-treatment center. The findings of these investigators, working in close relationship with severely disturbed and delinquent children over prolonged periods of study and treatment, have probably contributed more to the theory of delinquency causation and practice involving treatment and rehabilitation than is available from any other source. Working with exposed or delinquent youth in the open community, the various projects of Mobilization for Youth in the lower East side of New York City have also offered promising guides for prevention and control by expanding youth opportunities and by reinforcing home and family through self-help techniques.

Training personnel for work with delinquents.

Aid to the delinquent depends directly on the quality of the personnel trained for this task. Surprisingly little attention has been directed to the specialized training needs of workers who came into an intimate relationship with the delinquent and his family. Continuing in a traditional pattern, each discipline trains for its own narrow or comprehensive purposes and only incidentally, and sometimes accidentally, offers work in direct preparation for dealing with delinquents and their families. There is a growing conviction today that all personnel who carry responsibility for treatment and control of delinquent children have training for this special work. The need for providing more and better opportunities for training professional workers who will enter the field of juvenile delinquency or who are now at work in this area merits the immediate attention of the combined disciplines. Unless this problem is solved first, little improvement can be expected over and beyond the gains already made in the delinquency field.

This problem has been recognized by the President's Committee on Juvenile Delinquency and Youth Development; a number of training centers have been established throughout the United States.

Most of these centers have concentrated very heavily on short-term training programs for semi-professional or sub-professional workers. The problem of training the professionals as well as the sub-professional youth workers who will be engaged in prevention and treatment of the juvenile delinquent still remains to be faced by colleges and universities.

With this introduction to the problem of definition and defining agencies, let us take a look at a behaving—or misbehaving youngster, and ask the question: "When does a youth actually become a delinquent?"

5 When Does a Prank Become a Delinquency?

In examining the facets of norm-violating behavior, it becomes increasingly clear that where mildly overt and aggressive action is involved, there is a great deal of subjective judgment on what is delinquent behavior. Much depends on the attitudes and the degree of tolerance of the observer, and drawing the line between what may be defined as pranks and what is actually a clear case of lawbreaking is often difficult. In the following cases involving vandalism, the various degrees of behavior which may be termed offensive raise some important questions: What should our attitude be toward this incident? Which can be handled by the people involved? Which should be referred to the police or to the courts? What principles of child psychology will give us a better understanding of the behavior involved? How can these principles help us to diagnose the action? Which of these cases demonstrate delinquent behavior? What agencies and resources can be used to get aid?

1. Richard defaces a house.

Richard is a nine-year-old boy of average ability. He lives in the poorer section of a small town. His house is one of a cluster of similar dwellings built around the turn of the century and later converted into apartments. The grounds are unkempt, and inside is a general atmosphere of gradual decay; the floors slant and the walls bulge with layers of paper. Conveniences are at a minimum, and there is little care or upkeep given to the home.

There are five children crowded into the apartment, and between their constant activity and general neglect, the home has a depressing air of clutter and dirt. The father works for the town's department of public works, and the mother has part-time employment at a cleaning shop down the street.

One day on his way home from school, Richard marks with crayons on the white clapboard of a house he passes. The owner catches him after he has drawn his pictures and lettered the walls with "offensive" words; he takes the boy to his mother in a rage. The mother, tired out from her work and discouraged by her problems, is upset but does not feel that Richard did anything really bad. She wishes he had not done it, but feels that his action is typical of what many youngsters do. She scolds the boy and promises that he will never do it again, but beyond that she does not know what else to do.

> *Is Richard a delinquent or a pre-delinquent? Does the fact that there is so little respect for and interest in the upkeep of his own surroundings tend to put his action in the area of non-delinquent behavior? Or, is the defacing of property always demonstrably delinquent conduct?*

2. Three boys damage a country vegetable stand.

On their way home one summer afternoon, three boys pass a roadside vegetable stand whose owner is not in sight. They have no plans for doing damage, but one spies a crate of eggs and, on impulse, throws one of the eggs at his friend. Everyone thinks the idea is wonderful, and soon they are all hurling the eggs, smashing them at each other and on the walls of the stand. They add some ripe tomatoes to their weapons, and when the owner suddenly appears, he finds the stand spattered and smeared and much of his produce ruined. He catches one of the boys and tells the police; the other boys are immediately implicated, and all the parents are summoned.

The parents are angry at the boys' behavior, but do not feel that they have been guilty of a seriously wrong action. They offer to pay for the damages and to make the boys clean the stand. The boys feel guilty and ashamed; their contact with the police has frightened them, and they are glad their parents got them off with no worse punishment.

> *Are these boys merely exuberant pranksters, or are they delinquents? Should they be taken to court? Would it serve a useful purpose to do so? Is it right for their parents to pay for the damages? Will getting off comparatively "easy" tend to make them repeat this sort of action? In the minds of the boys, does the fact that their parents are assuming the responsibility for paying off the owner lessen the seriousness of their offense?*

3. *Four boys wreck an automobile.*

It is Halloween. Four boys from a depressed area in the town go to one of the better streets to see what damage they can do. They have often been in trouble for damaging property, breaking windows, and destroying unattended possessions, and they are known to the police as troublemakers.

On their way up the street, they see a car parked on a sloping driveway. They think it would be great fun to release the brakes and see what would happen. The car rolls down the back field, sideswipes a tree, and becomes wedged between two others; it is badly damaged.

The boys watch the proceedings while hiding in some thick shrubbery. They laugh excitedly when they hear the crash and feel they have had a good time. The police are called in, and, seeing the boys in the area, have a good idea who was responsible. They know the boys are usually in the same gang and that their peers consider such action smart and inventive. The boys are poor students in school and raise many problems for their teachers. They are acting according to the rules of their peer-group when they cause trouble and flout authority in school or on the streets.

Are these boys delinquents? Should they be referred to the courts? What standards in their own culture have had a bearing on their behavior? What can be done to make them aware of the seriousness of their actions? Will retribution through the courts make them see their behavior as wrong? If they are punished, will their actions cease once they are returned to their own environment?

4. *A case of spontaneous vandalism.*

A crowd of wealthy young teen-agers are at a party in a large summer home. There is some drinking, and suddenly one of the boys jumps on a large crystal chandelier and swings on it until it is torn from the ceiling. Everyone greets the loud crash with cheers, and it sets off a chain reaction; mirrors are broken, furniture is smashed, and the damage runs into thousands of dollars.

When the horrified owners discover the destruction, they call in the police. Some of the parents are upset, but many feel that the action was just the expression of high spirits. They are willing to pay for the damages but feel that it was wrong of the owners to inform the police. They remember many "wild parties" they attended when they were young, and think that this is merely a phase that all youngsters go through, that court action is unnecessary and harmful, and that it will merely intensify instead of solve the problem. Backed by their parents' attitudes, the teen-agers are defiant and feel that they have been treated too harshly.

Are these teen-agers delinquents? Should their actions be referred to court or settled by their parents? How have their attitudes been shaped by their parents? They have heard stories of some of the escapades their fathers once engaged in; have they been taught by these that it is all right to engage in this type of behavior just because they are young and high-spirited? Have they been conditioned to think that if money can pay for damages then no real harm has been done?

5. An organized gang sets fire to a school.

A gang of young boys from a depressed area in a large city has frequently engaged in norm-violating behavior. Some have records for stealing, and they all feel that violent and aggressive behavior proves their strength and intelligence.

One of the boys is angry at the principal of the school because he called the boy out for troublesome behavior in the classroom. The boys decide to burn down the school to revenge their friend. They break in one night and set fires in several areas of the building. By the time the fire is discovered and put out, there has been extensive damage; the building is almost totally ruined.

The boys are caught and placed in the local jail. Some have already spent time in the state industrial school for boys, so they know what to expect. They are not too concerned, but they feel it was bad luck that they were caught and swear that the next time they get together for similar action, they will be more careful. They know their confinement is only temporary and that they will soon be back on the streets.

Is there any question whether or not these boys are delinquents? Is it true that only adjudicated cases represent real delinquency? The police are glad they have caught them, and don't mind strongarming these toughies, but they know they will be engaged in the same type of behavior when they are again released. Is there any answer to this problem? Can these boys be deflected from a life of crime? Is there anything society can do for them?

The inadequacy of the personal and background data concerning these five cases makes it difficult, if not impossible, to render any valid analysis of the causative factors. Delinquent or bothersome behavior is seldom simply or briefly explained. Study, diagnosis, and treatment are not primary objectives, however, in relating these brief histories. These cases have been presented in order to raise certain vital issues. Each of these cases, individually (and all of them collectively) implies that there is no neat, simple, single answer to many of the questions raised for discussion. If the reader compares his answers with those of other readers, he may be surprised to find numerous contrasting and seemingly irreconcilable differences in opinion. Here is one of the foremost problems in building a community program of prevention and control. Members of the community find themselves divided into opposing camps concerning who is a delinquent and what course of action is most beneficial to the offending child and to society in general.

For example, in viewing these cases, a clergyman sensitive to moral principles may categorically state that all these acts are immoral and contrary to the absolute laws of God. However, even in more formalistic and highly organized religions, distinctions are frequently made between "venial," or excusable wrongdoings and "mortal," or unpardonable, sins. The distinction depends upon such factors as the spontaneity of the behavior as against the premeditated act. Hence, even from a strictly moralistic view of these cases, differentiating degrees of sin and guilt can be determined.

The police officer may indicate that, working according to the letter of the law regarding property rights, complaints could and should be made out in each case—although he might well hesitate before bringing in Richard, who marked the walls of the house. The officer might be content to leave Richard in the custody of his parents, after admonishing the youngster not to let it happen again.

If any of these cases is pursued into court, the presiding judge will insist, and rightfully so from the legal point of view, that none of these children—except for the boys on parole—can be considered delinquent until the court has adjudged them as such. According to this viewpoint, no child is delinquent until the court, after viewing all the evidence and studying all the background data, pronounces the child to be delinquent.

An important angle from which to view these incidents is that of the misbehaving child himself. While he may have little or none of a psychologist's insight into the meaning of his behavior, the behavior still has import for him. The angle from which he views his actions should always be of major concern. For example, the competitive, do-as-I-do-or-else compulsions in the case of the boys who destroyed the automobile indicate that what the adult disapproves of as a form ·of behavior, the peer group may regard with praise and approval. To deviate from the group's code of behavior, in the direction of adult-approved patterns, would be to lose the support and approval of the gang.

Many of the differences in opinions concerning the nature of a delinquent and how best to handle him stem from the varied perspectives and emotional climates from which the behavior is viewed. The attitude of the farmer who operates a vegetable stand, more interested in restoring his property than in rebuilding boys, is no doubt closer to the level of the community's attitude than is the more understanding and tolerant viewpoint of the psychiatric social worker, whose chief intent is to understand the meaning of behavior and to apply appropriate treatment. Many community programs of delinquency prevention and control stumble at the point of conflict between these varied, if not opposing, viewpoints. The professional worker, if he is to be effective, must show a high degree of acceptance toward the malbehaving youngster (but not of the malbehavior itself), and his motivation must be to help achieve a more effective personal and social adjustment through diagnosis and study of underlying causes. Yet he must constantly take into consideration the wide variance in viewpoints from which delinquent conduct is appraised. All too frequently professional workers have attempted to operate in a community delinquency prevention program as though their viewpoint was shared by all other community members. Such naïveté can isolate the youth worker in a professional vacuum. This problem of varying viewpoints concerning the nature of delinquent behavior—as seen in the thinking of the clergyman, the policeman, the juvenile court judge, the injured property owner, and the child himself—is one which must be considered in the legal definition of delinquency.

A consideration of the difference in degrees in delinquent behavior makes it possible to establish some criteria[1] of severity of norm-violating behavior. Stealing a nickel from mother once in a life time and snitching pennies daily bear different connotations. Likewise, stabbing a gang member is more serious than swearing at him. In order to understand the difference between major and minor violations, it is necessary to examine these four factors: *seriousness, form, frequency,* and relationship of act to *prior behavior and individual personality.*

Seriousness. The specific nature of the offense will determine whether it is a serious norm violation. Taking a used lipstick from a friend's

---

[1] Drawn from W. C. Kvaraceus, W. B. Miller, *et al., Delinquent Behavior: Culture and the Individual* (Washington, D.C.: National Education Association, 1959) pp. 43-45.

locker will not upset the community as much as theft of a payroll check from a jimmied mailbox; whispering in class may break a school rule, but it is generally considered as a lesser offense than smoking in the school building. In the adult community ignoring a STOP sign may result in traffic violation, but it is not considered in the same terms as driving an unregistered car. Thus, it is easy to see that norm violations may range on a continuum from minor to major, always reflecting the degree of seriousness of the act.

Form. Assaultive behaviors and destruction of and threat to property represent forms of norm violation that are regarded most severely by citizens and protective authority. This is particularly true for such acts as arson, sexual assault, breaking and entering at night. Or, to cite another example, the transgression of the sexually promiscuous high school girl who finds herself pregnant is a form of norm violation that alarms the adult middle-class community much more than truancy, breaking windows, loitering or swearing.

Frequency. Cheating on an examination once in a high school career and cheating on every examination and homework assignment have varying implications for both schools and individuals in the interpretation of the meaning of this norm-violating behavior. Some norm violation or another is a universal part of human life, as one's daily experience frequently testifies; this would seem to indicate that one transgression does not necessarily make a delinquent. Nor does the simple commission or noncommission of norm violation in and of itself automatically divide youngsters into delinquents and nondelinquents. Many studies of hidden and unrecorded delinquency have corroborated the assertion that norm-violating behavior is not the exclusive province of the "official delinquent."

Prior Behavior and Individual Personality. Norm-violating behavior will assume its full significance only when the act is viewed against earlier behaviors and the child's personal make-up. The implications of a single aggressive outburst against a peer by a hitherto apparently well-behaved and self-contained pupil, because of some real or fancied exploitation by the teacher or parent, may assume special significance in the light of his existing behavior patterns and modes of adjustment. The same kind of behavior on the part of another child may lead to a different diagnosis, because of the unique setting and background of his earlier actions and his habitual modes of adjustment.

Recapitulation. Recognizing delinquency as norm-violating behavior may clarify the issue as to *who* is the cause for concern in this report; still, it does not provide a precise definition of delinquency, nor does it simplify the problem. Identification of the delinquent involves a complex series of interrelated concepts and judgments on the form, frequency, and seriousness of the violations, and their significance in terms of earlier acts and individual personality. Whatever the kind of norm-violating youngster ultimately selected for diagnosis, study, and treatment, the school or other authority must take into account these four factors within the frame of reference or institutional system that serves as the most pertinent or essential reference point for the youngster himself. We will now take a closer look at some of these reference points.

6 The Subjective Appraisal: How Do Varying Rule Books Blur the Definition of Delinquency?

Since many communities, schools, and agencies display different attitudes and tolerances toward delinquent behavior, how can an exact definition be formulated? How does one family's unique standards make its concept of delinquent behavior different from another's? What of the varying codes in different classes of society? How do the youth's peers appraise status-achieving behavior?

Juvenile delinquency has been re-defined in the NEA report[1] as norm-violating behavior which brings the non-adult to the attention of official authority or agency. But this definition is not precise. We must raise the question: What norms or whose norms are being violated? The NEA report points out the wide variety of normative systems that exists in all communities in the United States, including street-corner society; lower

[1] *Delinquent Behavior: Culture and the Individual* (Washington, D.C.: National Education Association, 1959). This report was prepared by the NEA Juvenile Delinquency Project. The following members of the interdisciplinary team assisted in the preparation of the report: William C. Kvaraceus, psychologist; Walter B. Miller, cultural anthropologist; Milton L. Barron, sociologist; Edward M. Daniels, M.D., psychiatrist; Preston A. McLendon, M.D., pediatrician; and Benjamin A. Thompson, criminologist. This publication is available from the Publications-Sales Division, NEA, 1201 Sixteenth Street, N.W., Washington, D.C. The following materials have been drawn from sections of the report contributed mainly by Dr. Walter B. Miller.

45

class adolescent; middle class adolescent; Church A, B, C, to N; school; and, of course, the legal-societal system which is most strongly reflected in the way of life of the middle class. Each of these normative systems has its own rule book. While there is much overlapping among rules and regulations that may be found in the different normative systems, there is also much variance between the explicit and implicit codes for conduct.

Most middle-class adults are likely to view the delinquent through the peephole or the porthole of the middle class system. To these viewers, norm-violating behavior may appear as deviant and atypical behavior although it may be close to "standard" or even "demanded behavior" when viewed from the youngster's own primary reference group. For example, playing cards for money, shooting craps, drinking, truanting from school, swearing, and staying out all night may represent status and prestige-achieving conduct within a street corner milieu, although all of these acts may violate the rules and regulations of the legal-societal system. Most delinquents are not deviationists; they are out-and-out conformists, but conformists within their own group, not conformists to the legal-societal system.

In understanding the delinquent's behavior and in assisting him in accepting and living by the legal-societal rule book, professional and lay workers will need to be aware of the delinquent's primary reference group, of the interplay of forces within this milieu, and finally, of how the child and his family or gang can be weaned from their special rule book and helped to adopt the code of conduct of another reference group. Let us now examine more closely the dynamics of the subculture or milieu from which much delinquency stems in the large urban centers in the United States.

The existence of social stratification in United States society has been clearly demonstrated by many sociological surveys. The common knowledge of the existence of differing ways of life, each with its somewhat unique patterning of behavior, is readily reflected in the layman's reference to the "middle class," "upper-class," and "lower class." Publication of Vance Packard's *The Status Seekers*[2] represents an attempt to interpret for the lay reader some of the meaning and implications of class structuring in the United States. But what is the special significance of class status to norm-violating behavior?

Dr. Walter B. Miller,[3] working with street-corner gangs in Boston,

---

[2] Vance Packard, *The Status Seekers* (New York: David McKay Company, Inc., 1959).

[3] Walter B. Miller, "Lower Class Culture as a Generating Milieu of Gang Delinquency," *Journal of Social Issues* 14 (April, 1959).

has offered the hypothesis, with supporting evidence, that a large majority of norm-violators stem from *lower class milieu* and reflect in such behavior an interplay of cultural forces that generate illegal activity. Miller refers to the lower class culture specifically as a way of life which is followed by a large segment of the present-day population (from 40 to 60 per cent) whose concerns, values, and characteristic patterns of behavior are the outcome of a well-formed cultural system.

The dominant focal concerns of this subculture include trouble, toughness, cleverness, or duplicity, excitement, fate, and autonomy. These may be contrasted with the focal concerns of middle-class culture so evident in the PTA and related publications which lay heavy stress on child rearing, preservation of the family, ambition to get ahead, achievement through directed work effort, schooling and the improvement of the mind, deferment of immediate pleasures and gains for future goals, accumulation of material goods, and conscientious maintenance of property.

To illustrate the focal concerns of the family in lower-class culture, the lower-class parents frequently lament that they have "big trouble"; they may admonish their youngsters "to stay out of trouble"; a pregnant unmarried daughter may be described by the neighbors as "having gotten into trouble with a man. To "con" a stranger and to "take him for all he has" reflects a high duplicity I.Q.; sidewalk smartness is visible in verbal repartee and fast come-back. Physical prowess, ability to take it, power to endure physical hardship, as well as athletic skill, are held in high esteem and reflect the focal concern of force. Excitement may manifest itself in the urge to frequent the honky tonk and the penny arcade, or spend the periodic night out on the town with its standard mixture of sex and alcohol. And all the while Lady Luck prevails and provides a ready explanation for any mishap or good fortune that befalls a family member. Finally, the youngster, in his explicit concern for autonomy, may assert that "no one—but no one is going to push me around." However, all this does not imply any "single standard" of behavior for those who wear the lower-class label. The NEA report points out that there are many alternative behaviors that stretch along these dimensions in lower-class living. Much depends upon the orientation toward the focal concerns, for the lower-class family may be positively or negatively oriented to trouble, force, autonomy. At the same time, behavioral manifestations may sometimes reflect these concerns overtly, at other times covertly.

The youngster born and bred in a lower-class milieu who engages in serious and prolonged norm-violating behavior may do so for a number of reasons. First, he may be a daily witness to norm violations on the part of adults and other prestige figures in the neighborhood. Seeing the bookie or the number-pool operator openly at work can provide an imitative example soon to be followed and, at the same time, engender disdain or disregard for law and order. In other instances, the lower-class youngster may engage in norm violations because it enables "an easy out" or the achievement of some goal or object with the least energy investment. But, in most cases, the delinquent in this milieu turns to norm-violating behavior because he feels this to be the surest route to prestige and status with his primary reference group—usually the street-corner gang.

Although a strong psychic insulation exists between the lower class and middle class and between organizations such as the PTA and the lower class families, there is, nevertheless, some overlapping and interaction between these broad groups. This needs to be extended and broadened. The PTA needs to consider ways and means to contact and to include lower-class families in its membership.

At the same time, there is clearly discernible subgrouping within lower-class culture which has significance for much of the delinquency fall- out.[4] First, there is the "successfully aspiring lower-class member" who has the will, the capacity, and the means to lift his status. This is in the tradition of the American Dream. Second, there is the "aspiring but conflicted lower-class member" whose levels of aspiration exceed his realistic potential, or for whom difficult obstacles tend to thwart reasonable levels of aspiration. Friction, conflict, and frustration are inevitable in this "stalled" group. Such ferment frequently begets aggression, which may take on overt manifestations in the form of norm-violating behavior. The third segment has been described as the "stable" lower-class membership. This includes all those youngsters who either do not aspire or who do not have any realistic possibility of achieving such aspirations. This core group may represent the staying lower class.

It is in the second or thwarted group that many Negro and Puerto Rican youngsters may be found today. Lower-class Negro and Puerto Rican youth represent in the United States the largest upwardly mobile group—somewhat reminiscent of the European ethnic groups who emigrated earlier in this century. The severity of the frustrations of these aspiring but stalled ethnic groups has never been adequately appraised. A study[5] conducted in Elmira, New York, points out that the Negro youth in this northern urban community had high vocational

[4] Kvaraceus and Miller, *et al., op. cit.*, pp. 72-73.

[5] Aaron Antonorsky and Melvin J. Lerner, "Negro and White High School Youth in Elmira," *The Elmira Study* (State Commission Against Discrimination of New York, 1957), Mimeographed report.

aspirations, even higher than those of white youth from the same socio-economic level. In this survey, a very high proportion of Negro youngsters reported occupational aspirations that fall in the professional and semi-professional levels. The gap between what is hoped for and what is realistically possible produces ferment. So long as lower-class youth, white or non-white, are desirous of raising their own status but find themselves stalled in this process either because of cultural pressures or lack of personal attributes, the rates of delinquency for such conflicted segments will always remain potentially high.

Walter Miller has estimated that the majority (about 75 per cent) of youthful norm violations, defined as "forms of behavior which provide a base for legal action," stem in the main from lower-class cultural factors with little pathology or psychic involvement. The rest of the universe of all legal norm violators (about 25 per cent) represent psychologically-relevant delinquency.[6] Most of the latter stem from middle-class homes. These projected estimates infer that the psychodynamics approach via the Child Guidance Clinic and the one-to-one counseling relationship in treatment may be irrelevant to the genetic aspects of most delinquency as found in the universe of norm-violators. Conversely, any approach that aims to prevent and control norm-violating behavior must focus on the cultural situations and the way of life in the lower-class neighborhood. The singular lack of success in prevention and control of juvenile delinquency in most communities may be traced to the fact that the majority of lower-class youngsters who come to the attention of official agencies are simultaneously immune and allergic to psychological and psychiatric approaches. Instead of the individual, it is the neighborhood and the community that must be viewed as the patient. The key questions to be faced by those planning action programs are: "Can we change the way of life in the lower-class community?" "What techniques can be used to develop a law-abiding lower-class community?"

Miller's strong emphasis on the culturally determined delinquent does not minimize the need for more and better Child Guidance Clinics to help the individual and the family; it merely infers that only a small minority of delinquents (usually the middle-class variety) can be helped through this time-consuming and expensive approach. In fact, the theses presented in the NEA report[7] reaffirm a dependency on the Child Guidance Clinic both for diagnosis to confirm the extent of pathology that may be visible in the behavior of the norm-

---

[6] These estimates may need to be redrawn according to several recent studies which will be presented in the review and reappraisal in Chapter 8.

[7] Kvaraceus and Miller, et al., op. cit., Vol. I.

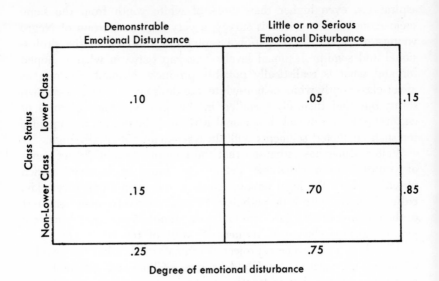

Figure 6.1. Distribution of "Delinquent" Individuals
(Adapted from Walter B. Miller).

violator, and for its strategy for approaching those whose problems stem from, or are complicated by, psychological and psychiatric factors.

Norms, Rules and Institutional Systems

As already indicated, there are many different institutional systems in the community. Needless to say, the community is not a "layer cake" with one class or group stacked on top of another; rather, its components overlap one another and are neither separate nor mutually exclusive. These systems include, among others, those of adult lower class; adult middle class; the streetcorner gang; adolescent lower class; adolescent middle class; the great variety of church systems—each with its own set of rules and regulations; the school; and the codified legal system itself. The school system may be subdivided into such sub-institutional units as the academic high school, the technical high school, and the comprehensive high school, with various hybrids according to suburban, urban, or rural locations.

Not only do these coexisting institutions have different rules and norms of behavior, but they may place differing emphases on the violation of the same norms common to several systems. Study of Table 6.1 will reveal the complication of a shifting system that can

Table 6.1. Delinquency as Norm-Violating Behavior (Adapted from Walter B. Miller).

Adult—Lower Class	Adult—Middle Class	Church A	Church B	School	Legal
Informs on gang members	Runs away from home	Receives communion without prior confession	Drinks, Smokes	Attacks Principal	Attacks person
Refuses to turn in earnings	Tells family's financial secrets	Tells lies	Plays Beano	Truants	Steals from dime store
Drinks the father's beer	Truants Tells lies	Doesn't attend Obligation Services Eats meat on Friday	Doesn't read Bible	Refuses to do lessons	Destroys property
Strikes the "old man"	Stays out all night	Fools in church Doesn't say his daily prayers	Swears	Swears in classroom	Drives car without license Truants from school
Stays out all night	Gambles	Skips Sunday school. Doesn't read Bible	Plays cards	Smokes in school Wears "DA" haircut	Drives car beyond speed limit Doesn't mind teacher
Comes in late	Fights with sibs	Swears	Wears lipstick Misses Sunday service	Talks back to teacher	Loiters on street corner
Tells lies Gambles	Swears and uses bad language	Drinks wine & beer	Doesn't attend Sunday school	Marks up building	Creates disturbance in public library
Truants from school Sasses back	Doesn't do homework.		Goes to dances	Smokes on playground	Spits in street car
Fights with sibs Swears	Wears DA haircut Sasses parents Skips Sunday school	Plays Beano		Plays rough on playground	
Hangs around corner	Hangs around street corner	Smokes			
Plays cards	Doesn't do his chores	Goes to dances		Reads comics & "true stories"	Drinks beer
Wears "DA" haircut	Doesn't bathe			Smokes	Smokes
				Swears	Swears
				Smokes at home	

"Criteria for Severity": Form, intensity, frequency, seriousness, prior acts and relationship to individual personality.

confuse both the "delinquent" who is picked out because of his norm violations and the person who is doing the picking.

"Beano" parties may be outlawed in one community and permitted in another; in one church system sponsorship of this form of "indoor sport" (gambling) may be considered as highly immoral, while in another denomination it may provide the main source of income for charitable work. This sliding scale of values, implied in the rules and norms of different systems, raises a number of troublesome questions for persons working with delinquent youngsters: Just which norm-violators do we work with? Which norm-violators are to be studied in research endeavor? Which norm-violators have been counted in the annual census of juvenile delinquency reported by the U.S. Children's Bureau? In examining the sampling of delinquents found in various research studies reported in delinquency literature, one soon comes to realize how pertinent these questions are. Results of otherwise carefully managed research endeavors are too often limited or conflicting by reason of poor definition or no definition at all other than the vague "delinquency" label applied either freely or with particular bias. Even in instances where more precise definitions are offered, the researchers seldom safeguard their conclusions by limiting them to the special categories of norm-violators selected for study.

Table 6.1 points out clearly that an individual who acts in conformity with the values and norms of his effective reference system may appear to be engaged in serious and norm-violating behavior to an observer (teacher, police, group worker) whose point of reference represents values of another system. Another observer, seeing the same acts, may take into consideration the implicit definition of the appropriateness of the behavior for the particular area or group. For example, there is the street-corner youngster who during the course of an evening spent in "hanging out" will use profanity constantly, thus breaking the law against abusive language. In continuing to hang out on the street corner, he may be regarded as a "nuisance" by the passers-by and the candy store owner. In doing this every night, he repeatedly breaks the law against ungainful and idle loitering. He frequently raises such a commotion that he is liable to be arrested for disorderly conduct in a public place. This pattern of activity, since it continues night after night, is repetitive behavior and, from one vantage point, could be considered serious violation, meriting arrest and adjudication. But this happens only infrequently, because the police in the cruiser have an implicit definition, as do the passer-by and the owner of the corner variety store, which recognizes this behavior as fairly appropriate for this time and for this place.

Figure 6.2. Swearing as Norm-Violating Behavior in Different Institutional Systems (Adapted from Walter B. Miller).

Street Corner Gang	Adolescent lower class	Adolescent middle class	School	Legal Code
Swearing habitual; use of terms "bastard," "son-of-a-bitch," "hell." No "dirty" connotation	Frequent swearing: frequent use of terms commonly accepted as routine	Habitual swearing; use of terms now considered vulgar and "dirty," except for occasional term and in certain place	Swearing not countenanced; repeated offense involves expulsion; language considered "dirty" and offensive	Habitual swearing against legal code; seldom used as sole basis for delinquency complaint

As a further illustration of this flexible and shifting value system which makes a clear, unequivocal definition extremely difficult, Figure 6.2 presents one kind of norm violation (swearing and use of "dirty" language) within several institutional systems: street-corner gang, adolescent lower-class, adolescent middle-class, school, and legal code. In street-corner society, swearing is a form or sign of membership-demand or identity; profanity is not very meaningful and hardly considered "dirty." In adolescent middle-class society certain kinds of swearing, if part of the habitual speech pattern, may be regarded with raised eyebrows but would not be a problem if used occasionally and in the "right" company.

However, as Figure 6.2 indicates, in this middle-class system swearing takes on "dirty" or "vulgar" connotations which it lacks in lower-class adolescent society where the ear is accustomed to this speech pattern. In the school-institutional system, a single instance of such language may constitute a major transgression and can result in expulsion or suspension, especially if repeated in front of a teacher and a class. But, on the playground and within the appropriate group, swearing probably would not appear as a serious norm violation. Although the legal code specifies "foul and abusive language in a public place" as an offense, few judges would be inclined to adjudge the street-corner citizen as "delinquent" on the grounds of this norm violation alone, recognizing implicitly the appropriateness of such speech patterns to the essential reference system of the street-corner society or even the lower-class adolescent system. However, a youngster who lives and works in any one of these systems *could* be adjudged an official delinquent by the court for this norm violation.

In summary, then, the problem of whether or not a specific act should earn the offender the label "delinquent" is an intricate one. Consideration must be given to a great number of factors both general and situation-specific before such a decision can be justifiably reached. With the heavy stress placed upon cultural and social forces, we also need to take an equally long look at psychodynamic aspects in delinquent behavior.

7 Psychodynamic Aspects of Delinquency

How does the internal system of the self help explain why some youngsters become delinquent? What is the pattern of "healthy" psychological development? What types of delinquents can be identified? How much pathology exists among delinquents? What are some of the psychological implications of the female-based household for child growth and development? How dependent or independent is the delinquent? What is a female-based household? How prevalent is it and what are its psychological implications? What factors and forces in adolescence reinforce patterns of delinquency and aggression? Can the teacher serve as an "ego ideal"?

Norm-violating behavior, whether or not it violates specific legal norms, always represents an interaction between the organism and the culture. Thus far this discussion has placed stress on the cultural and subcultural genesis of norm-violating behavior, and has often emphasized the fact that the delinquent act never takes place in a vacuum. It is now necessary to acknowledge the equally important concept that the "psyche," or psychodynamic factors within the internal system, must also be considered in an effort to understand why any youngster becomes involved in delinquent behavior.[1] But in doing so, one must avoid the implied false dichotomy that tempts many who are seeking causes and cures to think in terms of the two discrete headings of "cultural forces" and "factors under the skin." The reciprocal relationship and interdependency of the complex of vari-

---

[1] This chapter has been drawn from the NEA Juvenile Delinquency Project, W. C. Kvaraceus, Walter B. Miller, *et al.*, *Delinquent Behavior: Culture and the Individual*, Chapter 11, and reflects heavily the contributions of Dr. Edward M. Daniels, M.D., and Walter B. Miller.

ables with roots in both areas must never be overlooked and requires constant attention.

The present discussion is not formulated on an either/or basis, as in the case of the great but sterile debates *re* nature or nurture, heredity or environment, personality or culture. Rather, this discussion must turn on how the cultural concerns and the internal forces, as seen in personal make-up, interact and combine in the individual to create a pattern of norm-violating behavior. Delinquent acts represent biocultural-psychological phenomena. Therefore, in considering each delinquent act, the youth worker must raise the diagnostic question, "To what extent is this behavior a function of the internal system, including the biological, and to what extent is it attributable to the culturally based external system?" In the following section of this report, factors within the personal make-up of the delinquent will be closely examined.

Pathology in Norm-Violating Behavior: Incidence

The discussion of typology of norm-violating individuals identifies four major types or modalities. Most boys and girls, of course, fall into the quadrant of "the adjusted child" who does not habitually engage in serious norm-violating behavior. These are the youngsters who generally have a fairly clean record. This discussion, however, is concerned with those serious and persistent norm-violators who fall into the third category by reason of emotional disturbances which place them high on the pathology scale. Lacking any definite survey or census data, it is possible only to hypothesize on the basis of existing studies and current trends that this group of emotionally disturbed norm-violators embraces the smallest segment of the delinquent population, albeit it receives the major portion of the community's attention and assistance.

A number of factors have contributed to a false impression of a much higher incidence of delinquents in the category of the emotionally disturbed, persistent, and serious norm-violator than actually exists in any day-to-day count. Institutional and court statistics and impressions, on which most studies are based, represent specially screened (hence biased) samples of the population of norm-violating youngsters. The normal expectancy would be to find a spuriously high incidence of the emotionally disturbed in these samples. Likewise, studies based on cases in child-guidance clinics, which introduce a middle-class bias in terms of referral, as well as a constant focus and orientation to pathological elements in the syndrome, would be expected to yield data pointing to a high incidence of emotional disturbances

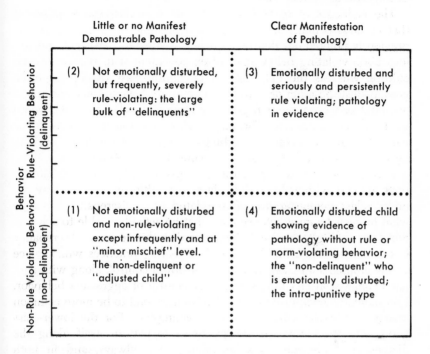

Little or no Manifest
Demonstrable Pathology

Clear Manifestation
of Pathology

Behavior

Rule-Violating Behavior
(delinquent)

(2) Not emotionally disturbed, but frequently, severely rule-violating: the large bulk of "delinquents"

(3) Emotionally disturbed and seriously and persistently rule violating; pathology in evidence

Non-Rule Violating Behavior
(non-delinquent)

(1) Not emotionally disturbed and non-rule-violating except infrequently and at "minor mischief" level. The non-delinquent or "adjusted child"

(4) Emotionally disturbed child showing evidence of pathology without rule or norm-violating behavior; the "non-delinquent" who is emotionally disturbed; the intra-punitive type

Figure 7.1. Typology of Individuals in Reference to Norm-Violating Behavior *(Adapted from Walter B. Miller).*

among serious norm-violating youngsters. Adding to the skewness found in the existing data available from institution, court, and clinic, the popular tendency in legal and professional circles has been to seek out causes and cures via the case-study and counseling method. Until very recently there has been relatively little visible interest in or concern with either the cultural and subcultural imprint or the sociology of the delinquent act. Again, the effect of this one-way orientation to norm-violating behavior has led to an almost exclusive focus on the pathological dimensions of delinquent behavior.

What is badly needed today is a carefully conducted census or survey to determine more exactly the true distribution of norm-violating youngsters within the modalities described in the simple typologies of youngsters. Such a survey would help to indicate that proportion of norm-violating youngsters who could be helped by the child-guidance clinic and counseling route and the number who must be approached through other methods in a directed effort to get at dynamic factors in the external systems rooted in culture and subculture.

The incidence of pathology, as it relates to class status, indicates that no class is immune to emotional illness and disturbances. It was previously pointed out that delinquency, defined as persistent and serious norm-violating behavior, is often consistent with the lower-class culture, whereas the behavior of the middle-class delinquent often goes against the grain of middle-class culture; hence, it becomes more obvious, and even more frightening, to middle-class parents, youth workers, and journalists. The middle-class delinquent is likely to be more disturbed and more disturbing. He appears more to be bucking his cultural milieu than to be acting consistently within it.

A somewhat different patterning of psychopathological manifestations appears within the middle class. Difficulties encountered by the middle-class youngster are often related to a discrepancy between what he feels he must achieve and what he actually is able to achieve. Some psychological research indicates that this sense of discrepancy is related to certain middle-class child-rearing practices which place strong emphasis on early and stringent bowel control, along with similar emphasis on cleanliness and early control of aggressive behavior. Consequently, compulsive types of responses tend to be more common among middle-class than lower-class youngsters. For the lower-class youngster, by contrast, pathology tends to pattern itself along the dimension of dependence-independence. But always, and in both classes, the possibility of pathology must be carefully checked out by the diagnosticians.

Disturbed youngsters within lower-class culture are often characterized as markedly impulsive. Many of them appear to evidence little impulse control in certain selected areas. This is probably related to the fact that parental child-rearing patterns do not emphasize the building-in of controls in these areas. These youngsters appear to reveal shallow super-ego (conscience) development and poor capacity to accommodate their inner drives in socially accepted ways (weak ego). In psychoanalytic terms, the id (inner drive) more easily gains control of them.

Moreover, the extent to which pathology appears in either class is a matter requiring attention and discrimination. A middle-class youth who persistently engages in serious violation of the law is more likely to reveal evidence of pathology than is a lower-class youth who is a chronic violator. But in neither milieu should pathology be hastily imputed to behavioral situations before the diagnostician is able to describe the behavior and what exists therein and thereout—in the internal system of the self and in the external system of the culture. In this check-out process care should be taken lest the diagnostician's own cultural values be unconsciously hidden in his set of descriptive terms.

Delinquent: A Useless Diagnostic Concept

There is general agreement among psychiatrists that, *diagnostically speaking, the youngster who violates norms can fall into any diagnostic category or into none at all, and that there is no diagnostic category of "delinquent" for youngsters who engage in or repeat illegal behavior.*

One cannot talk diagnostically of "a delinquent." When some measure of pathology is present in norm-violating behavior, many definitions of emotional disturbance or sickness are possible, and important symptoms of various types of disturbance may be found in delinquent actions. The pronouncement that a child is "a delinquent" is not the same as the clinical diagnosis that he is an epileptic. The concept of "a delinquent," then, may be ruled out as a useless and misleading diagnostic term.

In many instances, the delinquent act, defined as a violation of norms which brings the youngster to the attention of official authority, may be seen as representing a symptom. Truancy, a violation of school and legal norms, is an example of symptomatic behavior. In different situations, truancy may be: a symptom of the healthy rebellion of a normal adolescent who is willing to pay the price for this once-in-a-life-time indiscretion; a representation of demand behavior of gang members who hold the school in low esteem; a brief emotional recess period from a confining and unfriendly classroom climate; an indication of a serious conflict with parents who pressure a child to succeed and who are attacked by this act; or a symptom of a child's inability to face and cope with the realities of his daily life. Thus, behaviors which are very similar in form may fulfill very dissimilar functions for different individuals.

Brief Sketch of "Healthy" Psychological Development

A pattern of "healthy" psychological development is implied in the basic assumptions of the psychodynamic school of psychology. The developmental sequence it describes assumes the existence of a nuclear two-parent household of the type found in middle-class Western society. This pattern, as outlined by Dr. E. M. Daniels, is as follows:

The first person to whom the infant relates is his mother. During the postnatal period the child is gratified in his needs by feeding, fondling, and care. Some time around the age of four the boy becomes closely attached, as he was in infancy, to the mother, while the girl develops an attachment for the father. In this period, the boy resents the father, and the girl, the mother; each wants the opposite parent for himself (the Oedipal attachment). If the father and mother understand this process, they will be better able to tolerate the situation without excessive resentment and, at the same time, will let the child know he is loved. Gradually, around the age of six, the child gets the idea that the mother belongs to the father and that this must be accepted.

The first and fundamental stage of ego development is completed with the resolution of the Oedipal situation; the child now accepts the parent of like sex as a model, and, according to traditional theory, super-ego (conscience) development begins at this point. This identification of the child with the appropriate parent will profoundly influence the building of strong attitudes, values, and standards.

This is the pattern of "healthy" psychological development. Of course, the Oedipal attachment may begin earlier than age four; there is no conclusive evidence that the process may not take longer or that Oedipal conflicts will not reoccur during pubescence or in the young married adult, during pregnancy, child birth, or very early care of the new-born child. Here again, a satisfactory resolution will rest upon the nature of each earlier resolution.

Healthy psychological growth and development presupposes a "normal" or "healthy" ego and super-ego growth and maturation. Daniels describes this as meaning relative freedom from conflict among the three psychoanalytically conceptualized structural components of the personality: id, the seat of the impulses; ego, the correlating or integrating aspect of the personality; and super-ego, roughly equivalent to conscience. More specifically, healthy development involves the ability to resolve conflict so that a good equilibrium or balance of relationships among these forces results.

A healthy ego is capable of reconciling or resolving, without disruptive conflict, inner and outer demands. It is characterized by freedom from neurotic conflict, flexibility, and the ability to accept adult obligations. It is able to exercise control demanded by oneself and by one's social group. Finally, it is capable of achieving a successful adaptation to the changing demands of life.

In assisting the ego and super-ego to normal and healthy growth and development, as well as in repairing dysfunctioning of these components in rehabilitating the personality, much depends on the quality of the relationships between the child, his parent or parents, and those who stand ready to help him to better adjustment. These relationships involve important elements of positive identification and affection.

The dynamics of discipline, translated into psychoanalytic terminology, involve assisting and permitting the ego to establish limits. The individual must learn what is expected of him in the cultural milieu in which he is to function. A child brought up in a predictable manner at home, at school, and in the neighborhood has the best chance of building a personally secure ego.

The Dynamics of the Female-Based Household

Dr. Walter B. Miller, in his research concerning the street-corner gang, has identified a prevalent type of household unit in lower-class communities that frequently takes the form of a female-based household. This type of family unit has been described as "one in which a male acting in the 'father' role is either absent from the home, only sporadically present, or, when present, only minimally or inconsistently involved in the support and raising of children."[2] In this type of household, one frequently finds a grandmother (or other female relatives) and one or more daughters who are child bearing. Frequently associated with this type of household is the "serial monogamy" mating pattern in which the child-bearing female lives with a succession of mates or temporary "husbands." Figure 7.2 illustrates one variant of the female-based household. Living in this home are three females: grandmother, one child-bearing female, and her sister. There are three children: two of them (a boy and a girl), the children of the first husband; and one (a boy), the child of the second mate. This type of female-based household today represents a fairly stabilized form of household. It is much more common in large urban centers than most people suspect and is prominent in the lower-class Negro community. Miller has estimated that between 25 and 50 per cent of all household units in lower-class urban neighborhoods, particularly in and around the larger housing projects, fall into the category. This female-based household pattern has many implications for the psychological and social growth and development of youngsters reared in such a home setting.

The psycho-social implications of the female-based household point to a number of hazards to the healthy growth and development of

---

[2] Walter B. Miller, "Implications of Lower Class Culture for Social Work," *The Social Service Review*, XXXIII, No. 3 (Sept., 1959).

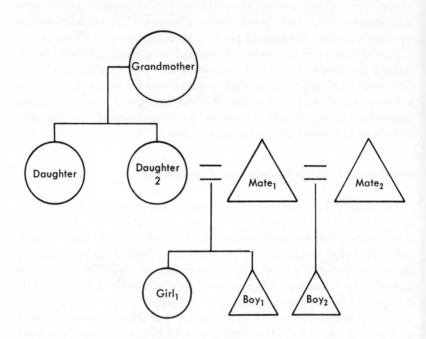

Figure 7.2. Typical Household Structure of Female-Based Household *(Adapted from Walter B. Miller).*

children and youth. Lacking a positive father figure, a young son living in such a family may experience more than the ordinary amount of difficulty in personality growth, especially when trying to resolve the Oedipal phase of the growth process. At the same time, the presence or the shadow of an inadequate, negative, or unsuccessful father figure may constantly beam the conflicting messages: "Don't be a bum like your father;" "All men are no good." What is presented here is a *model for non-identification* with the attendant problem of overt rejection or dissociation of the male-parent figure. This is particularly true of Negro households as the Elmira report[3] points out. In the dearth of positive male figures as found in older brothers or male kin, the Negro boy (or white lower-class youngster) may not be adequately sustained even by the traditional matriarchal family in which the mother plays the male role as well as she can. He may need to seek his male identification through association with his street-corner group. In testing and proving his maleness, he may engage in feats and episodes that involve norm-violating behavior and bring him to the attention of an official

---

[3] *The Elmira Study, op. cit.,* pp. 45-53.

agency or authority. Since personality formation rests heavily upon identification with the appropriate parental figure, the preponderance of the female-based household, as Miller has pointed out, may have special significance in the higher delinquency rates of lower-class culture.

This type of home is frequently contacted by the community social worker and the school visitor. In a recent visit to such a household, one welfare worker found a mother whose six children were the issue of different fathers. On the wall of the kitchen were pictures of Mates One, Two, and Three, each surrounded by his own children. Each child appeared to identify easily and correctly with his own father. The visitor urged the mother to marry the current mate and to offer the children an "intact and permanent home." In giving her reason for not marrying him, the mother said, "I've learned that once you get married to them, they become a lot less dependable. You know, they just run out and don't pay much attention to you or to the family. This way they stick around closer to the home and the family." Although a middle-class worker may find a home and a response like this difficult to deal with, the existence of this type of household can be neither denied nor seen as representing an extreme or isolated instance. It is more common than is generally recognized—comprising between 25 and 50 per cent of all household units in lower-class communities of major urban centers[4]—and its implications must be faced and taken into account, particularly in trying to understand the psychological development and the ultimate behavior of many youngsters reared under these circumstances.

What are some of the psychological implications of this form of household for child growth and development? It is important to recognize that a home like this is not predicated on the stable and dependable presence of mate or mates working together in the joint enterprise of rearing children in the pattern of the middle-class nuclear household. The absence or undependable presence of a father affects child-rearing practices and psychosexual growth patterns.

The mother who did not yield to the visiting welfare worker's pressures to marry her current mate may make an honest effort to be the best mother in the world, but she is only the mother. Both boys and girls lacking a father figure may experience difficulty in development by failing to resolve the Oedipal phase in the growth of their per-

[4] A. Hollingshead, *Elmtown's Youth* (New York: John Wiley & Sons, Inc., 1949), p. 117; U.S. 84th Congress, Senate Subcommittee on Low-Income Families, *Characteristics of Low-Income Population: Report of the U.S. Senate Subcommittee on Low-Income Families* (Superintendent of Documents, Government Printing Office, 1955), p. 48; Files of the Boston Public Housing Authority, 1957.

sonality. Dr. B. R. Hutcheson points out that problems of dependency, which first occur during early stages of psychosexual development, tend to recur, as mentioned above, during adolescence; if these problems are poorly resolved during earlier stages, the adolescent's reactivated dependency concerns may be a factor in certain kinds of delinquent behavior. Dr. Hutcheson's research also indicates that certain types of "crisis" situations, which occur more frequently in lower than middle-class families (e.g., drunken arguments, household disruptions due to illness, separations) may be an important influence in motivating certain kinds of delinquent acts.[5]

At any level of society and within any social milieu, there are always many different modes of reaction and adjustment, depending upon the particular situation. Within the type of lower-class household described here, there are a number of factors that will assist or handicap the child in successfully resolving the Oedipal problem, and this situation will be important in his psychological development. The following variables may be of particular significance: (a) the extent to which the mother herself has achieved maturity; (b) the degree to which she can fill both male and female roles; (c) the ordinal position of a given child; (d) the degree to which men have been painted as "no good" to the child; (e) the availability of satisfactory male figures with whom to make a positive identification; (f) the individual's basic biological endowment and perceptual equipment or tendencies; (g) the degree of conflict or consonance between those prescriptions which he gets through home, school, or church and the practices of his immediate surroundings; (h) the over-all nature of the neighborhood or community; (i) the presence of older and younger boys in the family; and (j) the success of the settlement house and the school in recognizing needs and providing an individualized program.

There have been notable attempts to develop an understanding of the "basic personality" of races, cultures, and even nations. Dr. Miller has suggested that the female-based household pattern may, in effect, tend to create a basic personality orientation for the lower-class individuals reared in such units.

Independence—Dependence Concern

Another basic vector of personality growth and development in lower-class culture relates to the strong independence concern. In ob-

---

[5] See: B. R. Hutcheson *et al.*, "A Classification of Delinquents Based on Treatment Needs." Paper presented to New England Regional Meeting of AAPCC, April 1958.

serving delinquents from this milieu, one frequently witnesses loud, overt manifestations of independence and autonomy in such expressions as: "Nobody is going to push me around"; "I don't need nobody to look after me"; and—as every teacher and principal will recognize—the familiar, "Make me do it. Just try and make me." But, at the same time, in the words and actions of these youngsters one can sense an implicit need or seeking for dependence, and the behavior of many delinquents indicates that they seem to act in such a way that they will be caught. In fact, many of them repeat their delinquencies a second and third time, almost as if they were trying to insure apprehension. Because a law breaker generally follows a standard, repetitive patterning in his acts, many police departments have found it profitable to build up and maintain "MO (*modus operandi*) Files" on individual law violators; this has frequently enabled the police to pick up the right youth, who seems to need to leave some trace of his identity behind him. Likewise, attention must be called to the high recidivism rate among young law offenders in most training schools, the returnees who swear, "They will never get me back in here again." In no time they are back.

This same factor can be seen operating in the constant search for excitement, thrill, and danger in street-corner culture. Whatever the consequences of these episodes may be, the youngster tends to attribute them not to self, but to the impersonal operation of "fate" or "luck." Youngsters in this milieu lean heavily on this explanation, showing why it isn't their "fault," why there was nothing that they could do about it anyway.

The building of the ego is dependent upon the kind of attention the individual receives, and this, in turn, defines the content of the super-ego—its models, values, and growth potential. The ego and super-ego of an individual grow not only on what he himself thinks he is and thinks he represents but also on what he surmises others think he is. Needless to say, these processes are subject to distortion, for not only is perception itself fallible, but often further distortion arises from psychological immaturity.

The act that is seemingly oriented to independence, while covertly reaching for dependence, is frequently visible in norm-violating behavior and may constitute the mechanism by which the delinquent youngster tests parent, teacher, police, and clergy in an effort to discover what they really think of him. At this point, the youth may accept whatever definition is given to him. In brief, there is a need to explore how much of the lower-class delinquents' norm-violating behavior indicating serious and persistent involvement with authority reflects a syndrome crystallized around a strong dependency craving. This craving is in marked contrast to the compulsive syndrome built around achievement and "getting ahead," which represents a different but parallel concern for middle-class youngsters.

Achievement and "Getting Ahead"

Unlike the strains and pressures experienced by lower-class youngsters in relation to the independence-dependence area, the middle-class child's major pressures and conflicts frequently emanate from the dominating concern for achieving and "getting ahead" and the ensuing sense of discrepancy between aspiration and achievement. This strong focus in the middle-class milieu may induce the whole perfectionist-compulsive syndrome, in which children have impossible ideas of what they should accomplish; the result for some individuals is a combination of neuroses built around the individual's inability to achieve internalized goals of various types; e.g., learning to read, being on the honor roll, or getting into the college of first choice.

Lest this generic pattern be overdrawn, it must be acknowledged that within the middle-class group there is a wide range of individual modes of adjustment or reaction, depending on a range of factors that includes the unique developments within the small family group and the impact on the developmental pattern of specific relationships within the family. The stresses imposed through the conflict over aspiration and achievement evoke a wide variety of symptoms. One of these symptoms may take the form of norm-violating behavior. However, the more solitary, introspective, and withdrawn the youngster, the more likely he is to become the nail-biting, frightened paranoid who is lost in his fantasies. And this type of child can also become a delinquency problem to the community.

Some Conflicting Directives

Dr. Daniels points out that youngsters in both lower- and middle-class levels experience conflicting directives beamed to them by their parents in regard to aspiration and achievement. Parental images speak out to the child, saying, "I will give love to you *if* you better me, and I will withhold love *if* you fail to better my mark." Frequently, the first-generation immigrant parent enlarges upon this by saying, "I will give love to you if *and only if* you best me and do better in life than me. I am going to sacrifice and give you all the opportunities I never had. My son isn't going to work and slave like me. He is going to be a doctor or a lawyer." But another wave length, less explicit but equally certain, also comes through to the youngster: "You'd better not best me, or I'll. . . ." The first invocation is seldom heard without the contradictory echo.

Many a youngster dares not go beyond his parent or his group; and if he does accomplish more than his father or the other youngsters on his street, he may suffer from strong feelings of guilt. This youngster may refuse to compete with his father, to best him, or to get a better job, although he may inwardly resent his father and may find other ways to compete with him. If, in the absence of healthy psychological development in self and family relationships, the ground has already been readied for pathology, the possibility of delinquent reactions is likely.

Faced with these two essentially conflicting and contradicting directives transmitted softly or loudly by the parents and picked up by the youngster in accordance with his "auditory acuity," the receiver must make accommodations within the complex of family, neighborhood, and school involvements. In attempting to make the possible accommodations, some youngsters follow the route of norm-violating behavior. In this manner the child may retaliate by a symbolic attempt to injure the parent.

Other types of conflicting messages are beamed to many youngsters often considered delinquent. For example, a father at the middle-class level, while intending and hoping that his son will become a pillar of the church and community, also seems to enjoy and to approve of pranks or mischievous acts (norm-violating behavior) that indicate that the youngster is definitely a real he-man and not a sissy. The lower-class mother in the female-based household furnishes an example of two conflicting, but simultaneous, messages on sexual behavior. The mother in this type of household, who expresses a clear concept of what a "nice girl" is and what constitutes a "good boy," sends out one set of directives to her daughter and carps: "Now, don't hang around with those bums at the drug store, and don't you go around with that Mary. She's not a nice girl, and I want you to be a nice girl." But, all the while, the mother is beaming another set of directives to her daughter which imply: "Prepare yourself to be the head of the family. Don't expect a steady man. Let me be a sister to you, and you be my sister." The implicit message tends to counteract the explicit message. The daughter, then, must work out some resolution to these two conflicting directives, and delinquent behavior may appear in the complex process of adaptation.

The Adolescent: Wearer of Many Masks

Aristotle once said that the adolescent is a player who dons one mask after another to see which one he likes best and which one fits best. At the same time, the youngster observes the reactions of others around him. He may even use certain masks to scare his elders. Today's adolescent tests alternative roles of a wide variety and with great rapidity. He senses, as he approaches adulthood, that he will have to make a decision to assume a relatively limited societal role.

This quick changing of masks creates much confusion for the adolescent as well as for his parents and teachers. Yet, the subject of his identify and future role must be seen as a primary concern to the growing adolescent. In this maturation process both the adolescent girl, concerned with "boys" and mating, and the adolescent boy, concerned with virility and masculinity, go through the process of testing and retesting a wide range of alternative behaviors. This can be disconcerting, even frightening, to parents and teachers, especially if they have forgotten or suppressed their own adolescent experiences.

Difficulties may arise when home and school try to protect themselves against this unpredictable adolescent. To crack down on the adolescent and to prevent him from trying out many different masks can interfere with the maturation process. School and home sometimes insist on an unreasonable amount of predictable stability. The ironbound parent and the institutionally rigid school that refuse to permit a necessary degree of flexibility may force out a defensive functional withdrawal of the child. It is this youngster who often becomes the sickest of the sick. He may, in the eyes of many offended adults, turn into the worst perpetrator of delinquent acts, acts which are engaged in defensively because the child does not know what else to do. This behavior is not thought out by the youngster but frequently represents a deep inner feeling that "This is the only thing I can do to get them to notice me."

This type of youngster is generally a solitary norm-violator rather than a member of a gang or group. An example is the child who sits in class and draws a lewd picture which he tries to hide when the teacher comes along. He sincerely doesn't want to exhibit it, but the teacher cuts into the instinctual fantasy which he carries on because he gets so little satisfaction from reality. An open clash can soon develop between the institution or the teacher and the individual. There may be little that is unusual about a child's drawing a dirty picture if not much is made of it. One teacher might say, "Why don't you get rid of that and come back to this job of . . . ," thus letting the incident assume its proper perspective. Another teacher, however, might shout, "Go to the principal's office!" or expose the child in front of the class, thus turning the incident into a major crisis.

The parent or teacher can err at either extreme; he can remain rigid and inflexible, or he can overempathize. The first type of adult may deny quite overtly that he was ever an adolescent and may insist on predictable stability; the second type may be found in the mother or teacher who tries to act as a "junior child" and thus reduces her own best potential. By trying too assiduously to act as a pal, a buddy, or a peer, the adult loses the peculiar role and effectiveness that can only come from a vertical parent-child or teacher-child relationship. After all, the child has many buddies and pals but only a few teachers and generally only one mother and father.

Most parents and teachers are protected and are enabled to function effectively in their adult roles by a certain degree of non-empathy and insulation that stems from an age-related difference in sensing and perceiving the vital concerns of adolescence. For example, the thirty-four-year-old mother may be reporting a measure of truth in her complaints about her fourteen-year-old daughter: "Really, I just don't understand Sally. She is so flighty and so interested in boys. Sometimes I think she doesn't act normal." Having forgotten much of her own behavior as an adolescent, having successfully repressed certain youthful tendencies, and having settled on certain limited alternatives in her adult role, she may be protected and insulated, in a functional way, from really close empathy with and understanding of the psychological set of her adolescent daughter. In fact, were these motives and feelings of the youngster fully evident to the parent, her effectiveness as a parent might even be impaired.

Nevertheless, the young mother or school teacher in trying to maintain discipline and in repressing her own deeper feelings, memories, and impulses with the complaint, "Why, I was never like that," may actually be pushing the adolescent in the same direction she once followed or would still like to follow. Internally, parent and teacher may be feeling, "I can't do this sort of thing any more. I am a pillar of the community." Many inner impulses, hidden or pushed down by the demands of the adult social role, can, when regarded in psychodynamic terms, hardly be "acted out." However, parent and teacher may be able to experience them vicariously. Through the "wild behavior" of the youngsters, parents and even teachers may find a way to thumb their noses figuratively at the "respectable" community or official authorities such as the school principal. In other words, the father or even the principal may subconsciously be feeling, "Boy, would I love to be driving that sports car with that cute little blonde beside me, and roaring down the street. That's living!" Sensing these things, though not consciously, parent and teacher may vicariously punish themselves for these forbidden impulses by cracking down on the young culprits who are "running wild" and "staying out late with different boys or girls."

Rebellion of the Adolescent

Rebellion is a time-honored and accepted characteristic of the adolescent, and it becomes especially visible when the fast-maturing boy and girl put on certain adult-like masks. In fact, the adolescent is almost expected to be rebellious, and, generally, this is considered a healthy sign in personality growth. Society in the United States seems to have little use for passive, pliant, and overly dependent youngsters who do not attempt to stand on their own two feet. Even the youngster who has lived quietly and who has never been in trouble until one day he suddenly picks up a book and throws it through a window may be regarded as showing a "delinquent" but positive development. Rebellion is a popular way of flexing growing muscles, of seeing what one is made of, and of testing how others see this emerging self. The boy who speeds in his dad's car or rides his motorbike fast and recklessly may, like a fledging, be trying his new wings. The louder the adult's "must not," the greater the rebellion. Perhaps in days gone by there was more tolerance for the proverbial sowing of wild oats than there is now, but today the machines and methods of rebellion are increasingly dangerous, particularly in urban life. Still, the youngster needs to find some way to prove to himself and others that he is becoming an adult. Such behavior is highly functional for the individual, and in order to help him on his way, the "whys" must be understood. Some behavior (it is difficult to estimate how much) of this "rebellious" type is frequently tossed into the "delinquent" category by irritated adults whose frustration-tolerance is low or has been lowered by these developments.

Mating Concern of the Adolescent

Violation of the norms relating to sex conduct haunts the delinquency field like a spectre, and parents and teachers have always been particularly alarmed and concerned when such violations are discovered. This is especially true of the girl delinquent involved in "business-transacted" delinquency.[6]

The basic focal concerns, involvements, and subjective perceptions of adolescents are, as previously indicated, quite different from those of adults. Moreover, as Dr. Miller has suggested, it obviously would be quite dangerous for the middle-class adult, obligated to support and maintain his family, to share the concerns which dominate adolescent culture. Were the young middle-class married woman to evince the same degree of sensitivity and receptivity in regard to mating as evidenced by the adolescent girl, the stability of her family situation would be severely threatened. The repression of the parent's perception of inner feelings of the adolescent creates a highly functional isolation that separates the two generations. The attempt to break through this insulation in order to obtain "more understanding of adolescents by adults and of adults by adolescents" may involve considerable danger.

Conversely, it would be nonfunctional for adolescents to feel and to adopt the set of focal concerns of married adults. A primary set of concerns for adolescents, especially girls, revolves around mating. Adolescence is the age period specifically designated by our culture for a primary preoccupation with mate-finding, and continuation of the race is predicated on this. Many parents today complain, "Boys, boys, boys —that's all she ever talks about, that's all my daughter ever wants to do, just go out with boys." It would be most unfortunate for future family life if boys and girls were to cut off or pull in their psychic radar antennae which scan the neighborhood, the school campus, and the youth group, acutely sensitive to every possibility in the form of a potential future mate.

Contrary to the recently proposed concept of "psycho-social moratorium," which implies that adolescents pass through a certain period in which they are disenfranchised from the basic concerns of their culture, the youngsters utilize this period most productively in preparing for one of their most important adult roles by finding an appropriate mate and getting ready for the establishment of a family unit. Here is a highly functional aspect of adolescent culture. This is not to deny that as discussed earlier, adolescent youth are to some degree "disenfranchised" from full involvement in the economic, technological, and political order, but this is true of all societies. Perhaps in the United States many adolescents are "too long on ice," and it is possible that problems may result for some in this kind of exile.

---

[6] Milton L. Barron utilizes this term to refer to delinquent behavior that comes under the purview of official authority.

Pathology: Some Variability and Differentials

It can readily be seen from this discussion that the degree of pathology in a delinquent act may range from little or none to severe and deep-seated pathological disturbance. Where pathology is present, psychiatric examinations of the delinquent may reveal evidence of psychosis, neurosis, or character disorder, which may be classified according to a range of subtypes within these broad categories.

Some emotionally disturbed, norm-violating youngsters are diagnosed as depressives. Delinquent acts may be committed to compensate for major defects the youngster sees in his own life or body image: he views himself as tremendously deprived, and his delinquent acts are attempts to get something—whether attention as in challenge to authority, or possession as in theft—to make up for his imagined inner deficiencies and to make him more of a real and respectable person. Another type of delinquent who evidences serious pathology is sometimes described as a "borderline psychotic." He has extreme difficulty in coping with his impulses—if he wants something, he may steal it; if he has the urge to destroy something, he may destroy it.

A third type of delinquent is the youngster who is mentally retarded; having difficulty in distinguishing clearly between "good" and "bad," he may commit serious blunders or needlessly engage in violent destruction. This youngster, if he has higher mental abilities and social competencies than many others in the retarded group, can present a special problem, in that he may tend to rely on violence as a direct means of attracting attention. For example, in schools for the mentally retarded, where the "brighter" youngsters receive more responsibility than the less able, members of the "brighter" group will frequently break windows, fight, or steal in an attempt to gain some of the attention and recognition given to the less able. Although the analogy is in no way exact, it might be pointed out here that similar patterns may develop in any school where gifted, average, and slow students are housed in the same classroom and where the teacher's pronounced concern for one group might cause the others to "act up" in an effort to gain attention.

In some delinquents, pathology may take the form of "hysteria," a neurotic pattern in which physical symptoms are substituted for repressed emotional conflict, and which responds quite readily to treatment. Factors relating to hysteria may underlie the behavior of girls who engage in promiscuous sexual relations to reassure themselves that they are sexually effective, but whose basic problem may derive from a deep-rooted fear of sexual inadequacy and possible frigidity.

Considering delinquent symptoms in terms of the broad spectrum of pathological typology frequently results in varying and even conflicting interpretations by competent and experienced medical authorities. In classifying one symptom of a single individual, diagnosticians often offer differing interpretations of the significance and meaning of the behavior for that individual. The existence of such disagreements during this period of varying interpretations should be recognized by teachers and other youth workers, but it is incumbent on them to understand and to be tolerant of the problems of medical and psychiatric authorities in their attempts to work out a system of diagnostic classification.

The Teacher: Ego Ideal

Positive identification is a major component of sound personal development. For a good many years of the child's early life, the teacher is a daily point of reference in the building of the youngster's ego and super-ego. It is difficult to prescribe a formula for a good model for identification. Psychodynamically, this ideal is dependent on many specifics in the teacher's relationship to the student and the student's relationship to the teacher. A few of the variables that make a clear-cut definition difficult would include the following: the age, sex, and social class of the teacher and student; the pattern of interpersonal relationships within the group; the degree of emotional and mental health of teacher and student; the consistency of disciplinary techniques employed by different teachers and by the same teacher, emotional climate of the school; home attitudes toward the teacher or teachers in general; and, more specifically, the personality of the teacher himself.

Defining the characteristics of the teacher as an effective role model is a complex but not impossible task. In Chapter 20 we shall present a list of proficiencies which have been endorsed by teachers working closely with the socially maladjusted and the emotionally disturbed and also by a committee of experts.

The Common Need: Setting Limits

Although symptoms manifested in norm-violating behavior may be similar in form, the underlying personality problems may be very different. If there is a common denominator, it is to be found in the idea that each child needs to be helped constantly to conform to limits which are reasonable for him and which are demanded by his community. This concept runs counter to the common myth that psychiatrists have urged complete self-expression; no sound psychiatrist has ever denied the need for the establishment of ego-limits.

Limit setting is a vital element in permitting and assisting every child to learn rules and regulations and to abide by them. The child must learn what is expected of him, and this is true in every culture and sub-culture.

The child can learn limits from many sources, including his gang. One difficulty is related to the fact that limits often become identified with maleness or femaleness, according to the emotional significance of persons with whom the child identifies in early life. This might involve a concept of "mother" in the lower-class type of female-dominated household different from that of the two-parent, middle-class household. Each situation presents its own variety of problems. A boy out on a window-breaking spree "for fun" may assess the relative weight of conflicting directives: "My mother (or teacher) says this is not the thing to do, but, hell, she's only a woman. The kids in my gang say to do it, so I guess I better."

A major basis for learning limits which one really accepts is identification. This concept has many implications for parents and teachers. It is central to the question of how best to establish a strong two-way relationship between parent and child, teacher and student. This means that neither school nor parent can hope to help the delinquent in setting and living by limits unless the youngster senses that the relationship includes important elements of real affection.

8 The Cultural Psychological Issue: A Review and Reappraisal

Current focus and funding in delinquency control and prevention have been directed mainly at community, neighborhood, and gang rather than on the individuals as seen in a clinical context. Federal and private support of programs for delinquency prevention and control through child-guidance clinics has hit an all-time low. The cultural rather than the libidinous origins of delinquency now hold the limelight. What are some of the factors concerning delinquency as a problem stemming from forces at work in the lower socio-economic milieu? Why is there a growing concern for middle-class and suburban delinquency?

A study made by the author in 1943 showed that the large majority of delinquents who turned up in research studies in America seemed to stem from the lower status groups. There was, for example, marked skewness in the social distribution of a Passaic, New Jersey, sample of delinquents as follows:

The Passaic data gathered on 761 delinquents reveal that significantly fewer parents of the sample population (delinquents) were earning their living in the professions by working as proprietors, clerks, and sales personnel, craftsmen,· and in services other than domestic. At the same time, significantly larger proportions were found to come from the factory operatives, W.P.A., other laborers and domestic services. It should be noted that these latter groups represent the economically and socially frustrated classes. It is highly probable that delinquent-aggression has its roots in the conflicts and frustrations that take place in the lower-lower, upper-lower, lower-middle and to some extent upper-middle classes, which are made up largely by families who earn their living in the manner of the Passaic delinquents.[1]

Another major statistical fact about the incidence of juvenile delinquency in Passaic strongly suggested the extent to which overt aggression in response to chronic and severe frustration and dissatisfactions arising out of certain negative school experiences served as a primary etiological factor in delinquency causation. Significant was the fact that the lowest number of referrals occurred during the months when schools were not in session, and the highest in the months of peak school tension during spring and autumn.

More specifically, the school picture revealed the following:

A significant difference was noted in the matter of nonpromotion. Almost all delinquents had repeated one or more grades. Many repeated several grades and were overage for their placement. Girl delinquents had repeated more grades than had boy delinquents.

The delinquents, almost without exception, received very low marks. Less than 2 per cent of the marks of the delinquents in the sample fell in the top A, B, C categories, as against 64 per cent of the marks received by their nondelinquent counterparts. Reciprocally, 30 per cent of the grades of the delinquents were in the failure category as against only 6 per cent awarded in the general school population.

A third of the delinquents were known to have been truant prior to their referral.

Two-thirds of the delinquent sample expressed strong dislike for school and classroom or for some person connected with the school program.

In general, the school picture of the delinquent presented an unsatisfactory, unsuccessful, unhappy, and hence extremely frustrating situation which preceded or accompanied law-violating behavior. While the delinquent child may be an inescapable headache for the school, at the same time it is true that the school is frequently an even greater headache for the child. How many youngsters actually drop out of school today and how many are really pushed out is still a moot question.

But these data were gathered in 1940. Now, twenty-six years later, the question of delinquency in relation to class status and school performance is again raised.

---

[1] William C. Kvaraceus, "Juvenile Delinquency and Social Class," *Journal of Educational Sociology*, 18 (September, 1944), p. 54; *Juvenile Delinquency and the School* (New York: Harcourt, Brace & World, Inc., 1945).

In regard to achievement behavior and norm-violating behavior, earlier investigators in the 1940's and 1950's perhaps overemphasized the social-class variable as a salient feature. More recent, and perhaps more sophisticated, studies, while holding the social-class variable as important, also take note of other intervening variables which tend to diminish or minimize the social-class factor. For example:

Brookover, Paterson, and Thomas[2] demonstrated that higher socio-economic status is related to academic achievement, but their sample included 40 per cent of high achievers who came from lower-income families. These investigators inferred that self-concept may, under certain conditions, have as much effect on academic achievement as does socio-economic status.

Still other researchers, Herriott, for example,[3] have indicated that academic aspirations are closely related to self-assessment and to expectations of significant or prestigious persons close to the learner.

Sexton's Big City study[4] offers another set of reasons why pupils from lowest socio-economic families often have the lowest rates of academic success. She reported that schools in depressed areas seldom received their equal share of school wealth and that they were seldom favored with the most experienced teachers, the newest materials, or the most recent educational innovations. They were truly deprived in the economics of teaching and learning.

The HARYOU Ghetto study[5] emphasized the importance of the intervening variable of mutually negative—even hostile—attitudes on the part of school staff and parents. There seemed to be no way out of the impasse in which teachers were convinced that the students could not or would not learn and the parents (and pupils) were equally convinced that the school couldn't or wouldn't teach them much of anything.

For the lower-class youngster in the inner-city school, the academic situation has probably worsened. Since the degree of retardation increases with school attendance, as HARYOU data dramatically and tragically point out, the schools can be accused of teaching the youngsters that they cannot learn.

---

[2] Wilbur B. Brookover, Ann Paterson, and Shailer Thomas, *Self-Concept of Ability and School Achievement* (East Lansing: Office of Research and Publications, College of Education, Michigan State University, 1962).

[3] Robert E. Herriott, "Some Social Determinants of Educational Aspiration," *Harvard Educational Review*, 33 (Spring, 1963), 155-77.

[4] Patricia C. Sexton, *Education and Income: Inequalities of Opportunity in Our Public Schools* (New York: The Viking Press, Inc., 1961).

[5] Harlem Youth Opportunities Unlimited, *Youth in the Ghetto* (New York: HARYOU, 180 West 135th Street, New York City, 1964).

This section reports some of the findings in two separate Massachusetts studies.[6] Both investigations have aimed (1) to estimate the distribution of norm violations among social classes, (2) to note the exact relationship between social-class mobility, norm violations, and academic behavior, and (3) to draw some implications for theory in the current concern for the social-class variable as a salient feature in the causation of delinquent behavior. Both of these studies indicate that norm violations are more evenly spread through all social strata, that class status *per se* appears a less important determiner of delinquent behavior than most theories now hold, and that the abrasive dynamics found in mobility—upward and downward—hold the more significant elements of causation. Achievement in reading, academic performance, occupational choice and aspiration, and educational aspirations all appeared to have a significant bearing on where the youngster fell on the norm-conforming and norm-violating continuum of behavior.

Old Colony Study

Gerald J. Pine[7] conducted his investigation in a New England community with a rich historical tradition, which will be referred to as Old Colony. The sample included 683 pupils in grades nine through twelve, representing the general school population of adolescents. The sample was stratified into three social-class status groups (upper-middle, lower-middle, and lower), three social-mobility status groups (up, down, stable), six occupational-aspiration groups, and three education-aspiration groups. In obtaining stratification data, the following instruments were used: Warner's ISC, a multi-factor mobility scale consisting of eight different factors, and a questionnaire entitled "Vocational and Education Data Sheet." Information regarding delinquent behavior was collected through the use of a self-reporting questionnaire coded to preserve anonymity. One hundred twenty items made up this in-

---

[6] The Rim City, Massachusetts, study reported herein was supported through the Cooperative Research Program of the Office of Education, U.S. Department of Health, Education, and Welfare; the Old Colony, Massachusetts, study was carried out by Gerald J. Pine in partial fulfillment of degree requirements for a doctorate and was submitted as a dissertation entitled, "The Significance of the Relationship Between Class Status, Social Mobility, and Delinquent Behavior" at Boston University, June, 1963.

[7] See also Gerald J. Pine, "Occupational and Educational Aspirations and Delinquent Behavior," *Vocational Guidance Quarterly* (Winter, 1964-65), 107-110 and "Social Class, Social Mobility, and Delinquent Behavior," Paper presented at the APGA Conference, San Francisco, 1964.

strument designed to obtain a measure of an individual's degree of involvement in several categories of norm-violating behavior. From the delinquency inventory, fifteen scores were obtained for each individual. The relationships between social class, social mobility, occupational and educational aspirations, and the fifteen delinquency variables were analyzed for statistical significance using chi-square.[8] Delinquency variables included: number of offenses, school offenses, delinquency treatment, gross delinquency score, property damage, misdemeanors, theft, truancies, family violations, alcohol offenses, collective participation, serious offenses, physical assault offenses, motor vehicle offenses, narcotics offenses. The .05 level of probability was employed as the criterion level for significance. Relationships between social-class status, social-mobility status, and delinquency variables were further tested by controlling the data for grade and sex.

No significant relationships were found to exist between social-class status and twelve of the fifteen delinquency variables (Table 8.1). Significant relationships were found to exist between social-class status and alcohol offenses, serious offenses, and collective participation in delinquent acts. Upper-middle-class students were found to be more involved in alcohol offenses and were also found to participate more in delinquent behavior as a collective activity than were students from the other two classes. Proportionately more members of the lower-middle class and lower classes were involved in serious offenses than were members of the upper-middle group. Among the groups controlled by grade and sex, one relationship was found to be significant.

No significant relationship was found to exist between social-class status and delinquency treatment scores. No differences were forthcoming as to what agencies had contact with the offenders from various classes, and no preferential treatment was accorded the offenders of higher status, contrary to general impressions that are frequently maintained.

Significant relationships were found to exist between social-mobility status and fourteen of the fifteen delinquency variables (Table 8.2). Students moving *downward* in the social structure were more involved in physical assault offenses, theft, felonies, school offenses, and alcohol offenses. Proportionately they had higher gross delinquency scores and delinquency treatment scores; they participated in more norm viola-

---

[8] The chi-square (X^2) statistical test rests on one sample error theory that enables us to discover whether or not some significant relationship, other than chance, had determined the distribution in the samples studied—in our case distributions between delinquent and nondelinquent groups on various factors such as class status, social mobility, aspiration level, etc.

tions; and their norm violations were more collective-type activities than individual. Students moving *upward* in the social structure were least involved in the offenses cited and had lower delinquency treatment scores and lower gross delinquency scores. Students in the stable-mobility position were more heavily involved in family violations than members of the other two classes. Fifty-one of the sixty relationships among the groups controlled by grade and sex were found to be statistically significant.

Table 8.1.   A Summary of Chi-Square Tests of Significance Between Socio-Economic Status and Delinquent Behavior—Old Colony Study, N 674 (F361, M320), Grades 9-12.

Delinquency Variable	X^2	P
Collective Participation in Delinquent Acts	109.711	.001*
Serious Offenses	27.665	.001*
Alcohol Offenses	16.246	.05 *
Property Damage	15.210	.10
Family Violations	14.398	.10
Narcotics Offenses	12.863	.20
Physical Assault Offenses	8.389	.50
Delinquency Treatment	7.335	.50
Theft	5.748	.70
Truancies	5.609	.70
School Offenses	5.423	.80
Gross Delinquency Score	4.855	.80
Motor Vehicle Offenses	3.569	.90
Number of Offenses	3.449	.95
Misdemeanors	2.489	.98

* Significant at or better than 5% level
8 degrees of freedom

Significant relationships were found to exist between educational aspirations and ten of the fifteen delinquency variables. Adolescents aspiring to enter college were least or moderately involved in the delinquency offenses; adolescents definitely planning no further education after high school were more heavily involved in delinquency offenses.

Significant relationships were also found to exist between occupational aspirations and four of the delinquency variables (narcotic offenses, family violations, alcohol offenses, and number of offenses).

Table 8.2. A Summary of Chi-Square Tests of Significance Between Social-Mobility Status and Delinquent Behavior—Old Colony Study, N 674 (F361, M320), Grades 9-12.

Delinquency Variables	X²	P
Number of Offenses	167.616	.001
School Offenses	57.700	.001
Delinquency Treatment	51.535	.001
Gross Delinquency Score	43.115	.001
Property Damage	34.431	.001
Misdemeanors	31.660	.001
Theft	30.982	.001
Truancies	30.131	.001
Family Violations	27.767	.001
Alcohol Offenses	27.280	.001
Collective Participation in Delinquent Acts	26.187	.001
Serious Offenses	24.477	.01
Physical Assault Offenses	22.308	.01
Motor Vehicle Offenses	16.586	.05
Narcotics	10.107	.30 *

* Not significant
8 degrees of freedom

Rim City Study

The Rim City Study was conducted by the author on the rim of the Metropolitan Boston area and represents an extension of a three-year delinquency prediction experiment started at the junior high school level (grades 7-9) in 1956.[9] During this three-year period, pupil behavior that ran counter to some established rule, regulation, or law in school and community was noted and recorded with the help of teachers, counselors, principals, police, and juvenile court officials. These reports were used to categorize the subjects in accordance with the type, severity, and persistence of the offenses. Four major rubrics were established as follows: 0—those subjects for whom no offenses of any kind were recorded during the three-year period of the study; 1—those subjects for whom only minor school offenses had been recorded; 2—those subjects for whom both school and community of-

---

[9] William C. Kvaraceus, "Forecasting Delinquency: A Three-Year Experiment," *Exceptional Children*, (April, 1961), 429-435. The research reported herein was performed pursuant to the contract with the United States Office of Education, Department of Health, Education and Welfare, Extension of Project No. 6403, Boston University, Boston, Massachusetts.

fenses were recorded, but for whom no "legal action" was taken; 3—those subjects who were engaged in serious and persisting norm violations and on whom some legal or official action had been taken by police or court. In a sense, these divisions represent a continuum ranging from "none" or "never" through "serious" and "legal offender."

Table 8.3 represents the initial breakdown by sex and degree of norm violation for the sample employed in the study. Following graduation from high school, actual decision data were obtained on nine variables believed to indicate some evidence of mobility (up, down, stable). These shifts in directions were based on multiple factors, including change of residence, school leaving, course selection, educational aspirations, occupational decisions, and participation in certain extraclass activities, as measured against the parental picture. For example, the son of a lawyer who failed in his studies and quit school and who obtained a job as a salesman was scaled as downward-mobile; the daughter of a truckdriver who became a practical nurse was classified as stable; the son of a factory operative who received a scholarship in a liberal arts college and who was planning a law career was listed as upward-mobile.

Table 8.3. Rim City Sample of Seventh-Grade Boys and Girls and Degree of Norm Violation.

Degree of Offense	Boys	Girls	Total
0 (no violations)	62	108	170
1 (minor in school)	49	30	79
2 (in school and community)	25	10	35
3 (legal offenders)	10	5	15
Total	146	153	299

Using the original seventh-grade sample, graduated from high school in 1962, all norm-violators, together with a sample of the "lily-whites," were stratified, using Warner's traditional ISC technique. The distribution for class status was dichotomized into "the uppers" and "the lowers." Approximately one-third of the sample made up the upper class and two-thirds fell into the lower-class category, thus reflecting the skewness estimated from 1960 census data based on parental occupation.

F ratios via analysis of variance were employed to estimate significance of differences between three criterion groups (minor offender in school, more serious in school and community, legal offenders) and those pupils who were never reported for norm violations against class-factors. Chi square (as explained earlier) could not be used in analyzing percentage differences on mobility dimensions because of the small numbers in certain cells. These data were inspected for trends, using graphic techniques. Currently a discriminate analysis is being planned between the never-offender vs. the combined 1 and 2 categories, with the exception of ultimately plotting the position of the legal offenders within a multi-variant analysis design.

No significant relationship was found between class status and degree of norm violation (Table 8.4), although a strong tendency toward significance is noted for boys.

Table 8.4.   Significance of Differences (F Ratio) between Four Rim City groups: Never norm-violating (M 62, F 108); minor norm violations in school only (M 49, F 30); more serious norm violations in school and community (M 25, F 10); legal norm violations (M 10, F 5).

Variable	Boys	Girls
Warner's SC Index	2.338	1.521
Dwelling Area (1956)	.839	1.554
Dwelling Area (1962)	.213	1.195
House Type	1.152	4.270**
Parental Occupation	1.564	1.993
Pupil's Occupational Choice	4.125**	4.103**
Income Source	.648	.489
Higher Scholarship Rank in Class	2.877*	.645
IQ CMM	2.450	3.498*

* Significant at 5 per cent level
** Significant at 1 per cent level

Girls living in less desirable houses appeared more vulnerable to norm-violating behavior. More significant, the occupational choices made by the student appeared as an important differentiator between the groups studied. The higher the level of occupational reach, the less norm-violating was the pupil. For boys, the higher the scholarship as reported in teachers' grades, the less likely were they to exhibit norm-violating behavior; for girls, those falling in the lower quartile on group measures of ability tended more often to show norm-violating behavior.

The data on mobility (up, down, stable) were less clear and definitive in the Rim City sample. Judging from trends using graphic techniques, the following tentative observations were made:

(1) Dropping out of school was more frequent with the norm-violating groups and tended to be associated more heavily with the downward movement of the uppers.

(2) Changes in residence area, up or down, showed little measured effect on the degree of norm violation.

(3) More movement and ferment were visible on occupational choice than on any other criterion. Heavy movement was visibile in both directions for all norm-violators, but the strongest trend was downward for the more serious offenders.

(4) Upper-class youngsters electing noncollege courses and who risked their status position tended to appear with higher frequency in norm-violating groups; conversely, high school seniors who actually entered college programs from either class (stable-upper and upward-moving lower) tended to be less frequently and less seriously norm-violating.

(5) Participation in extraclass activities for both lower- and upper-class pupils resulted in little differentiation among norm-violators.

(6) Lowest quartile performance in reading of upper-class pupils appeared to be more strongly tied in with degree of norm violation than did similar placement on group measures of mental ability.

Some Observations and Some Questions

Both studies tend to support the major conclusion that norm-violating behavior is less a function of the pupil's class status at the given moment and more a function of his class aspiration, vacillation, and dislocation. In the prevention and rehabilitation of minor or serious norm violators, it may not be as important to note what class the pupil is in as it is to know if he is securely located in the class, if he has just managed a toehold in the class, or if he is slipping down the rungs of the social-status ladder.

These data indicate that delinquent behavior is not the exclusive expression of the lower class; it cuts across class boundaries. Norm-violating behavior which is distributed nondifferentially among the social classes implies that delinquent behavior is not the inevitable product of any one cultural milieu. Although the factor of cultural milieu cannot be excluded from a consideration of primary delinquency determinants, the findings of the studies imply that it might be profitable to re-examine the weight of psychological factors in the development of delinquent behavior in all milieux.

Norm violation, as suggested by these two investigations, appears to be directly related to the psychological consequences of mobility. Theories of causation, prevention, and treatment may be in need of an overhaul in order to take into account the significance of mobility psychodynamics. Downward mobility, it appears, should be of special significance for those professionals concerned with the delinquency problem.

An individual's movement in the social structure plays a significant role in the development of his personality. In our culture, the personality of the child or the adult is linked in varying degrees to the competitive values of the quest for status and success. The individual has been taught to worship and evaluate his worth in terms of success goals, from the competition for marks in elementary school through the "status strain" of competing for a prestigious job, a suburban home, a car, a club membership, and other visible, measurable criteria of success as defined by the dominant value system.

Regardless of the cultural milieu one is nurtured in, it is most difficult to avoid shackling one's personality to these success goals. Communication media and the middle-class environment of the schools saturate the individual with the success ethic. His self-concept—the cluster of attitudes he has toward himself and his function or role in his primary reference group—is related to society's image of what constitutes the worthy individual, and in our schools and society one must succeed in order to have self-esteem.

One way to gain esteem—often the only way—is to do well in school. Going to school is an important business, and earlier research studies have confirmed that the delinquent has often been found to be academically bankrupt. Our two studies tend to reaffirm that adolescents who were terminating or curtailing their educational careers were more heavily involved in norm-violating behavior. Closely related to this is the low ceiling placed on occupational aspirations. Upperclass youngsters who did not go on to college and thus risked their status position appeared to be downward mobile and more vulnerable to delinquent behavior. The higher the scholarship for a boy, as reported by teachers' marks, the less likely is he to be found in the delinquent categories. Chronic subjection to failure experience with the attendant lack of any esteem from the school, the home, and the dominant community, particularly as seen with the middle- and upperclass youngsters, may be closely tied to the threat of loss in status and the development of a propensity for norm-violating behavior as a means of adjustment and even as a means of earning esteem. The terrible dependence on the diploma makes achievement behavior in school more and more a critical success factor.

For the adolescent, particularly, self-esteem is a crucial problem. The adolescent moving up in the social structure perceives himself more and more as a person of worth—a somebody—because he fits society's image of the worthy person. On the other hand, the adolescent moving downward while searching for a sense of personal worth finds this quest unanswered in his new and less-esteemed status. He acutely feels rejected by society's dominant institutions, not only because he is falling away from the defined success goal but also because he is failing to hold onto his present rung in the social-status ladder. Frustrated in his quest for status and attainment, and rejected by the "success-oriented" culture, the adolescent begins to think less of himself and experiences a devastating destruction of self-esteem. He may then resolve his personal-social-academic failure by adopting overt aggressive, hostile, or anti-social behavior.

If the intensity of the psychological consequences of social mobility varies with the degree of failure, then it is not difficult to understand the connection between downward mobility, low academic performance, and delinquent behavior. Downward movement can represent the greatest threat in the mobility process. For in a culture which highly esteems the success value, what constitutes a greater hazard than the failure to at least maintain one's own *status quo* in the social structure?

PART THREE

Early Identification and Prediction

9 Forecasting Delinquency: Some Assumptions and Prerequisites

Before being used to predict delinquency, the various tests, scales, and tables must be subjected to special validation checks. What are the flaws and blind spots in current prediction instruments? How can their weaknesses be eliminated or at least taken into consideration in order to provide a more reliable and valid prediction? What are some of the dangers in early identification of the pre-delinquent and what of the self-fulfilling prophecies?

Delinquent behavior is not a twenty-four hour malady; it develops over a long period of time, usually with the generous assistance of two or three adults. Since the future delinquent often presents many hints and rumblings of his coming explosions, are there any clear signposts for the early identification of the pre-delinquent? Apart from the primary and direct attack on delinquency problems via the general improvement in patterns of family living, in more effective school programs, in neighborhood value systems, and in leisure time offerings, delinquency prevention programs will depend heavily on the ability to identify at an early date (perhaps as early as the first grade level) the youngster who is prone, vulnerable, exposed, or susceptible to the delinquent pattern of adjustment.

Contrary to the usual depressed and depressing predictive validity coefficients reported in the literature on predicting success or failure in classroom achievement or on a job, it actually is possible to predict with 100 per cent efficiency the future delinquents in our society!

Considering the complexity and the pressures of modern living within the enveloping web of social taboos, regulations, town by-laws, city ordinances, and state and federal laws all trying to control the Adam still left in us, we can safely predict at least one good official or unofficial delinquency, and perhaps even more, for every man, during the growth and maturation process! Even many saints have had their histories of serious transgressions before they abandoned their sins to set their feet firmly on the path to beatification. But all this only raises the crucial question: *"Whom or what are we forecasting?"* The answer to this will be developed later; but first, what are the instruments currently available on the market and how effective are they?

There are at least seven instruments or techniques which are available to the test user and which offer some claim, and sometimes some data, to warrant mention—if not use—for early identification of the pre-delinquent. These include the following:

> Personal Index of Problem Behavior[1]
> Minnesota Multiphasic Personality Inventory[2]
> Porteus Maze Test[3]
> Washburne Social-Adjustment Inventory[4]
> Glueck Prediction Tables[5]
> Behavior Cards: A Test-Interview for Delinquent Children[6]
> KD Proneness Scale and Check List[7]

None of these items is infallible, nor has any one of these methods demonstrated sufficient forecasting efficiency or power to be used in

---

[1] Graham C. Loofbourow and Noel Keys, *The Personal Index* (Minneapolis: Educational Test Bureau, 1933). Winifred C. Riggs and Arnold E. Joyal, "A Validation of the Loofbourow-Keys Personal Index of Problem Behavior in Junior High Schools," *Journal of Education Psychology*, XIX (March, 1938), 194-201.

[2] Starke R. Hathaway and C. Charnley McKinley, *The Minnesota Multiphasic Personality Inventory* (New York: Psychological Corporation, 1943). Starke R. Hathaway and Elio D. Monachesi, *Analyzing and Predicting Juvenile Delinquency with MMPI* (Minneapolis: University of Minnesota Press, 1953).

[3] S. D. Porteus, *Qualitative Performance in the Maze Test* (New York: Psychological Corporation, 1942).

[4] J. W. Washburne, *Washburne Social-Adjustment Inventory* (New York: Harcourt, Brace & World, Inc., 1938). J. W. Washburne, "An Experiment on Character Measurement," *Journal of Juvenile Delinquency*, XIII, (Jan., 1929), 1-8.

[5] Sheldon Glueck and Eleanor Glueck, *Unraveling Juvenile Delinquency* (New York: Commonwealth Fund, 1950).

[6] Ralph H. Stodgill, *Behavior Cards: A Test-Interview for Delinquent Children* (New York: Psychological Corporation, 1949).

[7] W. C. Kvaraceus, *KD Proneness Scale and Check List* (New York: Harcourt, Brace & World, Inc., 1953).

a routine or perfunctory fashion. The best that can be said for some of them is that they are promising and that they merit perhaps another master's, if not doctoral, thesis by way of further or partial validation.

Basic Premises

The content of the test manuals does not need to be reviewed as it is available to any discriminating test user. Focus should be directed on the factors which tend to raise or lower the reliability and the validity of such instruments. These factors include the basic premises or assumptions on which prediction methodology in the delinquency field is generally founded (although not always acknowledged), and the special construction and validation problems that must be solved if delinquency prediction is to become a useful and practical reality, rather than a hopeful research fantasy.

Continuity of behavior.

In child study and rehabilitation, there is ever present the backward look to earlier life experiences of the subject in an effort to unlock the meaning of behavior. Prediction assumes a continuity in behavior or misbehavior, linked in a cause-effect sequence that is discernible by an observer. However, the sequitur of cause and effect may not be visible to the naked or untutored eye. Most observers today view behavior causally through the distortion of their own bifocals, thus reflecting the bias of their own theoretical frame of reference. The forecaster of delinquency might thus over-emphasize or under-emphasize data obtained through somatotyping, psycho-genic study, psychoanalysis or sociological inquiry that might pertain to the ultimate effect as seen in delinquent behavioral adjustment. Although much of the continuity of cause and effect in delinquency is to be found in the cultural and subcultural stream, there are, nevertheless, many contributing factors within the individual as well. At least, any forecaster today cannot afford to overlook either the cultural or psychological aspects of the delinquency phenomenon.

If some delinquency is spontaneous and accidental, this premise is weakened, or poorly maintained; if some youngsters prepare for their delinquencies quietly and pleasantly, as appears to be the situation in a growing number of cases, the observer, whatever his theory, may be hard put to spot the future offender.

Factor modality.

The forecaster assumes that there is a factor modality among enough variables that are commonly and peculiarly associated with delinquent behavior. These factor modalities represent significant differences that develop between those who become delinquent and those who do not resort to this adjustive mechanism. On the other hand, the singular and unique nature of each offender's syndrome tends to deny and to demolish any build-up of a useful common modality on which to base a forecast of malbehavior. In addition, isolation of a number of commonly observed variables in the backgrounds of delinquents as contrasted with nondelinquent counterparts involves an isolation and atomizing of elements that sacrifices dynamic aspects in causal relationship, hence reducing forecasting efficiency.

Unreliability of stimulus variables in class and subculture.

Whatever factor, stimulus, or variable is selected for use in a prediction schema, it is likely to fall victim to differential interpretation according to the respondent's value system, reflecting the ways of thinking, behaving, and adjusting in the subculture or class with which he is identified. Hence, love may be conceived as tender and may be identified with a lullaby in the upper class; love may be viewed by a lower-class adolescent as fierce and violent and may be identified with a family fight, thus proving the worth and importance of the young member in the family arena. A good example can be found in the use of the affection item in the Glueck social factors' table with a Maltese father, who culturally never displays open affection for his young, although the table expectancy is that he should do so. School achievement may be slurred in the lower-class home and praised in the upper-class family. Duplicity and cunning may be extolled in lower-class living and deplored in upper-class membership.

If delinquency is an essential and more typical aspect of life among the lower classes, these differential responses can be exploited in the forecasting game. However, as more delinquents tend to be drawn from the upper levels of community structure in the future, these stimuli and variables which invite differential responses among youth may only succeed in sorting them into the classes and/or subcultures from which they come, or with which they most easily identify. The value of such class identification would thus be lowered for prediction purposes.

Contingency in predicting behavior.

Prediction of future adjustment or maladjustment will always be made on a contingency basis. If the subject's situation improves, the prediction of delinquency will be weakened; if the situation deteriorates, the forecaster is more likely to be right. Hence the prediction made at a certain time must be viewed as relative to subsequent conditions which ensue. Failure to predict accurately may often reflect validation of the methodology, even though it depresses the validity coefficient.

Short-term vs. long-term prediction.

Some forecasters, particularly the Gluecks, have assayed long-term prediction working with the six-year-old or from the first grade level. Just as it is hazardous to plan a picnic or a skiing trip on the basis of long-term weather forecasting, one must be prepared for disappointments as well as surprises in this far more tenuous area. Obviously, predicting at the junior and senior high school levels, closer to the point of delinquency precipitation, should yield a higher level of validity coefficient than long range forecasting. A pertinent question arising is that of adequate time-allowance in the validation of any prediction scheme to insure adequate measure of delinquency fall-out. Current British studies reported by Mannheim suggest that 18 months may be sufficient to check the prediction power of some measures with older youth who have been institutionalized.[8] Beyond this, we do not know what constitutes minimal time duration in an effective validation design.

Special Methodological Problems in Construction and Validation

Assuming that a workable base can be squared off, the forecaster must still face the following special problems in the test construction and validation process.

Validation design.

There is no substitute for the before-and-after research design in validation studies of prediction tools. This means that the prediction technique must be applied to a sample of youngsters and forecasts

---

[8] Hermann Mannheim and Leslie T. Wilkins, *Studies in the Causes of Delinquency and the Treatment of Offenders. Prediction Methods in Relation to Borstal Training* (London: Her Majesty's Stationery Office, 1955).

made. A reasonable period of time for behavior and misbehavior to take place must be allowed, during which adjustment criterion data must be gathered according to some acceptable definition of malbehavior. Finally, the relationship between the forecast and the behavioral adjustment must be established and expressed in terms of prediction efficiency.

Many of the techniques now on the market depend too heavily, or even exclusively, on construct validity or concurrent validity. Many validation studies merely telescope the before-and-after design by using direct comparisons between available criterion groups, and still others attempt to validate forecasting effectiveness via retrospective analysis. Throughout many of these studies there is some confusion between what constitutes probability and what denotes predictive efficiency in a statistical design.

Before-and-after studies are expensive and difficult to manage. Loss of cases due to mobility alone is a serious stumbling block to the researcher in such long-term experiments. But there is neither a haven nor excuse in these difficulties for poorly executed research.

The criterion: Whom or what is being predicted?

The question was raised earlier: "Whom or what are we predicting?" What kind of criterion data are to be collected on each individual in the post-forecasting situation? Who and what is a delinquent? The omnibus concept *juvenile delinquent* can include the large bulk of our youth population, since everyone can, and does, easily fall by the wayside at one time or another in our more complex "Garden of Eden" society.

We must first observe that there is no dichotomy between delinquents and non-delinquents (except in terms of the court tag, but even here the dichotomy breaks down as one studies the informal and formal dispositions of cases). The implication is that the statistical design in prediction of malbehavior and delinquent behavior is not amenable to the expediency of a biserial correlation. Misbehavior exists on a continuum. What the researcher lacks is a graduated measure of the delinquency phenomenon on a malbehavior scale. Until such a measure, based on some system of habituation and seriousness of offense, is worked out, the unreliability of the criterion measure itself will seriously reduce the validity coefficient (assuming that a high degree of relationship exists between forecasting technique and adjustment).

All existing forecasting devices have attempted to predict any and

all kinds of delinquency without due regard for any diagnostic differentiation according to modalities or types of delinquents. This is
perhaps their greatest defect. Separate validation checks and prediction tables need to be evolved for the following types or modalities:
the *neurotic delinquent,* heavy with anxiety and guilt; the *socialized
delinquent* who has failed, for some reason, to internalize the value
system of dominant society and whose super-ego is already delin-
quency-identified; the overt-aggressive *unsocialized delinquent* whose
behavior represents a strong defense, even offense, against authority
figures conceived as hostile, threatening, and predatory. To these major
modalities might be added group-intoxicated type, traumatized delinquent, constitutional type, and perhaps others.

Refinement in validation experiment will await refinement in differential diagnosis in the process of gathering criterion data against which
to test the forecasting instrument, always working within the rubric
of each modality. Certain modalities of delinquents can probably be
predicted with greater effectiveness than others. For example, it may
be relatively easy to identify the future socialized and unsocialized
delinquents and relatively difficult to predict delinquents in the neurotic category. And it may prove an impossible task to predict the
traumatized offender because of the accidental nature of this
phenomenon.

One additional note bears mentioning. Convenient and undifferentiated criterion groups such as court cases or, worse, institutional delinquents on whom the community has given up or those who have
been removed from the community for special reasons should be
erased from validation studies aiming to set up prediction tables.
The special and hardy breed of screened delinquents obtained through
such sampling does not lend itself to fair test or experimentation.
In a sense, the cards are stacked in our favor. Without the use of
any elaborate device, most youth workers in any community can fore-
tell what youngsters are most likely to be banished to the training
institutions.

Need for local validation.

The delinquency problem varies from one community to another, and
in the large urban centers it will vary from neighborhood to neighborhood. Each community or neighborhood will show significant variations in incidence, type, and time of misbehavior, reflecting unique
elements in the population and in the culture and/or subcultures. Any
prediction tool that has been demonstrated as useful in a large urban

center with a mixed or heterogeneous population may prove to be of little or no value in the more homogeneous and monolithic culture of suburbia. Any promising instrument now available needs to undergo local validation rechecks. This will call for considerable research, interest, effort, and skill on the part of test users at the local level.

The need and necessity for local validation of prediction techniques is also pointed up by the problems presented by the class structure in American society. Sociological studies suggest that the average New England community, for example, might need at least three separate editions of a prediction scale or table: one for the lower class, one for the middle class, and one for the upper class. As one studies the items on some of the scales and check lists, the obvious irrelevancy of many of the stimuli for children of varying family status in our society is such as to render them useless and meaningless.

Observation vs. test situation.

In developing a methodology of prediction, we will need to favor the use of observation techniques such as check lists, graphic rating scales, and anecdotal records as against the use of test items or self-inventory questionnaires which place a heavy burden on the reading ability, trustworthiness, and seriousness of purpose of the respondent. The combination of low reading capacity, irrelevancy of response, and cultural duplicity of many pre-delinquents often tends to lower the reliability of the best of these instruments.

Furthermore, the technique that is evolved must be easily administered to large classroom groups. To build prediction tables assuming Rorschach testors, psychiatric interviewers, and trained social workers will not result in any usable or practical detection methodology as we contemplate ten million youngsters in the high schools of the nation. What we need, for example, is a handy method which trained teachers can employ as they come in close and continued contact with their students.

Whatever instrument is devised, it must face the practical test of serving as an improvement over what might be accomplished even now through the careful reading of a case-study folder or a cumulative record file. The professional worker, trained in child development and adolescent psychology, can generally anticipate a future delinquent through a careful perusal of a child's case record. Prediction methodology must provide a shorthand method that is at least as effective as this longhand approach.

How much hope can be extended to the community workers who are concerned with prevention and control of malbehavior through early identification of the potential nonconformer? If we can (1) strengthen the base on which prediction methodology must be built through a careful analysis of all our major premises, and (2) carry off our construction and validation processes with the refinements which have been indicated, it is likely that we can predict delinquency as well as tests of academic aptitude predict academic achievement (with reasonable success but with no phenomenal accuracy). Even then, we shall need to recognize that the prediction tool and the data gathered thereby have in no way relieved us of the urgency and the necessity of careful and deliberate judgment in drawing conclusions and of using all other available information concerning the child's exposure or proneness to malbehavior and delinquency.

10 Is It Possible to Construct a Reliable Prediction Scale?

A three-year experiment gathering validation data on the KD Proneness Scale raised these questions: Can test items be constructed to distinguish between delinquents and non-delinquents? Is the refined scale valid with junior high school students? Can it test the slow learner, the mentally retarded, the non-reader? Can a reliable non-verbal tool be constructed for youngsters in regular classes?

Because investigators have reported many significant differences between the backgrounds and personality development of delinquents and non-delinquents, a number of prediction scales, tables, and techniques have been developed to sift out and define these differences, and then to predict the delinquent pattern. But most of these tools are cumbersome or require highly specialized staff. There is a need for a valid, simple, and practical group-measure that can be used with all school children, including the slow learners, poor readers, and mentally retarded who frequently yield more than their expected share of delinquents.

In a three-year experiment[1] under a contract with the United States Office of Education, Department of Health, Education and Welfare, an investigation was made to gather validation data on a revised form of the Kvaraceus Delinquency Proneness Scale (Non-Verbal), which had been developed earlier and which had yielded some promising results on a limited sample. More specifically the experiment aimed:

[1] William C. Kvaraceus, "Forecasting Delinquency: A Three-Year Experiment," *loc. cit.*

(1) to reconstruct and/or to add additional picture items to the original KD Proneness Scale: Non-Verbal Form.

(2) to analyze the effectiveness of all items in distinguishing between delinquents and non-delinquents including boys and girls and within selected criterion groups of slow learners, non-readers, and mentally retarded pupils.

(3) to investigate the predictive validity of the refined scale with junior high school youngsters and also with selected categories including the slow learner, the mentally retarded, and the non-reader.

(4) to check the reliability of the refined scale.

(5) to investigate the relationship of the KD Non-Verbal Form (revised) with the KD Checklist, the KD Verbal Scale and with intelligence test scores.

Procedure

The experiment involved an actual tryout of the revised non-verbal scale using a before-and-after design. Prediction scores were obtained by administering the KD Non-Verbal Scale to all subjects and on the basis of independent teacher judgments of future delinquency based on a four-point descriptive scale. The subjects—junior high school students in grades seven, eight, and nine in one community, and pupils enrolled in special classes for the mentally retarded in two communities—were followed closely for approximately three years with the help of field workers, teachers, principals, counselors, police, and court officials. This behavioral adjustment feedback included all known violations, minor to major, and represented the afterdata. Relationships between scale scores and teacher ratings were then checked against the behavioral reports of norm violations in school, neighborhood, and community, using appropriate statistical techniques.

In preparation for the major experiment, an item analysis was carried out within the revision of the non-verbal scale. At the same time, two new scoring keys were developed based on the capacity of each item to differentiate delinquent boys from non-delinquent males and delinquent girls from their non-delinquent counterparts.

Correlations between the KD Verbal Scale, the KD Checklist, and an intelligence measure were also computed. The effectiveness of the non-verbal scale with slow learners, mentally retarded youngsters, and non-readers in addition to the general population was studied separately. And, last, the reliability of the revised non-verbal scale was estimated with several groups via the test-retest processes.

Description of the prediction scale.

The KD Proneness Scale (non-verbal) consists of 62 circles, each divided into quadrants. Each quadrant contains a stimulus picture. The subject is asked to select one of the four pictures which he likes the *most* and one of the four pictures which he likes the *least*. Responses are made on a separate answer sheet. Thus, a subject responds with a "most" and "least" answer to each of the 60 scoreable items. The first two items are used for demonstration and trial purposes.

The score for the test is obtained by the use of two keys: one key indicates direction toward delinquency and is called the "plus" (+) key (answering like the delinquents) the other indicates direction away from delinquency (answering like the non-delinquents) and is called the "minus" (—) key. The total score is the algebraic sum of the plus and minus counts added to 50 as a constant, thus bringing all scores within the positive range.

Each circle of four pictures (see Figure 10.1) was designed originally to contain one picture which the research literature suggests more delinquents would choose and one which more non-delinquents would select. The remaining two picture stimuli were considered to be neutral. The rationale for each picture is given in an earlier study of the original scale. Items that did not differentiate in the original study of the non-verbal scale were removed and new items were included in the revision. The revised scale was then submitted to an item analysis process in separate male and female studies.

The item analysis.

The method used in the development of scoring keys was to ascertain the difference in responses to each item made by a group of known adjudicated delinquents as compared to the responses to each picture stimulus made by a sample of non-delinquents of the same sex and age. An unselected sample of 289 boys and 277 girls was drawn from a total of 675 boys and 716 girls tested in the regular classes in the Fall River Junior Schools. The delinquent boys were the 255 residents of the Lyman School in Massachusetts and 54 boys who had been committed to the Rhode Island Training School. The delinquent girls were drawn from the following three state institutions: the Long Lane School for Girls, Connecticut (N 149); the Lancaster School, Massachusetts (N 100); and the Rhode Island School for Girls (N 32). The total of 281 delinquent girls represents all the institutionalized girls in the three state institutions at the time of testing.

The item analysis data were subjected to a chi-square test of sig-

Figure 10.1

nificance, the null hypothesis being that there is no significant difference between the responses of the criterion groups. The 5 per cent level of confidence was used as a cutting point in the selection of items and the establishment of the scoring keys. Six picture items failed to differentiate between the delinquent and non-delinquent boys, and only one picture item failed to differentiate between the female samples.

Teacher ratings.

In addition to the Scale score, Behavior Ratings were obtained on each subject at the start of the validation experiment. Teachers and/or guidance counselors used the following four-point rating scale in appraising the current status of each subject in the study:

1. Exemplary citizen: Highly regarded by all teachers; a force for good in the school; well integrated and socially adjusted; exerts his influence to improve living and working conditions in the school, neighborhood, and community; frequently assumes responsibility.
2. Average citizen: This youngster does not call attention to himself for any wrong-doing, nor does he call attention to himself as an outstanding leader for good; if infractions are committed by him, these are accidental, minor, or infrequent; gets along with his peers and teachers.
3. Marginal: This youngster is frequently suspected of wrongdoing and occasionally is involved in small offenses; has trouble with a few teachers and with some fellow students; considered to be a "discipline problem" by some of his teachers but not a serious or habitual offender.
4. Low morale: In serious difficulty around the school or on the playground; known to have been involved in any of the following: truancy, stealing, sex misconduct, hurting others, vandalism, cheating, breaking serious school rules, or has had contact with police or with courts. People in school or in community frequently complain about him.

The results of these teachers' ratings were used as a part of the before data.

The criterion or "after" data.

Juvenile delinquency in this study is defined broadly as "norm-violating behavior" or behavior that runs counter to some established rule or regulation set down by recognized authority. This includes all minor offenses, as well as offenses of those who were apprehended and legally labeled as "delinquent." This study regards delinquent behavior on a norm-violating continuum rather than as a dichotomy.

The behavior of all subjects in the study was carefully followed and recorded. School and community personnel made the observations which were forwarded to the study staff for posting and processing. Evidences of norm-violating behavior were recorded on special report forms by teachers, principals, guidance counselors, police, court and probation officers, and other social agency personnel. These reports were used to categorize the subjects in accordance with the type, severity, and persistence of the offenses. Four major categories were established as follows: 0 = those subjects for whom no offense of any kind had been recorded during the three-year period of the study; 1 = those subjects for whom only minor school offenses had been recorded; 2 = those subjects for whom both school and community offenses had been recorded but for whom no "legal action" was taken; 3 = those subjects who were engaged in serious and persisting norm violations and against whom some legal or official action had been taken.[2] It was felt that such a division of norm violations represented a continuum of offenses ranging from "no offense" through serious and legal offender.

The validation sample.

All the students enrolled in the three junior high schools and in special classes for the mentally retarded in Malden, Massachusetts, as well as all the pupils enrolled in the Fall River, Massachusetts, special classes were included in the study and totalled 2,414 subjects. The validation study was based on a statistical sample of 1,594 cases drawn from the initial total sample. Mobility, absenteeism, and school dropouts combined to reduce the total N. In drawing the statistical work-sample, care was also taken to include all those subjects on whom complete data were available. Check-out with IQ distributions and other variables indicated the statistical sample to be an adequate representation of the original sample.

The figure 1,594 included 1,379 students in the regular grades of the junior high schools, 123 students from the Malden special class, and 92 from the special class in Fall River. Distribution of numbers by sex and grade was as follows: 245 boys and 237 girls from grade 7; 212 boys and 216 girls from grade 8; 217 boys and 252 girls from grade 9; 77 boys and 46 girls from the classes for the mentally retarded in Fall River; and 59 boys and 33 girls from the special classes in Malden. Distribution of IQ's by grade and sex indicated that the scores were comparable and representative in the junior high groups. The

---

[2] A previous discussion of the application of these categories is found on pp. 81-82.

mean of the Binet IQ's of the Fall River special class was 70 ± 13 and the mean of the Malden special class pupils was 72 ± 11.

Statistical methodology.

Intercorrelations between teacher ratings, intelligence test scores, reading test scores and the Revised KD Proneness scale (non-verbal) were obtained for boys and girls and at each grade level. In a sense, six separate validations were conducted and offered a stringent test of repeated experimentation. Except for the reading score, the same statistical approach was taken with the variables obtained on both special classes.

The various data were next subjected to an analysis of variance. The technique as used here was to rank-order groups of subjects according to one of the variables (reading, for example) and to note if a corresponding rank-order and significant difference among means was found on other variables. Since the study proposed to investigate the predictive efficiency of the Non-Verbal Scale in relation to delinquency proneness, intelligence, and reading ability, analysis of variance included a study of all of these factors as well as the teachers' behavioral ratings. For example, in analyzing the reading scores of seventh grade boys grouped according to their quartile position on a reading test, the means of the behavioral ratings of the teachers were examined. A continuity rank-order of behavior rating according to levels of reading ability was uncovered. The best readers had the best behavior rating; the second-best readers had the second-best behavior rating, etc., down to the poorest readers in the fourth quartile who had the poorest behavior ratings. A statistical test (F-test) was used to check the significance among these four means with a 1 per cent level of confidence as a cut-off point.

Results

1. Correlations between the non-verbal prediction scale and the afterdata were obtained for each grade and for each sex. For boys correlations ran as follows: .114 in grade 7, .329 in Grade 8, and .045 in Grade 9; for girls the results were: .098 in Grade 7, .269 in Grade 8, and .235 in Grade 9.

2. Correlations between teacher behavior ratings and the afterdata generally were higher than for the Proneness Scale. For boys, the correlations were: .341 in Grade 7, .499 in Grade 8, and .371 in Grade 9; for girls the data yielded the following: .148 in Grade 7, .304 in Grade 8, and .299 in Grade 9. Several of these correlations

are significant enough to suggest that teachers' ratings can contribute much in a process of early identification of future norm violators.

3. Correlations in the special classes reflect the same trend in favor of teachers' ratings. For the retarded boys the Proneness Scale scores correlated —.095 in Malden and .199 in Fall River; for the mentally retarded girls the same correlations were as follows: .276 in Malden special classes and —.021 in the Fall River special classes. All these correlations may be considered almost negligible.

4. Results between the teachers' behavior ratings are more promising. The correlation with boys in Malden classes was .349 and .217 for Fall River boys; the same data for girls yielded a high correlation of .796 in the Malden special class but a low .081 with the Fall River girls. Since the teachers reported back on the subsequent behavior of the pupils whom they had rated, the halo of the self-fulfilled prophecy may be operative with the higher intercorrelations both within the special classes and the regular grades.

5. Correlations between intelligence test results and the afterdata are consistently low and negligible. For boys in the regular grades the correlations ranged from .091 to .250 and for the girls from .028 to .217. However, a significant negative correlation, —.405 was obtained for the Malden special class boys between their Binet IQ's and the norm violations. The Malden special class girls also reported a negative correlation but of much lower value, —.110. Fall River data reported out a correlation of .169 for boys and —.037 for girls with a Binet IQ as the predictor.

6. Relationships between reading test scores and the afterdata showed correlations for boys in the regular grades ranging from .179 to .238 and for girls ranging from .103 to .252.

Using the method of analysis of variance, the subjects in the study were arranged in rank-order groups according to one variable and then compared with other significant variables to see if corresponding rank-order prevailed, at the same time checking the significant differences among means. The following statistics report on the similarity in continuity of rank-order for the reading, intelligence, and afterdata as they are studied against the prediction variables and each other.

7. Reading scores of junior high school boys fell in rank-order agreement only at the seventh grade with significance at the 1 per cent level. The Proneness Scale results fell in rank-order agreement with significant differences between means only at the eighth grade level. The afterdata rank-order agreement was visible in Grades 7 and 9 with statistical significance for Grade 7 only. It is notable that the poorest readers who stood in the lowest (4th) quartile of every

grade had the worst behavior ratings (except Grade 9), the highest KD Proneness Scale scores (non-verbal), and the highest scores on the afterdata.

8. For the junior high school girls, the behavior ratings were similar in continuity of rank-order with reading but the F ratios failed to show significant differences. Teachers' ratings appeared to correspond more closely with the reading skills of girls than of boys. The prediction scale showed significant rank-order agreement with reading only in the ninth grade. As with boys, the afterdata reporting norm violations showed rank-order agreement with reading test scores in Grades 7 and 9, but the F ratio proved significant only for Grade 7. Again it was notable that the poorest readers in the fourth quartile group had the worst behavior ratings, the highest scores on the non-verbal delinquency proneness measure, and the worst records as to the norm violations reported in the afterdata.

9. In answering the question of the relationship of intelligence test scores to all other variables using the analysis of variance technique, the following results were obtained: for seventh grade boys the Behavior Ratings, KD Proneness Scale scores, and the afterdata reporting norm violations showed significant rank-order differences; a similar trend was visible with the teachers' behavior ratings for boys in Grades 8 and 9, but the mean differences were significant only for the eighth graders; the non-verbal prediction scale, other than for the seventh graders, failed to show any rank-order agreement with intelligence rank; intelligence test data for the junior high school girls did correspond with the behavior ratings at all grades but not always at a statistically significant level; the KD Proneness Scale scores did vary with the IQ rank for seventh, and ninth grade girls, but the mean differences were not significant. A trend among boys and girls was visible in which the duller students showed poorer behavior ratings; there was also a weak trend for the duller boys and girls to score higher (towards delinquency) on the non-verbal prediction scale.

10. Analyzing the IQ data in the special classes in both communities revealed that the "brighter" boys tended to get into more difficulties than their duller classmates. Similarly, the dullest special class girls in Malden had the best behavior ratings and "brightest" special class girls had the worst behavior ratings.

11. Using the criterion of norm violation as reported in the afterdata, a general trend was noted in the junior high school groups supporting the hypothesis that the brighter students are better behaved, have better behavior ratings, and score lower on the non-verbal prediction instrument. However, this trend was not strong enough to support the use of the measures for prediction purposes. It is notable among the junior high school sample that when the

subjects are ranked according to seriousness of norm violation, the rank-order continuity of means is broken for every variable by both male and female norm-violators in the "legal offense" category. It appears that the legal offenders fall closer to the middle of the distribution on the following variables: behavior rating; intelligence test score; paragraph meaning, and total reading score. In fact, the boys in the legal offenders category showed vocabularies better than all but the boys in the "no-offense" groupings. Also, their non-verbal Proneness Scale scores were lower than all groups with one exception of the "no-offense" category. These results suggest that the legal offender may be somewhat of an anomaly or maverick.

12. In the Malden and Fall River special classes, the boys who were reported as legal offenders tended to fall in the middle of the distribution when arranged by afterdata. Some conflicting results between the two special class sets of data were reported, suggesting that some of the malbehavior may be a function of the special school environment.

13. Reliability coefficients based on test-retests of delinquent and non-delinquent samples ranged from .873 to .776.

14. Intercorrelations between the verbal KD Proneness Scale, the non-verbal proneness scale, and the KD Checklist were all of a very low order, indicating the instruments were measuring unrelated aspects of delinquency proneness.

Conclusions

1. As a predictive instrument of delinquency or norm violations among junior high school students and mentally retarded youngsters in special classes, the KD revised Proneness Scale (non-verbal) failed to meet the stringent tests set up in the research design. Nevertheless, some statistically significant results were obtained at certain grade levels and for certain groups, indicating that the non-verbal Proneness Scale was not without some promise as a potential tool. However, the non-verbal scale cannot now be considered a functional tool that can readily or easily be incorporated in a school-community program of delinquency prevention via early identification.

2. The behavior ratings of experienced teachers showed more promise as a method for identifying the future norm-violators. It may well be that the theoretical premises implicit in the attempt to predict delinquent behavior from a thirty-minute psychological test situation are not tenable in view of the complex of factors in the child's psyche, in his culture and subculture, and in community attitudes, all of which interact to produce the delinquent act. The fact that teachers' behavior

ratings showed more promising results than the non-verbal prediction instrument also tends to substantiate the observation that "nothing predicts behavior like behavior." At the same time, the operation of the self-fulfilling prophecy in this study should not be overlooked.

3. The legally labeled norm-violator appears to represent somewhat of an anomaly or maverick on the intelligence and reading capacity dimensions. This group in particular failed to conform to the expected distribution as envisioned in the basic hypotheses that were tested. The operation of certain selective factors in the determination of who is to be handled officially and who is to become a legal delinquent is only suggested in this investigation and needs to be studied further. The implication of this observation can have serious ramifications for studies that sample delinquents as well as for census-taking and reporting of delinquency.

4. Junior high school youngsters who fall into the lowest or poorest reading group tended to show a heavy preponderance of norm violations. Reading ability, whether it be cause or effect, must be taken into account as a potential factor closely associated with the delinquency symptom. Attention to the poorest readers in the junior high situation may enable the community to focus on a group of youngsters who are already, or who will soon be, showing behavorial disturbances.

5. A perceptible trend was visible for youngsters with lower IQ's to get lower behavior ratings and to show more evidences of norm violations. However, in view of the intelligence test scores of the anomalous legal offender, a definite linear relationship between intelligence test score and delinquency was not established.

6. In the special classes for the mentally retarded, the "brighter" youngsters evidenced more behavioral difficulties than did their duller classmates. This may reflect, to some unknown extent, a degree of discomfort or conflict on the part of the borderline learners who are placed in special learning centers. However, some conflict in the results from the two special class centers was notable, indicating that environmental setting and individual teacher-attitudes may be prime factors in determining who really is the norm-violator or who will become the norm-violator.

7. The experiment reveals the fact that a reliable non-verbal tool can be constructed as a workable group measure for youngsters in regular grades as well as with those who have serious reading difficulties or who are mentally retarded.

11 Do Delinquents Share Some Common Characteristics?

Validation studies of the KD Proneness Check List suggest that delinquents do demonstrate certain common traits. What are the factors that seem most universal among them? Are they numerous enough and sufficiently significant to be able to predict the future delinquent?

A number of research studies[1] have reported a constellation of differences which typify delinquents when compared with their non-delinquent controls. Using these group differences, a *Delinquency Proneness Check List*[2] has been constructed as an aid for locating vulnerable, exposed, or delinquency prone children. The use of such a tool for early identification of vulnerable children in a community program of delinquency prevention and control would, of course, be invaluable.

The following study[3] reports the incidence of the checklist factors as found in the case records of a sample of 97 delinquents in one open institution. The study further indicates the extent of saturation of these differentiating factors

---

[1] William Healy and Augusta F. Bronner, *New Light on Delinquency and Its Treatment* (New Haven: Yale University Press, 1936). W. C. Kvaraceus, *Juvenile Delinquency and the School* (New York: Harcourt, Brace & World, Inc, 1945). William W. Wattenberg, "Boy Repeaters", unpublished study, distributed under the auspices of the College of Education, Wayne University, 1947. Maud A. Merrill, *Problems of Child Delinquency* (Boston: Houghton Mifflin Co., 1947). Sheldon Glueck & Eleanor Glueck, *Unraveling Juvenile Delinquency* (The Commonwealth Fund, Harvard University Press, 1950).

[2] William C. Kvaraceus, *Delinquency Proneness Scale and Check List* (New York: Harcourt, Brace & World, Inc., 1953, revised).

[3] I am indebted to Mr. Thomas O'Hara, counselor at Shirley (Mass.) Industrial School for Boys and to Miss Joanne Harris, of Brookline, Mass., for their assistance in this study.

as well as the relative frequency of each item. In addition, the correlations of the *K.D. Proneness Check List* with other measures are presented.

All adjudged delinquents in Shirley Industrial School for Boys whose grade placement was Grade 6 or higher were checked using both the *K.D. Proneness Scale* and the *Check List*. Table 11.1 reveals the number of delinquents, arranged according to frequency, whose case data showed the presence or absence of each factor previously reported in the research literature as differentiating delinquents from their law-abiding counterparts. These differences had been classified in three categories: (I) Personal; (II) Environmental (home and family); (III) School. The "?" column indicates that the case records did not reveal sufficient information to enable the investigator to check either way. It will be noted that some items were found in a very large majority of cases, whereas other items were noted rather infrequently.

The mean number of "Yes" checks was 31, indicating a strong saturation of the factors listed in this proneness measure. Only three delinquents showed fewer than 18 "Yes" checks.

Correlations between the *K.D. Check List* scores and the *K.D. Proneness Scale* scores, intelligence, and ages were as follows:

Check List *vs.* Proneness Scale   .254
Check List *vs.* Intelligence (Wechsler Bellevue)   —.45
Check List *vs.* Chronological Age   .007

These correlations indicate no relationship between age and items checked, a slight positive correlation between the two prediction instruments, and a rather significant negative correlation with intelligence test scores, as would be expected because of the presence of many items related to low ability and school retardation.

This study represents an inquiry into the case study records of older institutionalized delinquents as a partial validation technique of the *K.D. Proneness Check List.* The data suggest that many of the characteristics listed in the *Check List* do show up in the case records of apprehended delinquents with a high frequency, resulting in a saturation of factors associated or predisposing to the development of delinquent patterns of behavior. The study also reports that a number of items did not appear with any great frequency and might be omitted or de-emphasized in the use of the *Check List.*

In addition, the investigation indicates that the *K.D. Proneness Scale* and *Check List,* while positively correlated, render somewhat independent estimates of delinquency proneness and could be used as two separate measures with little overlapping.

Table 11.1 Incidence of Items from K.D. Proneness Check List Appearing in Case Records of 97 Delinquents Committed to Shirley, Massachusetts, Industrial School for Boys

Frequency			Check List Item—Number and Factor	Category
Yes.	No.	?		
92	5	0	10. Has previous record of delinquent behavior.	I
88	6	3	26. Poor home discipline.	II
88	4	5	65. Is indifferent to or dislikes school.	III
87	6	4	8. Shows lack of success in out-of-school activities.	I
86	7	4	25. Emotional conflicts between parents and siblings.	II
83	6	8	60. Has little interest in schoolwork.	III
82	4	11	5. Reacts to situations in overly-aggressive manner.	I
81	3	13	68. Intends to leave school as soon as the law will allow.	III
77	17	3	61. Is unsuccessful in schoolwork.	III
77	12	8	67. Is truant from school frequently.	III
73	8	16	70. Takes little or no part in extra-curricular or club activities of school.	III
71	15	11	13. Associates with others who are or have been delinquent.	I
70	3	24	9. Avoids positions and activities involving responsibility.	I
67	24	6	22. Relationships in family life unwholesome.	II
65	32	0	39. Family is large (five or more).	II
65	14	18	15. "Runs" with a "gang".	I
60	26	11	19. Seldom attends church or Sunday school.	I
60	37	0	21. Family broken by divorce, desertion or death.	II
58	19	20	30. Much nagging among family members.	II
58	34	5	47. Lives in multi-family dwelling.	II
57	5	35	69. Feels that he does not belong to the class group.	III
56	35	6	31. Evidence of neglect.	II
56	18	23	7. Never belonged to a club or organization.	I
53	29	15	66. Transfers frequently from school to school.	III
53	7	37	14. Declares he is afraid of nothing.	II
50	42	5	53. Lives in an under-privileged neighborhood.	II
47	45	5	38. Parents have court records.	II
47	42	8	29. Drunkenness in family.	II
46	43	8	23. Emotional conflicts between parents.	II
46	37	14	54. Lives in high delinquency-rate area.	II
45	8	49	11. Evidences a philosophy of "good" or "bad" luck.	I
41	33	23	62. Has repeated one or more grades.	III
39	49	9	45. Mother is employed outside the home.	II
39	53	5	59. Has below average verbal ability.	III

Incidence of Items from K.D. Proneness Check List Appearing in Case
Records of 97 Delinquents Committed to Shirley, Massachusetts,
Industrial School for Boys (*cont.*)

Frequency			Check List Item—Number and Factor	Category
Yes.	No.	?		
38	19	40	12. Is satisfied with self.	I
37	55	5	46. Inadequate living quarters.	II
35	25	37	58. Lives in racially mixed neighborhood.	II
34	42	21	44. Father is unskilled or slightly skilled worker.	II
34	59	4	2. Is below average in academic aptitude.	I
34	46	17	35. Extreme parental domination.	II
33	56	8	32. Is overprotected by family.	II
33	58	6	43. Record of family contacts with welfare agencies.	II
33	30	34	63. Grade placement too high for mental ability.	III
32	53	12	48. Overcrowding (more than 1-5 persons per room) prevails.	II
31	9	57	28. Feels disliked or unwanted.	II
29	60	8	49. Inadequate furnishings in home.	II
29	27	41	55. Has few facilities for play.	II
28	60	9	42. Family income inadequate for comfortable living.	II
27	64	6	57. Family rents home and pays less than prevailing average.	II
25	72	0	1. Is between 10 and 16 (if boy); 12 and 16 (if girl).	I
24	71	2	17. Has three or more siblings.	I
23	73	1	40. Family belongs to marginal group.	II
22	2	73	6. Attends movies at least twice a week.	I
22	60	15	27. Over-indulgence exhibited toward child.	II
20	74	3	51. Home unsanitary.	II
19	64	14	33. Intense rivalry among siblings.	II
18	63	15	64. Is in a special class.	III
17	80	0	41. Lives in other than natural home.	II
12	78	7	36. Cultural conflicts between parents and siblings.	II
11	82	4	16. Is the middle child in a large (five or more) family.	I
11	80	6	37. Delinquent brothers and/or sisters.	II
10	85	2	20. Birth unplanned or accidental.	II
10	82	5	52. Family is mobile or migratory.	II
9	83	5	18. Is slovenly or unkempt in appearance.	I
6	16	75	50. Family without automobile.	II
5	20	72	56. Lives over business establishment.	II
2	95	0	4. Has physical defect.	I
1	96	0	3. Is in poor health.	I

The Check List that has been discussed does not take into consideration the important distinctions that were made earlier between the genesis of lower-class delinquency and the origins of middle-class norm-violators. Table 11.2 provides a promising schemata that can be used to identify vulnerability of the lower-class or middle-class youngster. The screening procedure involves two major steps: *first*, identification of class status and, *second*, use of sub-indicators noting factors that are frequently associated with conflicts and frustrations that generate norm- and rule-violating behavior within the two milieux.

Table 11.2. Discrimination Level I: For Primary Reference Group

Parents do not belong to organized groups like PTA, Women's Club, Elks, Lions, Redmen, Lodges	Parents belong to several organized groups, such as PTA, Women's Club, Rotary, Lions, Redmen
Female based household	Flavor of female dominated household
School dropout: actual or intentional	
Speech patterns: Utilizes non-school supported grammatical features—*e.g.* "ain't," "we don't hardly"	Finish high school and intends to go to college
	Speech patterns: Utilizes school supported grammatical system
Low scholastic performance	High scholastic performance in school
Orientation on "being"	Orientation on "becoming"
Public property concern: to use and wear out	Public property concern: to maintain and improve
Family spends it and enjoys it now	Family saves and insures for the future
Male kin are tattooed	Plan and system
Sharply dressed, "hip" and jazzy,	Male kin not tattooed
Fate and luck	

Discrimination Level II: For In-Group Sub-Indicators

(LOWER-CLASS MEMBERSHIP)	(MIDDLE-CLASS MEMBERSHIP)
Runs with gang wherein prestige and status is geared to law-violating behavior	Poor school performance and failure
Shows high level of aspiration without means or opportunity to achieve	Withdraws with explosive potential
	Household pattern differs from nuclear father-mother household

Discrimination Level II: For In-Group Sub-Indicators (*cont.*)

(LOWER-CLASS MEMBERSHIP)

Has academic interest and/or performance, but runs the gamut of gang's criticisms

Uses school as arena for physical skill, force, excitement

Family or gang constantly getting into trouble with authority (school, church, police)

Shows smartness and good conning techniques

Shows "independence" by non-adherence to rules and regulations and by aggressive-overt attacking behavior

Social isolation from gang

Heavy pressure from friends and family against continuing in school

Finds excitement in vandalism, collective stealing

Reacts aggressively to conflicts between norms of home and values of school and society

Living in accordance with petty crime climate condoning law violations

Fights his problems out

Registers overt defiance toward authority

Takes it out on people and property

Identifies with female authority figure

(MIDDLE-CLASS MEMBERSHIP)

Interpersonal relationships among family members tense and conflicting, repressive, and/or over-protective

Intends to leave school early

Far below average for his grade

Truants from school

Low academic aptitude

Shows heavy guilt involvement

Inadequate identification with appropriate parent figure

Shows consistent patterning of norm-violating acts along the dimensions or concerns of lower-class society

History of enuresis (bed wetting), tics, nail-biting, persistent sleep disturbances

Passive and over-dependent

Characteristically anxious

Suspicious—fears the worst in a passive rather than in a belligerent manner

Ego weak—super-ego of inhibitors strong

After identifying the child's primary reference group, the sub-items can be used to note his proneness or vulnerability. With the lower-class youngsters, for example those who run with gangs and achieve prestige and status via law-violating behavior, who have high levels of aspiration but who lack the means or opportunity to achieve, who use the school as an arena to show their physical skill and force, who react aggressively to conflicts and frustration, and who show many of the other indicators can be screened off for a second look and a helping hand. On the other hand, the middle class youngster who is truant, who fails in school, who intends to leave school as soon as the law allows, who shows low academic aptitude, who withdraws with explosive potential, who comes from a psychologically tense home may exhibit factors that relate to potential norm-violating behavior. It must be pointed out, however, that this two-step differentiated check list must still face the empirical before-and-after test of validation. This approach does recognize that the factors that predispose lower-class youngsters to acts of delinquency often vary significantly from those forces that tend to produce middle class norm-violators. Of the various scales and check lists which have been discussed, this two-step differentiating prediction measure perhaps offers one of the most promising approaches to early identification of the future delinquent and, as such, merits further study and experimentation.

PART FOUR

Role of the School as a Central Agency

12 Stalled in the Shallows of Traditional Principles: Are the Schools Skirting the Realities of the Subliminal Curriculum?

What dynamic opportunities to shape behavior are the schools missing by clinging to time-worn patterns of education? Must classes be limited by clock and calendar? Why should age be the determining factor for student grouping? The inspiring teacher offering positive goals: how important is his contribution toward the growth of the adolescent?

The major purpose and function of the school is to develop new and improved behavior or to modify and change old and undesirable ways of behaving for the betterment of self and society. In this sense, learning as a product must be conceived in terms of specified and expected behavioral changes or acquisitions of new and improved modes of adjustment in consequence of school attendance.

A step in this direction has been taken by Will French and his associates in their Survey Study of Behavioral Outcomes of General Education in High School.[1] This work presents a general consensus of what high school graduates

---

[1] Will French and Associates, *Behavioral Goals of General Education in High School* (New York: Russell Sage Foundation, 1957), p. 247.

should be able to do and to think, and to feel and to act as a result of the common experiences in the general education aspect of their high school living and learning. As one reads through the illustrative behaviors and the developmental equivalents presented in this work, it becomes obvious that the much criticized driver-training course probably has more visible and measurable effect on the driving behavior of the young adult (witness the favored insurance rates for those who have passed such a course in Massachusetts) than the years of preoccupation with social studies have on the youths' attitudes toward citizenship. To date, these courses have failed to develop an enlightened and motivated citizenry willing and eager to exercise its prerogatives and privileges at the voting booth, judging from the turnout in any election year at the local, state, or national level.

The formal high school curriculum provides planned and systematic experiences through which expected behaviors or modifications will take place. This is the visible curriculum of the high school. In most high schools this curriculum operates in the monotonous routine and ritual of lesson assigning, lesson reciting and hearing, and lesson marking. But there is also a second curriculum which is to be found in the culture of the school. This is the way of life of the school, providing a normative structure of how to act and how not to act. This subliminal curriculum is, in a sense, a natural extension of the visible and formal curriculum of the school. Though hidden, it may represent for behavior and misbehavior the more formidable and even more effective —if not hazardous—aspect of the school's program in developing real and significant changes in the behavior of high school youth.

There is no such thing as "the culture" of the American public secondary school. A wide variety of cultures exist and can be found in different high schools and in different communities. The ways of life in the large high school in the big dirty city will differ substantially from the ways of living in the more homogeneous upper middle-class models found in the clean and neat suburban schools now fast disappearing from the rural scene. Margaret Mead has explored some of these significant variants in her Inglis Lecture at Harvard, *The School in American Culture*.[2]

---

[2] Margaret Mead, *The School in American Culture* (Cambridge: Harvard University Press, 1951), p. 48. See also Edgar Z. Friedenberg, *Coming of Age in America* (New York: Random House, 1965), for an insightful analysis of the culture of the modern high school which pictures the pupil as victimized and dehumanized by his school environment.

At the same time it must be recognized that the structure of school society, not unlike the structure of the society outside of the school, consists of a number of sub-groups, each with its own somewhat distinct cultural characteristics. In the high school these may cluster around class status of the family, college-going intentions, course elections, ethnic aspects of the neighboring community, and similar concerns.

Behavior and, of course, misbehavior frequently are only manifestations or reflections of the cultural imperatives of the school. The cultural imperatives of the secondary school are powerful and pervasive. They may and frequently do neutralize and even supersede the forces operating in the formal and planned experiences of the visible curriculum.

Some common imperatives culled from the cultural milieux of the secondary school that frequently tend to shape or determine personality (modes of adjustment) can be analyzed. It must be recognized, of course, that behavior and misbehavior represent always an interaction of the organism and the external environment referred to here in a cultural sense. Since factors within the culture are more often overlooked than are psychological and emotional forces in studying behavior and misbehavior in schools this discussion focuses exclusively on the more common cultural imperatives which have been distilled from many different secondary schools. All of these cultural imperatives can serve to predispose the high schooler to misbehavior and delinquency since they expose him to frustration, ego disintegration, stress, anxiety, weak imitative example, and lowered self-estimate. Nine cultural imperatives which represent serious hazards in the development of acceptable behavior will be considered.

Sex-crossed Activities of the School

The American high school is unique in many ways when compared with a number of its European counterparts. A point of greatest difference can frequently be found in the free-and-easy wheeling of boy-girl relationships, best symbolized by the insurance policy carried in the form of the steady date or the isolated couple at the school dance, united in romantic embrace.

One of the sexiest spots in many American towns today is its high school. This is especially true in smaller communities and most visible in suburbia. This theme was caught in the melodrama of *Peyton Place*, where even the high school principal is hardly immune to the

sexually oriented climate of his own institution and eventually ca-
pitulates. The identical theme has been burlesqued in a Grade B cel-
luloid excretion of Hollywood, *High School Confidential.* In this
caricature of the high school, seniors (maybe they were only sopho-
mores) speak frequently and glibly of the stag and stud roles of the
male "students."

In a sense the sex-crossed activities of the high school provide an
important part of the practicum for the future husband-wife com-
panion role, but without verbalization and without theoretical orientation to the phenomenon and meaning of sex. Hence, the young adult
may somehow master the developmental task and mature into an ex-
pert craftsman by the time the male or female family role is undertaken. But until the transition is made from the *how* to the *why,* youth
will seldom attain a professional level of competency in the full com-
pletion of their husband and wife roles. For example, there are many
victims of the Freudian syllogism, as seen in the disintegration and
disorganization of self, family, and society. What is sorely needed in
the American secondary school is the opportunity to talk it out rather
than to just act it out, even though the acting may be done without
injury and on the symbolic level. The heavy curtain of silence that
hangs around sex in an institution replete with sex-crossed activities
presents the modern educational paradox. It is hoped that talking it
out will develop restraint, good sense, and moral principle, rather than
further accentuate an already over-accentuated subject.

How much of this sex orientation is attributable to the unrealistic
adult romanticisms of youth and love could be explored profitably by
research teams from sociology, anthropology, psychology, and education. The fact that most private or independent secondary schools
continue in their monolithic sex structure testifies that they continue
to meet the needs of apprehensive parents who consciously or unconsciously seek out those school organizations which "protect" their
young adolescent from the sex-crossed activities of the public high
school. This is not to deny that there are other reasons, good and bad,
that motivate anxious parents to send their maturing youngsters to
private all-male or all-female schools.

The fact that American youth have made so minor and so insignifi-
cant a contribution in the creative arts may be attributable somewhat
to their exclusive preoccupation with sports and sex. It is frequently
difficult to state where sport leaves off and where sex begins. A long
litany of symbolic manifestations may be listed here: football, the juke
box, the coke bottle, current dances, and the mass identification with

popular singers. Talcott Parsons[3] has suggested similar reasons why American youth have seldom (and only recently) shown any strong or rebellious movement in the political life of the nation in contrast with the youth of other nations. If the governmental structure of our nation collapses, one of the reasons may be because grown boys or men prefer the comforts of the bath and the bed to the discomforts of the smelly marketplace, the slanderous political arena, and the bloody battlefield—as in ancient Athens, in Rome, and in Byzantium.

Delayed and Postponed Responsibility

Contrary to the practicum in relating to the opposite sex with its lack of information and discussion, the rest of the school's program at the high-school level can best be described as information without application or implementation. For the period of his high school career the learner is cut off from the stream of real life problems. He finds himself in a deep freeze. The activities in which he must engage appear irrelevant to the student's past, present or future—especially the present. Since the high school is careful to detour around real life problems and controversial issues involving race relations, alcoholism, materialism, religion, politics, collectivism, or consumer competencies, it involves the learner in a type of artificially contrived busy-work and shadow-boxing that either lulls the adolescent into a stupor or drives him in his resentment to overt aggression in the delinquency pattern. In protecting youth from real life problems, the school enters into a tragic conspiracy of irresponsible retreat from reality. The perversion of the high school curriculum to neutral and petty purposes emasculates the school program and disintegrates the ego. The complaints of the delinquent today are that school experiences are stale and flat. Boredom in school is what drives many youth to retaliatory and nonconforming behavior, to chronic truancy, and eventually to withdrawal. The best therapeutic device available for the noisy and sick part of our adolescent society is an interesting, meaningful, and vital high school curriculum.

Nowhere is the listless play-acting more visible than in the so-called student governments in the high schools. Seldom are youth trusted to make their own decisions and to experience the learning that can

---

[3] Talcott Parsons, "Age and Sex in the Social Structure of the United States," in *Personality in Nature, Society, and Culture*, eds., Clyde Kluckhohn and Henry A. Murray (New York: Alfred A. Knopf, 1950), pp. 269-281.

come from making moral choices on their own. The direction and supervision exercised in student government make a mockery of the democratic processes. Neither does the high school appear effective in finding any honest or real work with which to preoccupy the fast-maturing adolescent. The result today can be seen in the young adult who is convinced of his low status. He is a nobody, a nothing. He suffers from the lack of any utilitarian function (except that of serving as a perpetual scapegoat for the adult members of society who heap upon him all the debris of their own inadequacies). There is no more unimportant member of society than the adolescent. He is the outraged personality of the twentieth century, as indicated by the eloquent testimony of the mounting rebellion visible in the delinquency trends of any large city. Herein is frequently reflected the aggressive inferiority of modern youth. The dysfunctioning curriculum of the secondary school, coupled with compulsory school attendance, is rapidly turning the American public high school into an adolescent ghetto.

The Compulsory Nature of the Adolescent-School Relationship

There are many captive students in American high schools. What proportion of its clientele would the secondary school lose if the compulsory school attendance laws were revoked and the attendance officers were taken off the job?

In the educational mythology of compulsory secondary schooling, the public institutions have promised to educate every child of every parent, but considering the group aged 21 to 24, the *Current Population Reports* of the Department of Commerce based upon a sample of the 1960 Census returns, indicated that approximately 40 per cent of the population in this age range did not bother to complete high school. In other words, even with the present compulsory attendance laws, the high schools still are losing close to one-half of their clientele.

Current estimates[4] indicate that there are about eight million youngsters of high school age, of which one million have dropped out of school. Of this group, one-half of the 16- to 17-year-olds are unemployed, and two-thirds of the 14- to 15-year-olds are also without jobs. These youngsters, caught in the school-to-work vacuum, are waiting for something to happen. Many of them through delinquency are making things happen. It is estimated that soon 1,600,000 boys and girls 14-17

---

[4] *Youth Employment and Juvenile Delinquency*, Report to the Committee on the Judiciary, United States Senate, made by its Subcommittee to Investigate Juvenile Delinquency, 84th Congress, 1st session, p. 7.

years of age will be out of school and that more than one-half million of these will be unemployed. This exiled group represents a real threat to the future of our society. If the reactionaries in the basic education camp have their way, this number, a mere half million, may represent a very minimal estimate of future unemployed youth who will have left school. It is interesting to note that during the past ten years the drop-out rate has been cut by only 7 per cent and that during the past five years it has been cut by a mere 3 per cent. These figures would indicate that the holding power of the present high-school program (graduating sixty of each hundred persons 17 years of age annually) has probably reached its peak—even with compulsory legislation.

The mass drop-outs provide school personnel with some idea of the inner conflict of the adolescent concerning this minor decision with major consequences, "to quit or not to quit the high school," once the mandatory attendance age has been reached. Studies of drop-outs and studies of delinquents reveal that the two samples are overlapping on many traits. There is little doubt that the school drop-out annihilates the high school in this last gesture of retaliation and contempt for the agency in which he has endured much and has himself almost been destroyed.

Learning by Clock and Calendar

The tempo and rhythm of learning in the high schools is fast, brief, and staccato. The student studies by clock and calendar. Learning stops for frequent holiday and vacation periods. Entrance to school and withdrawal from school are based on birth certificates rather than on any measure of ability or achievement. Learning is always short-timed, truncated, and operates in fifty-minute periods in which teacher and pupil study to beat the clock. All of this is alien to a studentship and a scholarship which is continuous and permeating, and which must race in the long arduous marathon rather than the fifty-minute dash in a five-period day. Much of the pseudo-intellectualism of our day can be traced to the "quickie" nature of the school's learning-teaching process.

Organizationally, the high school program sorts out classes (not individuals) among teachers about every fifty minutes. The frequently-shifted youngster belongs to no one. Even with a "homeroom period," he suffers a feeling of rootlessness and impersonality. As a member of a class he may achieve the status of a pupil but seldom that of a person. When the adolescent calls attention to himself as a person through misbehavior, help may be extended to him but through the impersonal bureaucracy of the guidance department.

Secondary schools have shown a complete lack of imagination and ingenuity in developing programs that would insure the establishment of strong and extended teacher-pupil and pupil-teacher relationships on which instruction and learning can be anchored. Attention should be given to the possibilities inherent in arranging programs in much longer time patterns by spending a half day or full day within each area of instruction, or even a week with the science teacher followed by a full week with each of the other teachers in other areas. High-school programming will make learning and scholarship pervasive only when schooling itself is pervasive. Obviously this means that the calendar year must become the school year and that there can be no long holidays from learning.

Grouping on the Age-Grade Principle

High school classes are very tightly grouped on the age-grade principle, with subdivisions according to interests in different curricula which reflect, in turn, educational and occupational levels of aspiration. Grouping tightly on the age-grade basis can affect behavior and misbehavior two ways:

First, it implies to both teacher and pupils an equality and homogeneity that actually does not exist and in consequence of which instruction is undifferentiated through the slavish use of the single text and the identical lesson assignment. This invites the problem of the bored learner at the upper levels and the frustrated learner within the lower ranges of ability and achievement. Only by individuating instruction within the classroom can the great educational superstition that all children of the same age who come to school can learn the same things, at the same time, at the same pace, and to the same degree, be broken. High school students taught under this American superstition of equality are bound to suffer the trauma of a bad hangover once they leave school and meet the competitive climate in the world of work.

Second, grouping in tight age brackets tends to reinforce the already overly strong youth culture which is so often irresponsible to anyone but itself. The teen-ager notoriously would rather be wrong with his peers than right with his family or other adult authority. When this happens, as Margaret Mead has pointed out, American youth tend to surrender some moral autonomy for the comforts of the irresponsible crowd. This is the inherent nature of the delinquent act, particularly of the "group-intoxicated" and "socialized" types.

How much leeway is possible in grouping more broadly but within the chronological age span of the secondary school presents a real problem. Surely more could be done in the six-year secondary school by overlapping membership in some classes such as music and art, and by adhering more closely to an ability-achievement criteria in others, thereby breaking the solid age-grouping that now prevails. At the same time, the pressure to differentiate instruction for extremes will be lessened.

Contrary to some fears and even to some evidence that pre-adolescents, adolescents, and post-adolescents cannot be effectively grouped for instruction, careful observations of social and emotional situations on the ski slope, or in the swimmiing pool, or on the stage of the little theatre (where instruction is frequently imparted to groups having very wide age ranges but in accordance with a continuous growth principle), will reveal many positive outcomes, particularly in terms of a reciprocal respect and a camaraderie rare even in closely knit pressure groups.

The Cultural Surrogates of the School

When Kahlil Gibran speaks on teaching in *The Prophet*, he describes the teacher walking in the shadow of the temple among his followers, giving "not of his wisdom but rather of his faith and his lovingness." The emphasis here is probably not so much on subject matter as it is on the kind of warm personality who could relate easily to others through trust and affection. But let us not dispense entirely with wisdom or even subject matter, especially at the high school level!

Teen-age behavior can be strongly influenced by any glamorous figure with whom adolescents so easily identify. But who wants to identify with the teacher? The painful "mirror, mirror on the wall" self-inquiry that every teacher should undergo in searching out his own self-concept should be, *Who wants to be like you?* If the general public and the teacher himself are disenchanted with the teacher's status and role, the high school will not be highly populated by influential or glamorous imitative examples. Is it true that teachers are, as Phyllis McGinley portrays them in her cruel sonnet on the PTA, "apprehensive mentors of the young."[5] Are those who are hired to teach others all

---

[5] Phyllis McGinley, "Sonnets from the Suburbs, P.T.A. Tea Party" in *Times Three* (New York: Viking Press 1962), pp. 133-134.

too often uninspired and uninspiring? Yet teaching conceived as changing the behavior of others can be an exciting, glamorous, even dangerous occupation as one works on the critical frontier of human influence.

In this periodic self-inquiry the teacher should also raise one other allied question: "Why am I in the teaching profession?" The high school learning situation cannot be very hopeful if teaching is elected only as a secondary or tertiary choice. In these and the coming days of spiraling high school enrollments, will we be luring and pressing into service large numbers of workers whose basic motivations are extraneous to living, working, liking, and especially abiding as well as enjoying adolescents—workers who see themselves only as harassed and temporary hired hands in this vineyard? Some of these same teachers, who may render a higher quality of service strictly in the line of duty, may still fail to influence the behavior of others for the better so long as duty remains duty without love.

One last question on the school parent surrogate. What effect have recent debates on public education had on the classroom teacher in the high school? If the teacher is frightened, insecure, and jittery, it is certain that the pupils in his classes will also reflect some measure of this insecurity. If the teachers are not sure of themselves, their training, and their community roles, the result will again be seen in jittery pupils. Evidence can be found in the high rates of truancy, expulsion, withdrawal, and delinquency (particularly in the large city high schools where relationships are apt to be impersonal and anonymous) that the level of frustration tolerance of the school staff has been significantly lowered. Unless the teacher emerges from this exciting and promising period of debate and criticism as a stronger and more secure person, irreparable harm will have been done to large segments of the youth population. It is platitudinous to preach, but nonetheless true, that the high school cannot be any better than its teachers. Whatever role and status the high school teacher now enjoys or suffers is partly attained and partly attributed. But the limits of what can be attained are set only by the teacher's own self-concept.

The Undetermined and Unspecified Goals

While there is much learning activity visible in every American high school, not every teacher and student is always aware of the goals toward which the activity is directed. Rarely does the high-school staff explore and examine with the rest of the community, including the students, just what they want the secondary school to perpetuate beyond the simple and comfortable vagary of "the healthy and good citizen of a democracy." The result is that students, through their daily activities and assignments, aim only to please teacher or, stated negatively, to avoid the displeasure of the teacher, rather than to achieve some worthwhile objective *per se*. The extrinsic rewards of the mentor's smile, the marks on the report forms, and the honor roll can be unhealthy substitutes for real goals.

School personnel and the lay community need to arrive at some consensus on those issues basic to our American way of life that will help describe the kinds of persons we want and need in our fast-changing world. In arriving at some statement of desirable school outcomes we will need to know more about the kind of society we want now and in the future. How nationalistic or internationalistic should the future citizen of the United States and of the world be? How religious or non-religious? How competitive and how cooperative? How leisure- and how work-oriented? How individualistic and how socialistic? Unless the school and community can look ahead with some clarity of goals in what is a rapidly changing and perhaps unpredictable world, secondary schools—goal-less and directionless—can become educationally anachronistic. In transmitting the culture and heritage of the past, the high school may stand rooted in the past, but the high school must also face up to its full responsibility for improving the way of life of the future.

Success in Academic Achievement

Status in school is always linked to successful achievement in the classroom. For the adolescent, one source (often the only source) of teacher-parent approval can be found in academic achievement via the report card route. Unless the student shows a satisfactory level of attainment, he is not apt to find himself surrounded by smiling and approving adult faces.

School failure is frequently a concomitant and forerunner of deviant behavior. Studies of delinquents and non-delinquents[6] indicate a wide split between the educationally bankrupt and the educationally affluent. Delinquents frequently make a success of failure by using this means to thumb their noses at the home and school.

It is easy to understand how failure can be used to strike back at

---

[6] William C. Kvaraceus, *Juvenile Delinquency and the School* (New York: Harcourt, Brace & World, Inc., 1945), p. 337.

the teaching authority or to demolish the school, by students whose neighborhood or peer group value system is contrary to that of the school or of the dominant society; it may not be so easy to understand how the upper middle-class child can use failure as a powerful weapon to cut down his parents. When school success becomes a paramount issue to the parent who draws selfishly his own brand of personal satisfactions from the achievement of his youngsters, academic failure can prove a subtle and satisfactory boomerang for any youngster. In fact, this is one of the few ways that many high school adolescents have of getting back at their own offensive parents.

How to insure success for the less academic or "non-academic" pupil in the high school presents a difficult curriculum problem. Until this issue is met by the secondary school of the future, many of the students who must enter high school will run the risk of breaking their backs as they reach for unattainable goals. When satisfactions that come only through achievement, success, and approval are not attainable, the youngster may well resort to other means to achieve some measure of these satisfactions. These means may frequently follow the antisocial route of misbehavior.

External and Formal Discipline

The future high school, if it is to diminish deviate behavior, must aim to develop inner behavioral controls that will make its graduates less dependent on the supervising, monitoring, and policing authority. Self-discipline, as contrasted with external-control dependency, has been the aim of the secondary school, but this aim can hardly be attained so long as the school culture continues to dominate with adult controls and continues to tell the student what to do, when to do it, how to do it, and whether it is right when done. Such heavy dependence upon forces of external and formal discipline tends to deepen already existing misunderstanding and resentment between youth and adult and to intensify the hate and hostility now manifest in much of the deviate behavior in youth culture. Both the sociologist and the psychiatrist have independently come to the conclusion that the culture of formal and external controls, when it succeeds, frequently creates a reluctant and recalcitrant conformist living close to the letter of the law. When it fails, it creates "the outlaw" best exemplified by the overt, aggressive delinquent who is a member of an "outlaw gang" in the depths of the big city.

These and other cultural determinants found operating in most public secondary schools will continuously precipitate crises, tensions, and frustrations for the high school student. David Segel[7] has pointed out three kinds of behavior solutions that can follow frustration in the high school: (1) regression as exemplified by leaving school; (2) aggression as seen in disorderly conduct, overt attack, and vandalism; (3) fixation as found in the sitting out of school activities or going through the motions.

Of all these behavior solutions to inimical school situations, perhaps the most wholesome or promising will be found in the overt-aggression pattern in which the delinquent is doing something about it. He is putting up a fight. He is adjusting in the best and usually the only way he knows how. He is calling attention to himself and to his problem situation. He is not retreating, nor is he giving up, nor is he resorting to fantasy in solving his terrible problem. There is much that is positive—even wholesome—in the delinquency phenomenon. Needless to say, this is not well understood generally and can be readily misunderstood.

Knowledge of these cultural contingencies of behavior and misbehavior in the high school will enable the professional youth worker in school and community, together with the parent and the pupil, to plan cultural change. By changing the behavior of large masses of young people, the great American secondary school of the future may even be able to change and influence the culture of the community. If the secondary school fails to have any widespread effect on the behavior of the masses of youth, it will suffer the awful tragedy of being the most expensive irrelevancy of the mid-twentieth century.

---

[7] David Segel, *Frustration in Adolescent Youth*, Bulletin 1951, No. 1 (Washington, D.C.: U.S. Office of Education, 1951).

13 Do Large City Schools Contribute to the Development of the Socially Inadapted?

Since the rate of delinquency seems to be in ratio to the size of a city and its schools, can the attitudes of big urban institutions be turning young people to norm-violating behavior? Where can the teacher in a large school be given help and support? Is concern for academic reputation resulting in the removal of students who may lower the standards? What of the emotional needs of the students, as separate from their intellectual requirements?

Children and youth who live in the big city and attend schools in crowded urban centers tend to be more exposed and more vulnerable to social inadaptation and delinquency, according to a number of recent studies reported from different countries.

Evidence of the delinquent gang as a fast-growing social urban institution is provided in the French investigations by Ceccaldi (1961),[1] who reports that in the period between 1950-58 a 124 per cent increase in gang delinquencies was noted in cities of more than 100,000 population, whereas cities with less than 50,000 showed only a 28 per cent increase for the same period. A finer breakdown of figures for small and large communities reaffirmed a significant correlation between gang delinquency and the factors of the compressed and industrialized areas, although the correlation does not represent a straight line relationship.

In a controlled follow-up study of delinquents in Finland,

[1] Pierre Ceccaldi, "Le Phenomene des Bandes, Manifestation actuelle de la delinquance Juvenile." *Revue Penitentiare et de Droit Penal*, No. 50 (April-June, 1961), pp. 1-54.

Saari (1951)[2] has reported that the recidivists included the highest proportion of moving individuals and also that such persons tended to move to more densely populated districts.

In a Norwegian study by Christie (1960),[3] in which one thousand young offenders were compared with a sample of their non-delinquent counterparts, it was noted that two-thirds of the offenders had no education beyond the primary level. Yet the offenders lived in the densely populated parts of the country where there was easy access to extended education and better schools. It was also noted that school achievement and marks were considerably lower for the offenders. Christie emphasizes the fact that since the school agency has taken over many of the functions of the family in modern industrialized Norwegian society, these differences in school background between offenders and non-offenders become a matter of special reference in view of the similar home and family backgrounds from which the groups came.

The youngster who is most in need of help and reinforcement by the school agency is precisely the one who is most apt to reject or to be rejected by the school. Yet for many of these young people the school represents the only positive and constructive experience that may offer help and assistance. How to keep such city youngsters in school to the benefit of themselves and society should be of major concern to authorities in large urban centers. There is some evidence, for example, in a study by the National Education Association,[4] that the school staff may be too inclined to relieve itself of the inadapted or delinquent pupil by early rejection or dismissal. In this study, almost half of the teachers and principals argued for the early expulsion of misbehaving children as a means of coming to grips with the problem. This is merely evasion of the problem.

In the United States, sheer bigness of educational enterprise and trouble with pupils seem to go hand in hand. The National Education Association, in the previously mentioned study, noted that "Teachers in big school districts, in big schools, and with big classes reported significantly more trouble with pupils than teachers in small districts, in small schools and with small classes." This was one of the most definite relationships established in this study.[5]

The big-city slant in juvenile delinquency is further accentuated by

[2] E. Saari, "Delinquency as a Symptom of Later Social Maladjustment." *Acta Academiae Paedogogicae Jyvaskylöensis,* VI. (Jyvaskyla: Jyvaskylan Yliopistoyhdistyksen Kustantama, 1951).

[3] N. Christie, *Ung Norske Lovovertredere* (Oslo: Universitetsforlaget, 1960).

[4] National Education Association, Research Division, "Teacher Opinion on Pupil Behavior, 1955-56," *Research Bulletin* (April, 1956), pp. 51-107.

[5] *Ibid.,* p. 104.

a report by the Illinois Youth Commission (1959). In Illinois, the 14 counties in which the principal industrial and urban centers are located were found to be responsible for 91 per cent of all boys committed in a single year to the state training school.

The research studies cited reaffirm the greater vulnerability, exposure, and opportunity for delinquency and social inadaption of young city-dwellers. At the same time, they underscore the school's responsibility and opportunity as the one agency that constantly comes in contact with the city child and is in a strong position to assist him in his growth and adjustment.

For the many city children who come from disrupted and unstable homes, who live in neighborhoods lacking cohesiveness, whose value systems are in conflict with those of the dominant adult community, whose parents are ignorant or neglectful, and who find no moral, social, or psychological roots in the neighborhood, the school generally represents the one positive and supervised experience that can steer them in the direction of personal and social well-being. The school has a singular opportunity to turn youthful energies, often pointed in destructive fashion to self and society, towards more wholesome ends.

Maintaining the School as an Ego Institution

Children in the big city who enter the public schools in heavily populated neighborhoods are immediately absorbed in a massive educational system. Although the big city school system accepts all children, it does so on its own terms. These terms frequently demand some renunciation of differences—personal, social, and cultural—and a constant submission to the processes of conformity and standardization. Most schools achieve their goals at the price of some loss of privacy, personal identity, and individuality. They require a submission to external controls and to the pressures of the group; they invoke the severe competitive processes of selection and survival of the academically fit; and all too frequently they produce an artificial separation between the classroom and the life stream of everyday problems and activities.

These demands of the large city school system may be destructive to the ego. Children and youth who are unable or unwilling to submit frequently join the ranks of the school failures, the troubled and troublesome, the truants, and the early school drop-outs. They may even set up their own ego-supporting institutions in the form of the juvenile gang. It is imperative that the school, in working to achieve its goals, operate always as an ego-supporting institution.

The destructive nature of the school experiences of many delinquents and socially inadapted youngsters shows up vividly in Kvaraceus's (1945)[6] controlled studies of delinquents and their nondelinquent counterparts. School case histories of delinquents reveal them to be most often in bad school posture. Their school reports indicate low achievement or failure in many subjects. They are overage for their grade. They register a strong dislike for school and for the people who manage it. They are frequently truant. They intend to leave school as soon as the law will allow. In short, while they represent a headache for the school, the school represents an even greater headache for them. There is little evidence of status, prestige, success, security, or acceptance in the school experiences of most delinquents. What these school experiences point to is a succession of severe frustrations that beget aggression toward self or toward society.

The Teacher as a Person and a Professional Worker

The most direct and effective way to strengthen the school as an ego institution is to improve the interpersonal relationships between teacher and students. It is the individual teacher who generally enjoys the most intimate and continuing relationship with the child outside the home and family circle. Through the powerful instrument of this relationship, the teacher can do much to promote, via the normal educational processes, better mental health and emotional growth. To achieve this he must be a mature adult, committed to his responsibility of helping children and youth, presenting a positive image with which to identify. He must be aware of conscious and subconscious motivations and be able to communicate with others. Here is where those responsible for teacher preparation and in-service training of staff can make their most telling contribution—by seeking to improve teaching personalities and teacher competencies.

Every teacher faces the same basic problem. He must define and maintain his role as a mature professional adult. Teachers in the big city school system usually operate in a cumbersome bureaucracy. Surrounded by administrators, supervisors, and specialists, they often become uncertain of their own functions and the extent and direction of their own responsibility. Of particular significance is the previously cited National Education Association study which indicated that a substantially larger proportion of teachers in large school districts than

---

6 William C. Kvaraceus, *Juvenile Delinquency and the School* (New York: Harcourt, Brace & World, Inc., 1945).

of teachers in small school districts felt that they lacked the rights and authority needed to maintain effective control over pupils. This same study found that those teachers who felt that they had the necessary authority did have better-behaved pupils and fewer trouble-makers in their classes.

It may well be that teachers in larger school districts, as compared with those in smaller districts, are less likely to have an important voice in determining the discipline policies of their school. Consideration should be given to including teachers of larger school units in any discussions related to policies and practices for handling problems of school discipline and social inadaptation.

On a generally subliminal level, teachers constantly face the problem of resolving conflicts arising between their school organization role and their teacher-helper role. The organization commitment pulls in the direction of the enforcement and maintenance of standards of achievement, speech, dress, and behavior; but the teacher-helper commitment demands the assistance of the young learner in terms of his basic needs within the reality setting of his milieu.

For example, in assisting the slow learner or near-failure, the teacher-helper provides the pupil with individual instruction and emotional support, but at the end of the marking period, the organization role may force the teacher to fail the pupil in spite of the learning effort expanded or the extenuating circumstances of the pupil's learning difficulties. Such a situation may lead to hostility directed at the very pupil the teacher has been trying to help, but who also precipitated the role-conflict. In working with socially inadapted youth in particular, the teacher must be conscious of the problems he faces in experiencing this type of role-conflict.

Many teachers in big city systems today indicate strong job dissatisfaction and low self-concept which often tends to reduce their frustration tolerance. It is difficult to tell whether the figures on pupil misbehavior in big schools and big districts reflect, in fact, a true difference in the incidence of social inadaptation between big city pupils and small city pupils or whether they merely reflect significant differences between irritability levels of city teachers and teachers employed in smaller schools and smaller communities. Many teachers today appear in an angry and hostile mood. This is especially manifest in the teacher's relationship with the reluctant and recalcitrant learners. The frequent cry heard for sterner and harsher measures in dealing with these pupils and for their removal from the regular classroom or exclusion from school would indicate that too many educators are now more concerned with the academic reputation of their school than with the welfare and well-being of the offending students.

Some teachers subconsciously fear their disturbed or disturbing pupils and resent their presence on the classroom. In relating to these children, the teacher may have forgotten fears of the past suddenly unlatched by a chance remark or episode. These unresolved threats and hidden anxieties can blind and deafen the teacher to classroom realities or can paralyze him temporarily. Sensing the precipitant of this recall process, the teacher may strike back at the pupil, using him as a symbol of the earlier offender. At times, the teacher may try to work out or resolve his old problems through the problem behavior of his students.

Emotional Needs of Pupils and Teachers

In most classrooms the cognitive aspects of life experience and the learning process are played up and the emotional aspects are played down. We understress the emotional life of the pupil until his difficulties are so pronounced that this dimension can no longer be denied. The teacher generally does not trust emotions—his own or those of his pupils. He only seeks to repress or deny them.

Alfred North Whitehead has stated in the *Dialogues,* "Intellect is to emotion as our clothes are to our bodies; we could not very well have civilized life without clothes, but we would be in a poor way if we had only clothes without bodies."[7] Teachers act in many classrooms today as though their pupils were clothes without bodies. In fact, the classroom is often used as a sedative to calm down creative feelings, as though the school's aim were to produce dispassionate young adults. The result is often a boring ritual of learning and teaching that drives many an alive and feeling pupil into a stupor or into rebellion.

Teachers who work with many disturbed and inadapted pupils are apt themselves to experience strong emotional difficulty. Someone must help them resolve the personal difficulties arising from work with these children. In the big school systems, aid can be provided through therapeutic counseling by psychiatrists, psychologists, and psychiatric social workers operating as mental health consultants. Help can come from a positive and understanding school administrator or supervisor who lends his ear to the troubled teacher. The principal of the school

---

[7] *Dialogues of Alfred North Whitehead,* ed., Lucien Price (Atlantic Monthly Press, 1954) p. 232.

may even use his office as a way-station in which the teacher can freely express his innermost anxieties and fears. To this end, consideration must be given to a much needed shift in focus on the part of school-centered child guidance clinics, whose effectiveness may be strengthened and broadened by becoming more and more teacher-guidance clinics. The classroom is seldom without mental health hazards for the teacher. Unfortunately, most teachers have little direct or easy access to mental health aids.

The teacher, seeing the child in his continuous day-to-day relationships and for a long period of time, can carry out the screening and identification responsibility that may help prevent emotional disturbances and social maladjustment through early identification of incipient difficulties and symptoms. Screening and early identification are feasible, as several studies have indicated, through the careful use of teacher observations and ratings, peer-group ratings, and self-reporting devices. But it is the problem of communicating in the referral process which often presents the more difficult and crucial step.

It is always hard to communicate to the parent and to the child himself that psychiatric or psychological help must be sought. The problem facing the teacher can be stated as follows: "How best can I describe clearly and comfortably the pupil's emotional disturbance or social inadaptation?" Frequently the teacher's over-concern and anxiety only disturb the parent and child. The parent picks up the message—"Something is wrong with my child; the school says so." But, on reflection, he is unable to recall exactly what the school said. Guidelines need to be drawn, and skills in communication need to be developed by the school staff in the referral-communication process after the pupil needing help has been identified.

The bigness of today's schools can breed impersonality and isolation. Although many teaching machines are useful and important, the schools should be aware of the students' needs for human relationships. The time saved by the machines should be used to increase the opportunities for warm personal exchanges in the classroom.

Special Services for Pupils and Teachers

The big city school, with its large enrollment and broad base of financial support, can economically provide many special personnel services including guidance, counseling, remediation, and health services. Teachers have real limits to their competencies in diagnosing and helping the socially inadapted pupils. There are also limits to the time that can be spent with the many individuals who need help. To this end the big city can offer to the teacher the services of the school psychologist, psychiatrist, case worker, vocational counselor, school nurse or doctor, home visitor, etc. Too often such services tend to cluster at the secondary school level. They need to be equally available to the primary school staff who are better able to put forth preventive effort in dealing with incipient problems.

The large urban communities did not invent the delinquent and the socially inadapted child. However, the fact remains that city schools now hold, and are likely to continue to hold, the largest segment of a nation's disturbed and disturbing youth population. In helping these youngsters find more acceptable modes of adjustment, municipal authorities will need to work more and more through the schools and classrooms. This will demand teachers who are more effective as persons and as professionals.

14 How Can the Superintendent Be a Top-Level Guide?

At the head of the teaching pyramid, the superintendent accounts for over-all policy and shapes the structure of the entire system. How can he inject vitality and meaning into the school atmosphere? What must he look for in the teachers he hires? What kinds of curricula are best suited and most meaningful to his students? What must he do to direct, help, and train his personnel? How can he work with the community and parents to create an understanding attitude toward both school and students?

The superintendent occupies a kingpin position for helping norm-violators in school and community. What is of prime concern to the administrator will be reflected in the prime concerns of the school staff. The superintendent must fulfill his responsibility to the troublemaker at two levels: (1) on the community level he must be concerned with and participate in the over-all community planning and coordination involving all youth and family agencies; (2) on the school level he must show concern for improving the school program for all children, including those youngsters who need special provisions and services if they are to learn because of some mental, emotional, or physical dysfunctioning. However, the school superintendent must be alert lest the school stray from its unique and special function: *teaching and learning*. The school is not a hospital for sick children; it is not an open warehouse to store children up to a certain age; it is not a convenient incinerator for difficult and unwanted youngsters. The superintendent will meet his responsibilities at the school and community levels only when he fulfills the following normal school functions:

Finds, employs, and trains the most effective and wholesome teaching personalities. No official act that the superintendent performs has more ramifications than the hiring of a teacher. An effective and well-adjusted teaching personality can prevent and control troublesome behavior; the ineffective and especially the maladjusted teacher can create behavioral disturbances for himself, his pupils, and the administration. In his search for teacher-talent, the superintendent must be alert to the personal characteristics requisite for good teaching; he must make sure that the teacher he hires really wants to be in the classroom, that he really wants to live and work with all types of young people—even irritating and offensive youngsters.

Assigning each teacher to a school and a classroom needs to be done with careful concern to match the teacher to the subculture in which he will work. The superintendent will need to take into consideration the teacher's social status, his self-concept, his willingness to work with certain types of youngsters, and his ability "to take it" and not just "to dish it out." There are many teachers who are unable or unwilling, for example, to work with *lower-class youngsters* whom they find threatening and even offensive. Matching the teacher to the total job setting may help prevent many behavior disturbances and may enable the more sympathetic handling of bothersome cases when they arise in the school and classroom.

Obtains the facts on school and community troublemakers. In acting to prevent and control norm-violating behavior, the superintendent must act on all the facts—not on hunches and impressions. This calls for a research emphasis. In planning the school program, he must know who the truants are and be familiar with their home and family backgrounds; he needs to know what type of youngsters drop out of school and why; he needs to know how many youngsters are failing and in what subjects and classrooms; he needs to know the neighborhood story on the truant, the delinquent, the school drop-out, and the failing student. Lacking such essential data, it is not possible to approach the problem of the bothersome pupil with a preventive program that will be truly relevant to the complex factors that frequently underlie norm-violating conduct. In short, the administrator must be research-minded and must plan his improved program on the basis of carefully gathered information that relates significantly to the phenomenon of the troublemaker. Lacking the essential data, the school's efforts to help the troublemakers may prove irrelevant to the factors which generate such conduct.

Works to reduce class size and teacher load to reasonable limits. One way to reduce the number of troublemakers is through the organization of smaller classes. Bigness breeds behavioral problems. Anonymity, impersonality, and assembly-line teaching, which generally are associated with large classes, tend to impair or limit the quality of the pupil-teacher and teacher-pupil relationship. Effectivenesses of the learning-teaching process as well as the emotional climate of the classroom depend upon the quality of this relationship. Teachers who do not know their pupils, and who are prevented from establishing a close working relationship with every pupil based upon mutual respect and liking, will suffer the consequences of many troublemakers. Smaller classes will demand greater expenditure, but there is no cheap or easy solution to preventing and controlling norm-violating behavior.

Plans and promotes continuing education programs for the total staff. In-service training programs must be carefully planned to meet the individual needs of the teaching staff, just as the teacher must meet the needs of his pupils. Greater stress must be placed by administration on training via the human relations laboratory approach. Most teachers fail in their handling of the bothersome pupil because of lacks in their own personal make-up and equipment rather than because of any lack of knowledge in either the substantive or methods areas. To be effective, in-service training experiences must be positive and therapeutic and they must leave the teacher with a strong sense of personal security and satisfaction with his teaching role and his daily contacts with boys and girls. Too often the in-service training program tends to make teachers insecure and distrustful of their classroom role. This, in turn, invites classroom disorder.

Sets up committees to work out a variegated curriculum to meet the needs of all pupils. The adequacy and range of the school curriculum— all the planned experiences which have been geared to stated objectives—need to be re-examined annually at all grade levels and in all subject matter areas. Most of the youngsters whose troubles originate in school merely reflect inadequacies in the curriculum. These youngsters, via their non-conforming behavior, reject a poorly planned or severely limited school offering. It is unreasonable to expect that different pupils, whose needs, as found in their abilities, special aptitudes, interests, occupational objectives, and cultural backgrounds, are widely divergent, should take the same courses at the same time and at the same pace. *Failure and boredom* are the twin-consequences of a one-track, one-book, and one-purpose curriculum and teaching method.

The administrator who fails to provide the leadership and the stimulus in establishing teacher-citizen committees to study, revise, and reconstruct the school program to meet the needs of all pupils must assume a measure of responsibility for the troublemakers in his school system. The school system with little or no curriculum activity on the part of its staff will harvest the largest crop of school troublemakers and will report the heaviest school drop-out rate.

Develops a special program for early school drop-outs. Compulsory education within the framework of an undifferentiated school program tends to produce the "sitter" who awaits impatiently his school-leaving birthday as an escape from an unbearable and frustrating situation. As we indicated earlier, those youngsters who intend to leave school as soon as the law will allow include many troublemakers within their unhappy ranks.

Retrospective and follow-up studies need to be made locally in an effort to uncover reasons—cultural, personal, curricular—why youngsters leave school. If these antecedents can be dealt with by school, home, and community, the resulting increase in rate of retention will also mean a drop in the number of troublemakers in school and classroom.

For the terminal student who still persists in dropping out before graduation, the administration must establish a terminal pre-employment curriculum. Such adaptations should include work-study programs at the secondary school level and must be worked out jointly by school, labor, industry, and child-welfare organizations.

Joins with all other community youth and family agencies in coordinated effort to identify, study, and treat the troublesome student. The school agency, in helping the norm-violator, cannot afford to work in isolation. There are two reasons why the school must look to other agencies: first, many of the problems of the troublemaker stem from factors outside the school's sphere of influence; second, the school is not an omnibus agency—it is limited in its function and resources.

The school administration must work to unite and coordinate its efforts with the activities of all other youth and family serving agencies in the community. The administrator must help his staff to know and to use all the resources in the community in systematic fashion; he must open the school doors to other professional workers; and he must provide the leadership in the community to coordinate all existing facilities and services that affect children and their families.

Makes available needed and essential services to help in diagnosis, remediation, and rehabilitation. There are limits to the teacher's competencies and classroom responsibilities. The teacher cannot be expected to be all things to all pupils. Frequently he will need to lean on school and community personnel for advice and help in meeting the needs of troublesome cases. The administrator must take steps to make available and accessible to every teacher the specialized skills of the school doctor and nurse, guidance counselor, psychologist, consulting psychiatrist, social worker or visiting teacher, remedial reading specialist, and speech therapist. Without these resources it is unreasonable to expect the classroom teacher to understand and to help adjust many of the more serious cases that are to be found in today's classrooms.

Since all such essential services cannot be procured overnight, the administrator, working closely with the school staff, will need to establish a priority list of needed services. Such listings should be prepared with due consideration for similar services which may be available from other organizations and agencies within the community, county, or region.

Establishes with his staff a workable policy regarding discipline, suspension, and expulsion. Suspending or expelling the bothersome pupil from the classroom will seldom solve the youngster's problem although it may rid the school of a minor headache. Operational principles and procedures for handling discipline problems and for separating bothersome youngsters from school must be available in the form of a workable guide for action. Teachers, like their students, need to know where they stand and what the philosophy and point of view of the school is for handling minor and major offenders.

These school policies should reflect research and thinking on personality growth and adjustment. They should provide for child-study and diagnosis as a first step in the adjustment process. When it becomes necessary to separate the youngster from school temporarily, the conditions for re-entry in school must be stated; if the bothersome pupil is separated permanently, a contact with some out-of-school agency is made to help the youngster and his family. Care should also be taken lest the school hold on to the youngster too long, thus depriving him of help and treatment which might be forthcoming from placement with some appropriate institution or agency. And finally, the school guides for action should enable, or even force, the teacher to view the bothersome pupil's norm violations in terms of the primary reference group or subgroups to which he belongs as well as in terms of the rule book of the school. When schools lack a definite and lucid policy, action that is followed in discipline and expulsion can be inconsistent, arbitrary, and contrary to good mental hygiene practices.

Makes plant, equipment and space available to other agencies in an all-day, year-round program for youth. Schools represent a heavy community investment in plant, equipment and space. They seldom wear out; more often they merely become obsolete. Many superintendents have helped all youth, including the norm-violator, by developing the concept of the neighborhood or community school open the year round on an all-day basis.

Encourages and advises parent-study groups and the local PTA. Few agencies in the community enjoy the natural relationship with parents and children that is found in the concept of the good school. By working closely with parents and other adults interested in child growth and youth welfare, the school administrator can do much to improve parenthood and at the same time improve school-community programs for all youth via the strong public support that is forthcoming when youth and youth problems are understood.

Interprets the school's role and function in the community. How far should the schools go in helping the young troublemaker in school who may be emotionally and socially disturbed? In view of the unique and special function of the school—teaching and learning—it is imperative for the administrator to interpret for the public where the school's responsibility begins and ends. Many of the school's critics are complaining that the schools are trying to do too much, that they are departing from their main purpose; other critics expect the schools to take on any and every new responsibility in the interest of child and community welfare.

The schools have been given the mandate to educate all the children—even troublesome and difficult ones. But to do so effectively, the schools will need the support—moral and financial—of the greater part of the community. This will demand a skillful interpretation of the schools' commitment to its youth and an objective evaluation of the local school's efforts in carrying out this commitment.

15 What Is the Role of the Principal?

As guide and counselor for the teacher, the principal can offer positive support for the members of his staff. How can he best demonstrate his willingness to help the teacher function effectively in the classroom? What must he understand about the social structure and environment of his school? What helpful attitudes can he develop in order that the teacher may understand and take advantage of his role as helper? What mental climate should he cultivate in the school? How can he develop in-service training so that the teachers may learn the best ways to deal with youngsters? What outside agencies are available to him?

The principal's key function is to help the teacher work more effectively in the classroom. According to a report made by Kenneth R. Brown,[1] director of the NEA project on working conditions of teachers, the two most frequently cited problems center around the size of the class and the presence of "unwilling and unable" students in the classroom. It is also significant that 48 per cent of the principals and 45 per cent of the teachers in an earlier NEA study urged that the reluctant and recalcitrant pupil be banished from the classroom and that some other provisions be made for him. There is real danger in such widespread protest that instead of helping the norm-violator, the school may be trying to rid itself of a major headache—and a major responsibility. There are many preventive and rehabilitative actions that a principal can take before resorting to such radical measures. The following recommendations to principals should be considered:

[1] Reported by Kenneth R. Brown at Annual Meeting of the National Education Association, St. Louis, Mo., July 1, 1959.

Study the social composition of the school-neighborhood. The social composition of every school presents different kinds of behavioral and adjustment problems to the school staff. The principal and his teachers need to study the implications of the social and cultural backgrounds of the students in his building. Some schools house an heterogeneous population reflecting lower, middle, and upper middle-class families. Other schools are more homogeneous and enroll mainly lower-class youngsters or pupils who come chiefly from middle-class homes. Troublesome pupils from lower-class milieux more often represent culturally-determined problems; troublesome students from middle-class homes frequently include a larger number of emotionally disturbed learners. The staff cannot understand or help these norm-violators without due recognition of the primary reference groups to which they belong.

Develop a wholesome climate in which to live and work. The principal sets the tone for school living. He must help the staff to look at bothersome behavior from an objective, diagnostic, and positive viewpoint. By imitative example he must show that troublesome behavior has causes, that it is the school's job to accept and to help the youngster without becoming emotionally involved with the young offender or his parents.

Provide therapeutic counseling for the staff. Teachers are persons and, like their pupils, they also have problems. When a problem-laden teacher meets a problem-laden pupil, behavioral explosions may occur. Teaching a large class of different and often difficult pupils day in and day out makes unusual demands on the teaching personality. When the going gets rough, teachers need ready access to an accepting and understanding administrator to whom they can take their problems. If principal-staff relationships are positive and of a non-judgmental nature, the principal should be able to play the therapeutic-listening role of the good administrator. His office should be a comfortable listening post for the over-worked, hard-pressed, harassed, and unhappy teacher. This is the easiest form of counseling and one that can do the least damage. If no one on his staff ever voluntarily comes by to discuss his school problems with a principal, the administrator is the one who probably needs help.

Don't tie the teacher's hands. There are many approaches to excellence. A principal should not force all the teachers to act and think in a single mold when handling young offenders. Troublesome youngsters who show the same symptoms often have different causes for their overt behavior. The teacher must feel confident and secure with his own methods. The principal must check out the methods used by his staff in disciplining and helping those youngsters who persistently and seriously violate the norms of home, school, and community.

Play a leadership role in conducting case conferences and in coordinating special resources. When a pupil continues to show serious and persisting norm-violating behavior, the cooperative thinking of the staff should be enlisted in diagnosing the youngster's difficulty and in outlining treatment. Case conferences should be scheduled, involving all staff members who have a contact with the youngster and who might be brought in to help in the treatment phase. In addition to helping the youngster, this case conference technique may serve as an in-service training device.

The limitations of the school in helping all troublesome youngsters must be recognized. A principal needs to know what services are available from other agencies and institutions in the community, county, and state. By making systematic and scientific use of all community resources focused on the individual needs of the norm-violating pupil, he can bring order and meaning to the vast network of social and recreational agencies that are available, especially in the larger urban centers.

Keep the communication lines open. In helping troublesome pupils, the research and treatment focus has been exclusively on the quality of the relationship between teacher and pupil or between counselor and patient. However, what help the youngster and his family receives also depends upon the relationships between teacher and teacher, teacher and principal, teacher and school nurse, teacher and guidance worker, teacher and parent. At the same time, help that may be forthcoming is determined in part by the quality of relationships between the school and other community agencies: police, court, church, clinic, etc. By improving the interpersonal relationships among his staff members and by strengthening the school's contacts with other agencies in the community, the principal can keep the supply lines open to the troublesome pupils.

Help teachers inventory and appraise their competencies in working with the norm-violating pupil. Individual differences exist among teachers just as they do among pupils. A principal should confer with his staff individually and give it the benefit of his insights. A constructive and positive point of view should be taken with the staff, just as the teacher takes a positive and constructive point of view with his students. Teachers should not be made to feel inept and guilty. Most teachers can improve their competencies in dealing with the emotionally disturbed and socially maladjusted youngsters, but they will need the help of an insightful and sympathetic administrator.

A principal and his staff may be helped by studying the U.S. Office of Education report[2] on the competencies, skills, knowledges, and abilities needed for success in teaching socially and emotionally maladjusted children; these have been summarized in Chapter 20.

Help evolve a meaningful curriculum for all youngsters. The cause for much of the bothersome behavior in school can be traced back to the curriculum. The student who is failing, who sees little value in schooling, who intends to drop out as soon as the law allows, often bases his disturbing behavior on an inadequate or ineffective school offering. The principal can make his major contribution in preventing norm-violating behavior by developing a variegated curriculum that enables all youngsters, regardless of their interests, abilities, and cultural backgrounds, to make sense of the school program and to succeed. Even within the traditionally academic curriculum he can help his teachers to adapt their instruction to the varying needs of the pupils in the classroom. A restricted and one-track curriculum that keeps some pupils in a perpetual state of educational bankruptcy will continue to force out the disturbed and disturbing pupil.

Protect the teacher and the pupil from the hostile and avenging adult critics. In every community there can be felt a continuous stream of hostile and vengeful expression aimed at the bothersome and often frightening norm-violating adolescent. This public hate and hostility often overflows and engulfs the professional workers, including the teachers, whose role is to help the bothersome ones. Wild complaints aimed at "progressive educators" and "permissive teachers who mollycoddle the undisciplined pupils" abound in every community and often set the teacher up as an arch-villain aiding and abetting the young norm-violators.

A principal must protect his staff against community diatribe and and pressure that would turn a teacher into a punitive and avenging mentor of the young. He must constantly interpret and reinforce the teacher's major role as a helpful guide and friendly counselor. If the principal and his staff yield to the adult tendency to use youth as an institutionalized hate object, the school-agency will abscond from its primary and unique function—to help growing boys and girls.

---

[2] *Teachers of Children Who are Socially and Emotionally Maladjusted,* Bulletin 1957, No. 11 (U.S. Department of Health, Education, and Welfare, Washington, D.C., 1957). Note in particular the teaching competencies Check List, pp. 52-61.

16 Integrating the Guidance Team: How Can the School Personnel Worker Increase His Effectiveness?

In dealing with students, the personnel worker must learn to see his functions realistically without expecting to perform every possible service for any and all applicants. How many cases can the personnel worker handle? How must he limit his work load and circumscribe his area of responsibility? Shall the "hard-core" curriculum solve his problems or multiply them? Should we focus on the needs of the non-academic student in constructing the curriculum? What are the dangers of herding youth into conformity? Where and when should the counselor dare to encourage deviation? What is the essential and unique role of the teacher in guidance work?

Although current statistics point to a leveling-off in school drop-outs in America, the figures also seem to indicate that the holding power of the public schools has probably reached its peak. The problem of retaining pupils concerns all educators and guidance personnel, but it is unlikely that the public schools will do much better either in retaining pupils through the secondary school or in helping them to achieve in accordance with their potential without a drastic shift in focus and a strengthening of the school and pupil personnel services, especially at the secondary school level.

School and student personnel services in the larger communities include a wide variety of functions of which the central activity is guidance and counseling. Included under this heading are: child accounting, attendance service, medical and nursing services, psychological and psychiatric help, and case work. All these services tend to focus on the individual pupil. Personnel services are distinguished from instruction but are intimately related to the instructional program. They should not be thought of as "special services"; rather, they should be considered as "essential" services. Their aim is to insure or enable all youngsters to profit from schooling. In this sense, the personnel worker must be regarded as a handmaid of the teacher in the classroom.

The school-student personnel worker is a constant reminder of the inadequacies and malfunctioning of an overcrowded and overambitious school agency. He represents a community gesture to repair the wear and tear of an inadequate curriculum, of bigness and impersonality, of poorly trained and listless teachers, and of the sociology of the school. However, it is not enough to keep providing more and better personnel services in a valiant and expensive effort to prop up the classroom; it becomes imperative to shift the focus of the personnel services and to attack the basic causes that result in a demand for these services in the first place. The chief goal of school and student personnel services should not be more and better services; it should be the elimination or solution of the school-community problems that create the need for such services. How can this objective be attained?

Most personnel services represent relatively new functions in school practice. As new workers in a new field, most personnel functionaries tend to suffer from a terrible urgency to succeed. Many workers, particularly in the guidance, counseling, and case work area, posture a high success rate and suffer severe neurotic anxieties when their subjects fail to learn or to readjust. They are anxious to prove themselves and to please. Consequently, they take on every difficult task that is sent their way. They become omnibus functionaries—a school wastebasket of unsolved and unsolvable problems. Promising more than they can deliver, they become false prophets. If the pupil personnel worker measurably affects the learning, behavior, or adjustment of one out of three of his clients, this might be considered a "good batting average." But the summary and evaluation statements of these workers imply a 100 per cent batting average in their annual tabulations of the number of cases served, the number of interviews held, the number of families contacted, the number of pupils examined, and the number of tests administered. What is sorely needed are evaluative criteria that would help to indicate the improvement and growth—physical, mental, emotional, or social—that has taken place in consequence of an extended relationship between pupil and personnel worker.

Personnel workers should start by being more selective and discriminating in the cases they undertake to serve. They will also need to call a halt to the number of youngsters that are added to their mounting case loads. This will demand a clear understanding of their own competencies for dealing with certain types of cases and a more realistic concept of the rehabilitation process. Talking with a disturbed youngster two or three times a month may mean that he has been seen but not necessarily served. Indiscriminate case referrals and heavy case loads involving several hundred clients water down the effectiveness of most personnel workers today.

Many of the problems of the nonlearner and the norm-violator take root in the curriculum. In trying to assist these youngsters many counselors, case workers, and psychologists suffer severe job frustrations. Lacking a comprehensive and balanced curriculum, the best they can hope to accomplish is to persuade the disinterested and failing pupil to return and to adjust to what is basically an unsatisfactory and unpromising learning situation. So long as the school lacks a varied curriculum to meet the needs of all youngsters, the effectiveness of the counseling, social work, psychological, and attendance services will be severely circumscribed. A major and primary prerequisite to effective school and pupil personnel services is a balanced and varied curriculum that accommodates all levels of talent, that meets a wide range of interests, and that prepares for the job requirements of the current labor market, in addition to getting a youngster into a college of his choice. School and pupil personnel workers can best serve their present and future clients by addressing themselves to the improvement of the curriculum of the school.

The curriculum of the school includes all those planned and directed activities which are aimed to achieve agreed-upon objectives. This includes all those learning experiences through which the school personnel guide their pupils so that certain changes in behavior will take place or new behaviors will be developed.

In a rapidly changing social-economic-political scene, the schools must remain experimental, flexible, and fluid. Many critics of the schools are urging change and improvement by regressing to the college preparatory curriculum riveted to the "hard core subjects" of mathematics, science, and languages. At most, only about 25 per cent of the youth have the ability to profit from this traditional emphasis. The highly recommended science-math-languages diet will foster defeat and frustration for many a youngster and will turn him into an early school drop-out. It is this group of youngsters, incapable of coping with a stiff and inflexible curriculum, that occupies much of the time and energy of the attendance personnel, the psychological staff, the counseling and case work functionaries.

With the school critics in hot pursuit, many schools now appear to be more concerned with their reputation than with their pupils welfare. As Salinger's Holden Caulfield ruefully explains: "They give guys the ax frequently at Pencey. It has a very good academic rating, Pencey. It really does."[1] We might also add that it keeps school and student personnel workers very busy.

To get at the roots of much of the learning and adjustment problems of school youth today, school and student personnel workers will need to focus on the improvement of the curriculum. The imbalance in the courses of study in the public schools today favors the academically talented middle-class youngster and is highly prejudicial to both the nonacademic and the lower-class child. We need to ask, "What are we educating for?" and to re-examine the objectives of the school against the needs of all pupils as well as the needs of technological society.

It would not be worthwhile to try to indicate what should constitute the breadth and scope of a balanced school program for a local community. This can be done only by the local school staff and citizen groups after a careful study of local youth needs and the ability of the local district to finance a comprehensive school curriculum. The addition of more and better personnel services alone will have little effect on the basic learning and adjustment of the courses of study that make up the curriculum. Limited and inadequate curriculum offerings will always keep the school and student personnel staff busy. Instead of working with consequences the entire school staff should focus on the antecedents of the learning and behavior problems.

Both the teaching staff and the school and student personnel workers have tended to ignore or slight the cultural determinants of behavior. They have operated almost exclusively on the principle that nonlearning and misbehavior were to be explained solely by psychophysical factors in the student. Their attention needs to be directed to imperatives embedded in the cultural milieux of the school and neighborhood that strongly shape the pupil's modes of adjustment. If, for example, the reports[2] of the National Education Association Juvenile Delinquency Project are close to the truth in the estimate that the larger bulk of the norm-violators represent predominantly culturally deter-

---

[1] J. D. Salinger, *Catcher in the Rye* (Boston: Little, Brown, and Co., 1951).

[2] National Education Association Juvenile Delinquency Project, *Delinquent Behavior: Culture and the Individual; Delinquent Behavior: Principles and Practices* (Washington, D.C.,: The Association, 1959).

mined delinquency and that a minority of norm-violators suffer demonstrable pathology, much of the effort of counseling-testing-casework teams may actually prove irrelevant to the antecedents of this type of behavior. There is little doubt that such factors as disinterest, educational anesthesia, school failure, truancy, and early school-leaving in many instances are the results of strong cultural factors rather than forces from within the psyche.

Impoverished parents, realists that they are, rarely spin out all the likely fantasies of what is possible in our democratic society. They foreclose on themselves and their young. While most children from favored homes can be heard to say—even before they enter the first grade—"When I go to college I will . . .," the economically and socially handicapped can be heard saying, "As soon as I quit school, I will . . . ."

The success of the program directed by Dr. Samuel Shepard, Jr., in the Banneker District of the St. Louis Public Schools illustrates how achievement and intelligence levels of youngsters can be raised if the problem of parent and teacher foreclosure is attacked in an aggressive manner. Even teachers often give up on underprivileged children much too easily. Consciously and unconsciously, they do not believe the needy child has a chance or that he will ever make it. They feel the cards are really stacked against him—and indeed they may be—and it is here that the school must enter in and insure a fair deal for every child.

Most student personnel workers have failed to adapt their counseling methods to the less-educated parent. They have slavishly followed counseling principles that accommodate more particularly to middle-class homes and to middle-class intellectuality. Parents from unfavored socioeconomic strata need to be reassured over and over again as to what is possible, and their children need to be told explicitly how to go about staying in school and getting into college. The passive and client-centered counseling methods must to be shifted in the direction of a more aggressive and active involvement of the school staff in demonstrating, convincing, and informing parents of poor but able students of the opportunity structure that exists within the school and community. This cannot be achieved by inference or with long-term, passive intellectual exposure.

This discussion points up the need for another type of school service in the office of a social analyst. Such a worker, drawn from the disciplines of sociology and cultural anthropology, would enable school personnel to understand the society of the school and the subcultural currents within school and community. The social scientist concerned primarily with the dynamics of behavior as they germinate in the individual's milieu, under extremely varying social and cultural conditions, would serve as a strong complement to psychological and case work methods.

In *The Vanishing Adolescent,* Edgar Friedenberg points out that guidance and counseling services, even under the guise of therapy, may only serve as temporary sedatives whose covert function is "to keep the young minds and hearts in custody till they are without passion."[3] Here, indeed, we are faced with a great danger, lest the atypical or maverick student be herded into conformity and branded with ordinary markings. Paradoxically, this cutting back to "normal pattern" via the routine guidance to conformity may actually defeat the counselor in his major aim: to develop each individual in accordance with his unique talents. Digression from the pedestrian pattern should be encouraged in the guidance process. One shudders to consider what the school counselor might have done with young Ben Franklin in the modern high school. Ben's esoteric experiments would not have endeared him to his instructors or counselors. If he could have survived the standardized set of laboratory experiments, it is more than likely that his advisor, armed with the results of the Kuder Preference Record and the Otis I.Q., would have pointed him to a career of teaching science in a Philadelphia high school.

Personnel workers must be alert to exploit the unusual talent and the bizarre interests of youth rather than prune them back to conform to classroom ritual and routine. Most guidance workers have fallen into the soft trap of uniformity and conformity as an ideal toward which all students are to be trained. There is little space or sympathy for digression in the secondary schools today.

School personnel services should point their efforts to strengthening and multiplying the contacts between teacher and pupil at the classroom level. Guidance counselors in particular should remain alert lest they cut out or cut down the classroom teacher's feeling of personal concern or responsibility for all individual pupils in his classes. All school and student personnel workers need to orient their services to teachers as well as to individual pupils.

The U.S. Office of Education reported that for 1964-65 there were 1500 full-time counselors in the elementary schools of the country and 31,000 in the secondary schools. This represents a tremendous increase since 1959 when the total number of full-time counselors was 12,000. However, there were also about 11 million high school students enrolled in the nation's schools during 1964. The implication is that, judging from the small number of cases that can be handled in office-oriented counseling situations by the very limited number of available

[3] Edgar Z. Friedenberg, *The Vanishing Adolescent* (New York: Dell Publishing Company, Inc., 1964).

guidance personnel, individual pupil counseling will have little effect on the incidence of failure, school-leaving, and social-emotional problems of high school youth.

Guidance workers and others must spread their influence to more pupils by working through the teaching staff. This can only be accomplished if a mutual relationship of trust and respect exists between teachers and personnel workers. Many social workers, psychologists, and guidance workers could make their influence felt on a school-wide basis by conducting group therapy sessions for staff and by creating opportunities for individual counseling of staff members. Barriers to this broadcast role exist both in the concept the teacher may have of the counselor and in the counselor's self-concept of his own professional role. The greater problem is perhaps in the counselor's self-concept, in his own lack of confidence in this wider potential role, and in his own less than professional concept of the guidance functions. Whatever the role that is attributed to him by others, the counselor is the one who, through his self-concept, sets the ceiling as to the limits of what status can be attained.

Neither school nor classroom can rise above the high-watermark set by the quality of its personnel. If reluctant and recalcitrant learners are to be helped, they must be assured of the highest quality of professional personnel who themselves have been given a clean bill of health. It is true that the sick frequently attract the sick. Those adults who work closely with difficult and disturbed youngsters in school and classroom must show emotional maturity and an honest desire to work with young people.

Those who are elected to work closely with the persisting and serious norm-violators need to be carefully screened by means of psychiatric and psychological interviews; while on the job they should have easy access to supporting therapy to enable them to maintain their own mental health and balance on a job that presents many difficulties and emotional hazards. School officials will need to face up to the problem of the worker who fails to see that he needs help, even when help is nearby.

School and student personnel workers still tend to fly solo, or they act out their roles in discrete circles under the tent of the school. They need to fly in tight formation with other school personnel as well as with professional workers in the community who come in close contact with school youngsters and their families. This is in recognition of the interdisciplinary approach to understanding, diagnosing, and treating the youngster needing help. Becoming a member of a school and community team will mean giving up some degree of autonomy of function; it will mean leaving the building during school hours; it will mean meeting on off-school hours with non-school personnel; it will mean opening the school doors to other community workers. There is little promise of success in professional or agency isolation.

Finally, the personnel worker, if he is to be a practical and effective operator, must be research oriented—both as a consumer of research and as a director or participant in action research. Keeping up with the significant research and fact gathering is not an easy task, especially for the busy practitioner who must do this on the run, or on a marginal work basis. However, whether the treatment and action programs merely reflect time-worn palliatives and panaceas or actually culminate in successful attainment of the school's goals depends upon the awareness of the results of research at three levels. First, at the level of theory, the worker must conceptualize and integrate a theory of learning as a process, and a theory of personality as a form of adjustment; second, he must know the local school-community situation in which pupils and staff live and learn; and third, he must know, using case study techniques, the individual youngster whom he is trying to help. Lacking any of the facts at these three levels of knowledge, he will run the risk of proving himself an impractical practical worker. Not only must the school and student personnel worker develop his practices according to implications of research, but he must always be willing and ready to change or modify his practices when new data shed additional light on techniques and methods, on causes and precipitating conditions.

Actually, school and personnel services take on meaning and justification as they contribute to the basic educational objectives, thus insuring that more—if not all—youngsters can achieve optimum growth and development. But this is not enough. School and pupil services must do more than repair and rehabilitate. They must shift their focus from consequences to antecedents of poor school performance and maladjustment. They must be directly concerned with the underlying factors that compel or beget academic and social problems. This will mean greater concern for the improvement of the curriculum; it will require a study of the society of the school; it will call for exploitation of individual pupil differences; it will demand strengthening and increasing interpersonal relationships between pupils and teachers; it will require better selection and upgrading of professional staff; it will call for more effective teamwork; and it will require an awareness of implications of research for school practice. With this orientation, we can no longer regard school and pupil personnel services as special services; they represent activities essential to the operation and, especially, the improvement of the school agency.

17 What Kind of Help for the Teacher and from the Teacher?

Self-knowledge and self-appraisal are paramount in the effective teacher who will deal most successfully with his students. Understanding of the youngster and his problems is of parallel importance. What must the teacher do to gain this self-knowledge? What attitudes and habits must be cultivated in order to maintain a positive, dynamic approach to the classroom? How can the teacher help his students to see their problems and to start working them out? How can he appraise the young person's background and discover the various forces that shape him? What outside aids are available to the teacher? How can the report card and marks be used to help the pupil?

All the future troublemakers and delinquents are now sitting in the nation's classrooms. Every predelinquent has continued and close contact with one or more professionally trained teachers charged with the responsibility for developing well-integrated, useful, and socially effective citizens. Hence the teacher's role in the prevention and control of norm-violating behavior can be powerful and pervasive. However, the full impact of the school in curtailing the inflationary trend in misbehavior will be felt only when all the teachers in the school system evidence the following insights and skills:

Have fun in the classroom and don't get "run-down." What a teacher is, is what a teacher does. Jittery teachers produce jittery students. The instructor who is unhappy with his job or with himself will precipitate rather than prevent troublesome behavior in his classroom.

If a teacher does not like his job, or dislikes the pupils in his classes—especially the disturbing and disorderly ones, if his mental and emotional health is below par, he should stop and take personal inventory of himself and his goals or talk over his problems with his principal or supervisor. There are plenty of mental health hazards facing the pupil in home, school and neighborhood. A teacher need not be an additional one.

Working with thirty (more or less) different, often difficult, youngsters all day long, week in and week out represents a severe test of personal and professional adjustment. To remain effective in the classroom a teacher must protect his own mental and emotional well-being. If he no longer feels any security or satisfaction on the job, he may be in need of a mental-health check-up.

Researchers are pointing out that classrooms with a high incidence of troublemakers can often mean that the teacher has fallen into the convenient trick of working out his personal problems and frustrations through the norm-violating behavior of his students.

Preserve a positive and diagnostic attitude. There is much hate and hostility expressed toward the offending youngster in school and community today. A teacher should not join the attacking pack. His job is to help. In court he may be the only friend that the child has. By accepting the youngster as a person, by offering him a helping hand, by enjoying him, a teacher can establish a positive relationship—the only firm base for learning-teaching and therapy.

There are always reasons why the youngster behaves as he does. A teacher should look behind the behavior and ask himself the key question: "Why?" in order to find the real answer. When he develops the diagnostic habit, he will begin to show the professional attitude.

Let the youngster solve his own problem. Only the student can solve his own problem. But a teacher can help by hearing him out, by giving him insights in his behavior, by showing his faith and belief in him, by letting him weigh and choose alternatives, by letting him make a mistake, by helping him build up his self-concept, by enabling him to start to succeed in school, and by enlisting the help of specialists in school and community.

Don't try to go it alone. There are many kinds of norm-violating behavior that arise in the classroom which can be handled by the teacher himself; these are some problems, however, that will necessitate outside help. It is necessary to know what special resources exist in the school and community. When a teacher is in doubt, the specialists: the principal, guidance worker, psychologist, visiting teacher, should be consulted. This should be done without feelings of guilt or failure and not as a last resort. Many of the youngsters' behavioral difficulties may be deep-seated or they may stem from factors in home, neighborhood, peer group, or subculture. These problems cannot be solved in the classroom.

Determine the locus of the difficulty. All behavior and misbehavior must be viewed as an interaction of inner and outer forces. Teachers and other school and community workers have developed a strong inclination to search for causative factors that are exclusively mental and emotional. They tend to overlook the compelling forces that are frequently found in the youngsters' milieu or subculture. If the generating forces which are largely responsible for the youngsters' problems are in the cultural milieu, the focus of forthcoming treatment will need to be on changing the value system and the way of life of the group. Here the teacher may feel limited. However, he should remember that as he changes the behavior of many youngsters, he can also change the culture or the way of life.

Note what rule book the child is using. The teacher lives and swears by the middle-class rule book. Frequently this is not the rule book that the young offender carries with him. There are many rule books available in the community; in understanding and helping youngsters from a lower-class culture, a teacher should know how the various rule books read. He will need to sell his system of values and to get the norm-violating youngster to discard his manual of behavior—even in the face of pressures from his peer group. This is never easy for the youngster who must now substitute the jibes and snubs of his gang for the smiles and approval of his middle-class teacher—a "square" in the eyes of the gang.

Local schools and agencies need to give more attention to the early identification of the potential delinquent. As previously discussed in the sections on prediction and early identification, the teachers in one three-year experiment did a better job of identifying the future delinquents than the psychological measures which were being tested out. The experienced teacher will recognize that the check lists and scales which were presented earlier tend to reaffirm and systematize much of his own observations in the classroom.

Use the report card with care. It can be a dangerous weapon. A teacher should be careful when distributing report cards to the members of his class. Depending on the youngster, his home and family background, and his peer group, he may be receiving a hand grenade which will explode in the living room of his well-ordered middle class home. The teacher may be giving him a bankruptcy notice which will insure an early school drop-out, a passport to an Ivy League College, or a badge of honor (or dishonor) to be worn in street-corner society. To the teacher the report card may mean painstaking appraisal; to the students it represents or symbolizes many things. Nothing will break the calm of a middle-class household like a "bad" report card. Achieving, going to college, and improving the mind represent dominant concerns of the middle-class family. The terrible story of school failure spelled out in the report card when aired at supper time will contaminate the evening meal. The dining room table becomes a verbal arena.

Failing in school in this type of family may mean letting the parents down. Most middle-class parents take their child's failures personally. They fear the terrible consequences of loss of status when the report card indicates that their youngster may not be able to get into any college—let alone the college of their choice.

The apprehensive, crestfallen, and defeated middle-class parent will counsel, beg, admonish or cajole the youngster: "Please, please bring up your marks." The parent will point to the future and paint it as bleak and foreboding: "If you don't do better, and if you don't get better marks, you get no allowance, you can't have the family car (or bike according to the pupil's age and grade), and you can't watch TV."

One of the few "safe" ways that the middle-class student can strike back at his parents is through failure in school. For this youngster three failing marks can mean three stab wounds in the parent's back. In this way, the report card can become a lethal but concealed weapon and the predatory parent had better watch out.

On the other hand, the middle-class parent whose youngster brings home "all A's and B's" basks in the reflected glory of his offspring's achievement. In fact he may quickly drain off most of the pleasure that comes from scholastic attainment by showing off the youngster's school report to his fellow employees at the office or to his neighbors at the bridge table. And usually, rewards—in accordance with the family's socio-economic level—are forthcoming. An A can be worth a dollar or a dime, depending on the current state of the family exchequer. In this way the school report may become a vehicle for barter or blackmail.

By way of sharp contrast, the teacher's report to the lower-class home carries radically different symbolic overtones for Harry, a member in good standing with the street-corner gang.

On their way home from school, the gang—all thorns in the side of the school staff—compare their marks. Gleefully they check to see who has the most failures and absences. Harry, with five failures and a sharply written comment from his homeroom teacher complaining of his inattention and low achievement which "is far below his ability level," earns the prestige and approval of his confreres as they show their contempt for school with their multiple failures. In fact, Harry tops the gang's "honor roll."

But woe to any member of the street-corner group who finds himself on the teacher's honor roll. His reputation and his status with his peers are immediately jeopardized. The fact that his report card also shows a perfect attendance record for the last quarter sets him up as a target for the jeers and jibes of the gang. The "professor" will have to be tough indeed to endure the climate of the gang and the rigors of their criticism. There is no high honor for him in his street-corner society—only dishonor. Soon he will discover that he has betrayed them and will soon be betrayed himself. His report card, like the deciding Greek ostrakon, has banished him from his group—never to return again.

The report forms are not without their symbolic overtones for the school staff. The special marking system employed by the teachers will often reveal the school to be suffering acutely from institutional schizophrenia. Most reporting devices today, especially at the elementary school level, optimistically attempt to appraise growth and development of "the whole child." This is consonant with the broadened objectives of the modern school. The result is a six-page report form (replacing the 3 x 5 card) with a long list of personal and social traits and habits in addition to the traditional skills and substantive headings. The switch to a more complicated system is proof of alert administration eager to change or to implement lessons learned at the Institute on Appraisal during the past summer session at State U. But changes are not always synonymous with improvement.

At the same time, the new school reports reveal a personality-splitting ambivalence in marking or rating. The appraisers waver between marking the pupil's performance in terms of his own capacity and appraising his achievements in terms of the modal performance of his grade or age-group.

A glance at the report forms now in use would indicate that the mental hygienists have won out and most youngsters, particularly in the elementary grades, are being evaluated against the criterion of their own potential or individual capacity for learning. The result is a school report that informs the parents that the pupil is doing what is a "satisfactory job *for him.*" Ultimately, this kind of appraisal will only confuse the youngster and his parents, since he must still face the comparative appraisal against the performance of others in the competitive market of the outside world. The student should not be protected from comparison with his peers. The world outside the class-room represents a highly competitive culture which, at its worst, approaches a "dog-eat-dog" rivalry as best seen in the Wall Street and Madison Avenue tradition of the business world or in the arena of organized sports.

The only way the evaluators in school can solve this personality-splitting dilemma is to provide two marks: one indicating the level of the pupil's performance measured against his potential; the other reporting his achievements against the performance of other pupils of his own age or grade. A few schools have already moved in this direction. But a study of the appraisal and reporting methods in any one school system will usually reveal that the elementary schools are using the criterion of individual capacity whereas the secondary school tends to rate in terms of the average or modal performance of all the pupils in a grade.

In a recent cartoon by a well-known artist who is given to comment-ing in two panels on "the good old days" vs. "the modern way," an "old" pupil is depicted quaking with fear as he carries his report card home. In "today's panel" the parent is shown fearful and trembling as his youngster brings the report in to him for signature. It is true that the report cards sent home by the modern school have become more complicated and much more elaborate. Many schools have felt the need for supplementing the written report with a "parent conference" to make sure the complicated message is not misunderstood. In one school system the teacher carries the report card home to the parent and confers with them regarding the meaning of the written message. And in other communities the written reports to the home are being re-placed entirely by the teacher-parent conference. Doing away with written reports to the parents runs the risk of destroying the one pipe line that exists between many homes and school.

Call them what you will—Progress Reports, Home-School Com-munications, Achievement Reports or just old fashioned Report Cards —they provide a real-life experience of being judged and evaluated. Not the worst thing between teacher, student, and parent is the communication device reporting growth and progress that has or has not taken place. Unfortunately, in the periodic nature of such report-ing, there is much that partakes of the Day of Judgment. Every day should be report-card day. And every teacher should remember that in his appraisal of his students he appraises himself.

18 What Is the Real Meaning of Discipline in Today's Classrooms?

Many methods of maintaining discipline in the classroom have been proved destructive rather than helpful to the students. What is good discipline in the school? What does the punishing, threatening atmosphere do to an individual's growth? What intelligent practices can reduce the number of discipline cases in today's classrooms? In understanding his complex role as a motivator, guide, appraiser, and group leader, how can the teacher make an effective impression on his students? How much does the teacher's own emotional stability influence the course of good discipline? Can student government ever be useful in teaching the student self-rule? Is punishment ever an effective device?

Today it is difficult, if not impossible, to approach the topic of discipline by way of a mild or lukewarm discussion. This is true whether we are talking over the backyard fence, around the bridge table, or across the principal's desk. We suffer from no shortage of opinions concerning discipline. These opinions are usually strong and conflicting. In a sense, we have too many opinions and too few facts.

No professional group has suffered more from the free and easy use of undefined terms than has the teaching profession with the word "discipline." One way to send a teacher off to professional oblivion is to dub him a "poor disciplinarian." If one were to ask critics of the schools and teachers to name the outstanding characteristics of the modern school, the stereotype comment of "lack of discipline" would not be long in coming.

What sets the style for discipline in the classroom today? Is it merely the inevitable pendulum swing to the opposite extreme in handling or approaching pupils? Is it personal or professional caprice or whimsy as with milady's headgear which is now "flowered, furred, or feathered, according to the season?" Is it merely tradition as found in time-worn, if not time-honored, practices? Or do our current practices emanate from those stylists—the professional educationists—who hold sway at the various summer sessions—those educational fashion centers where new and modish vocabulary can be picked up?

Whatever practices the school follows in its effort to achieve order and to help youngsters to order themselves ought to be set firmly on two basic principles: (1) *the prestige and worth of the individual personality,* and (2) *faith in the rational method or in the methods of scientific research.* The modern school recognizes that pupils are persons; that the school exists for them. We say that there is no such thing as human rubbish. We believe in the inherent dignity and right of every human being, even of pupils.

In the modern school, practices related to disciplinary situations reflect what the research literature tells us about how children learn and how personality growth and development can be fostered. At the same time the lessons learned from those youngsters who experience special difficulties in the routine of daily living are applied with profit to other children. In assisting children to grow, the modern school carefully combs and culls from the research literature those promising practices and adaptations which have been shown to have positive or beneficial results, and sheds those practices which serve as palliatives or which have negative or even harmful effects on child growth and development. The following comments, suggestions, and observations have been carefully sifted through these two screens.

First, what do we mean by discipline? All school people accept the concept of discipline as *order.* Our complex social structure could not endure long without order. Instruction cannot be rendered nor can learning take place in a wild blackboard jungle devoid of any order—meaning cooperative freedom and responsibility. Our chief question is, "What methods help and what conditions hinder achieving and maintaining reasonable order in the classroom?"

The experienced teacher knows that discipline is not an entity in itself. The teacher does not teach *and* maintain discipline. Rather, discipline is an integral and pervasive part of the teacher's total job, and in a sense it may be a measure of his effectiveness in directing the learning-teaching process.

A number of authorities have pointed out that discipline is concerned with all those conditions under which the group in the schoolroom lives and works together. There is *good* discipline in a classroom when the relationships between individual pupils and between pupils and teacher make for maximum growth and development of all. There is *poor* discipline in the classroom when growth and learning are hampered rather than helped by the relationships of the pupils with each other and with the teacher.

Good discipline in the classroom simply means good ways of living and working together so that the highest development of all is insured. We should note that the classroom ridden and ruled by fear, threats, punishment, or failure may show order and even some academic learning, but the highest development of all may be jeopardized on the personal-social side by way of exclusive dependence on outer controls. Hence, we have an unpromising disciplinary situation even though order is visible.

There are three key words that characterize the approach to discipline in the modern school. First, the instructor manages the teaching and learning situation so as to *prevent* discipline problems from arising. Second, when problems do occur, the teacher's approach is *positive* in a search to *help* the pupils in the adjustment process. She asks the question *why?* rather than "What exactly did he do?" Third, the ultimate goal in the classroom is always *inner control* or *self-discipline*, in marked contrast to the exclusive dependence on outer controls which so characterizes both the traditional school and adult society itself.

The following school practices can help to reduce the high incidence of discipline cases that are being reported in many schools today.

Providing meaningful and successful experiences through an improved curriculum. The greatest disciplinary hazard will always be located in the everyday boredom and monotony of the listless classroom. Many discipline problems in the classroom represent a rebellion against what is, from the child's point of view, a never-ending procession of meaningless and purposeless activities. The curriculum problem has many facets, ranging from the difficulties in providing a school offering which remains reasonable within the limits of the individual differences presented by compulsory education laws, to the more complicated problems of varying value systems wherein some children learn at home or on the street that going to school is a "waste of time" and nothing in the school program has any appeal. Out of the American dream to educate all children regardless of their talents, interests, and needs, has frequently been spawned a nightmare of discipline cases.

Every school system must bend its efforts to review, revise, and improve its curriculum offerings so that all children may find some value and success in the school program. So long as the school persists with a single-menu offering, it can expect an increase in disciplinary cases arising from a perversion of standards such that the least able must constantly find failure and defeat, and the most able encounter only boredom and effortless achievement. The constant revision and improvement of the school curriculum should involve all members of the community, including teachers, parents, and even youth themselves.

Improving the quality of instruction. Effectiveness in the classroom will depend upon the skill with which the teacher plays the following roles: a motivator, a guide in the selection of the learning activities, an appraiser, and a group leader. A preponderance of disciplinary problems in a classroom frequently means that the teacher is not handling one or more of these roles effectively.

As a motivator, the teacher tries to excite the child to learning. Too often the height of motivation, from the learner's point of view, is "to please the teacher" or to keep him happy and quiet. Unless the teacher relates the learning to the past, present, or future needs of the child, what goes on in the classroom will fall in the realm of random or purposeless activity. Learning activities become time-fillers if not time-killers.

If the teacher has really bothered his pupils and has set up a series of queries or problems which the class sets out to solve, he must now be ready to play the role of a guide in the selection of the learning activities through which answers will be forthcoming. A field trip is conducted; reading materials are gathered and read; experiments are arranged; films and pictures are viewed; surveys are conducted; and reports are prepared and shared by the class. This is the "excess and varied behavior" of the learning process in which pupils actively engage in a large variety of learning activities searching for the answers to their queries and problems. The instructor seldom "tells or gives the answers"; rather, he engages the class in different activities through which they will uncover the answers for themselves.

As an appraiser, the teacher must be able to say how much learning has taken place with each individual in the class and with the class as a whole. In this role he judges the product of learning, particularly as seen in terms of the objectives of his grade and subject area. Earlier, at the beginning of the teacher-learning situation, the teacher inventories the pupils, using available tests of achievement, ability, and special aptitudes. The problem of individual differences has little meaning for instruction until the teacher has come to know the prior achievement and the present potential of every student. By gearing the learning activities to the abilities and achievement of the individual pupils, he insures initial success as well as continuous growth on the part of all learners.

At the same time, the teacher does not lose sight of the fact that he is the leader of the group. A class is more than an aggregate of thirty or thirty-five individuals. It has form and structure. There is a kaleidoscopic set of interpersonal relationships between all class members, including the instructor. Living and learning in the classroom is aided or impeded by these relationships. The teacher in this role of a leader seeks to identify the isolates as well as the others, and leaders or "stars" who influence others, and to uncover the cliques and sub-groups in the class. It has been estimated that 30 per cent of the usual run of discipline cases are dominantly group-conditioned, and that another 60 per cent are partially group-conditioned and partially developmental. Only about 10 per cent of discipline cases are free of any group factor or involvement. Since discipline problems are so frequently an outcropping of some disturbances within the structure of the group, the teacher would be well advised to concern himself with methods and techniques of studying and guiding group actions.

Lending a sympathetic and listening ear. The least expensive and the least harmful approach that the classroom teacher can use in working with a young offender is to lend a sympathetic and listening ear to his problems. The teacher must recognize that he cannot solve the youngster's problem for him. The young offender must solve the problem for himself. In addition to finding acceptance and belonging in the classroom relationships with his teacher, the child must gain insight into his own problem situation and must undertake to find his own solution. To berate a child, to plead with him, to cajole and beseech him, or to shame him will serve no good purpose; more likely it will only further complicate his problem for him. Techniques of moral suasion or verbal blasting coat the child with new problems, burdens, and anxieties. The teacher, by talking less and listening more, can often achieve the opposite effect of helping the child peel down to the core of his underlying problem.

Making more judicious use of punishment in the form of natural consequences. Beating a child is neither a causative nor a humane approach of helping a child with his problem. But there are more sadistic forms of punishment than whipping or flogging. It is generally recognized that the following methods of punishment are not only profitless but frequently destructive: shaming a child, making him feel inferior, creating fear, developing a highly competitive climate, exacting emotional blackmail, giving the child a deep-seated guilt feeling, demanding apologies.

Because certain forms of punishment have been shown to have little positive value and often to run heavy with negative effects, many teachers have abandoned the whole principle of natural consequences. As Ernst Papanek has pointed out, "No child is legally responsible for his misdeeds and he should not be punished for them; but educational consequences can help him understand better what makes his behavior intolerable to society." Further, he states, "punishing teaches the child only how to punish; scolding teaches him how to scold. By showing him that we understand we teach him understanding, by helping him we teach him to help, by cooperating we teach him to cooperate.[1]

The free and easy use of punishment is not only destructive in terms of its negative learnings and in its non-causative approach, but it frequently presents to the child concrete proof that he is in the way, that he is unwanted, or that he is a most offensive member of a group. The teacher who strives to build self-confidence, self-respect, and self-control will not do so with a punitive approach.

The traditional school (this probably includes a large majority of our learning institutions) still strives to achieve order by maintaining many outer controls through watchful supervision and through punishment. These institutions will only suceed in producing adults who are heavily dependent upon the police uniform, the nightstick and the threat of reprisal; they will fail to produce an adult citizenry with a high degree of inner control as seen in self-discipline. Yet, somehow, the blame for the "lack of self-discipline" has been placed in stereotype fashion on "the progressive school."

The hope for more effective inner controls and self-direction can only come from within the school that gives as little supervision as possible at all ages and in all situations, from the school that practices the self-control that it teaches, from the school that makes discipline by punishment less often necessary, especially in the upper grades.

The modern school (yes, the progressive or scientific school) today undertakes to understand why the child behaves as he does, to study motives and causes. Most of all, it seeks to prevent maladjustment and behavioral disorders through early identification of children who are prone to, or who are exposed to, the development of undesirable patterns of behavior. At the same time, it manages its total school program in such a way as to insure the highest degree of personal and social development of all its pupils as can be found, not through blind obedience or conformity, but through self-discipline.

---

[1] Ernst Papanek, "The Training School: Its Program and Leadership," *Federal Probation*, XVII, No. 2 (June, 1953), p. 18.

19 Will the Push-Button Classroom Develop Persons or Thinking Machines?

Is the growing use of auto-instructional devices turning the school into an educational automat? Will these tools diminish the need for the teacher? How much can automatic tools for learning accomplish? Should not teaching be more than mere communication of facts and information? What are the assets of the various self-teaching devices? How can the teacher use them most effectively?

The embodiment of the ethos of our age may be found in automation processes from vending machines to washing machines and, on the most grandiose scale, IBM installations. All these automatic devices save time and labor—and of course money—and with their ubiquitousness, perhaps it is inevitable that the classroom of the future will increasingly take on the efficient and economical appearance of an educational automat. If so, what is likely to be gained, and what is likely to be lost to the young learner through the fast-growing trend toward this type of self-teaching process, which uses projector, record player, tape recorder, TV screen, and teaching machine?

How impersonal can the classroom get and what are the effects—immediate and long term, good and bad—of seeding the classroom with mechanical aids that enable or even insure effective self-instruction and learning? (The term "teaching machine" is much too perjorative to be used in this discussion and makes too difficult a fair and objective consideration of this topic. Equating even a part of the teaching function to a mechanized gadget presents to many workers in the educational vineyard a threat to the worthiness of the human teacher and even to the teaching profession as a whole. *In what kind of business have we been engaged, if much or most of our function can be programmed more effectively on some mechanical gadget?* Such a train of inquiry can interfere with the teacher's fair consideration of the real promise and the real problems inherent in auto-instructional devices.)

The answer to the major questions that have been raised will come only from a consideration of two subsidiary queries: (1) What part of the educational process and product can be effectively programmed for self-teaching devices? and (2) what is the unique role and function of the teacher in today's classrooms?

Before considering these two essential questions we must recognize that the modern mechanized aids can hardly be considered innovations. They have had their counterparts and their critics in earlier times and in less technological cultures. The abacus, the Hornbook, the tachisto-scope and the more recent paper-back work book were all devised to assist the pupil to engage himself in worthwhile learning experiences and, at the same time, to release the teacher from the class as a whole, enabling him to apportion his time and energy more effectively.

Accepting the mounting evidence that auto-instructional aids can and do abet certain types of learnings in certain subject areas, the basic issue does not center around the question: "Shall we use them?" Rather the issue turns on the more discriminating query: "When and how shall we use these aids?"

What we need to do at the outset is to review and set down a concise statement of the ultimate purposes of the educational processes and to mark out those particular outcomes which can be programmed for machined learning. There is already some consensus along the line that self-teaching devices can handle learning outcomes which consti-tute factual material that can be atomized. Such learning products must be clear, simple, and categorical; what is to be learned must be cut up into small, discrete, but interrelated elements. Learning on this basis generally falls at the levels of recognition and recall. Unfortu-nately, few personal, social, economic, or political problems that are met in everyday living tend to be clear, simple, or categorical. Further-more, the more crucial and far-reaching outcomes of learning will always be found at the level of interpretation, application, apprecia-tion, and invention. These levels are still outside the reach of most self-learning devices and thereby place a low ceiling on what is to be mastered.

Taking a hard but honest look at the nature and levels of the learning product that preoccupy the combined human-teacher and pupil effort in most classrooms today, the impartial observer would be forced to admit that the self-teaching devices could be used to replace at least 75 per cent of the teaching function as played out in the typical classroom. This in itself is a most serious indictment of learning in the school agency.

If learning product and outcomes of the school operation are viewed (as they must be) in terms of desired changes and modifications in pupil (and ultimately adult) behavior, or in terms of new and desirable adaptations or ways of behaving, the limitations of what learning outcomes can be programmed become readily apparent. To know, to recall, and to verbalize represent important and initial objectives of education, but they are seldom the ultimate goals. Living out the objectives of the school in play, on the job, and in home and community endeavors represents the real test of the educated person. Homes, neighborhoods, and nations of the world do not lack "educated" persons who can pass or have passed advanced tests and examinations in the hard subjects so much as they lack persons who can and do aspire to the *Summum Bonum* of the Judeo-Christian tradition. There is still around us today ample and tragic evidence in the products of schools that the factual teachings of the classrooms are falling on barren ground and among tares. Too few learners have been inspired to selfless behavior.

As Goethe pointed out at the turn of the nineteenth century, "A teacher who can arouse a feeling for a single good action, for a single good poem, accomplishes more than he who fills our memory with row on row of natural objects, classified with name and form." The young learner is much more than a memory drum on a computer. He is a living, growing, feeling person. How he *behaves* is as important as what he can memorize and verbalize.

On this basis, the teacher has a unique role and function in the development of his charges which, it would seem, no machine can fulfill. In fact, as a director of the learning process and as a "mediator of culture" the teacher plays many different roles.[1] He is a botherer, motivator, or stimulant; he is a person who knows; he is a guide in the selection of learning activities; he is an evaluator; he is one who maintains order; he is the creator of a "moral atmosphere"; he serves as parent surrogate and character model. Many of these roles will be affected by self-teaching gadgets. As "a person who knows" the mentor

---

[1] *Teacher's Role in American Society*, Fourteenth Yearbook of the John Dewey Society (New York: Harper & Row Publishers, 1957), Chap. 6.

will need to know more, if he supplements his teaching with automatic aids. He will need to be more informed in learning theory and the communication processes. He will need to discriminate among different kinds of subject matter content and to supplement programmed learning. And he will need to know each student's readiness for the various steps and types of programmed and unprogrammed learning. Even with a full bin of programmed concepts in his subject matter field, it is highly doubtful that the teacher's need to know subject matter will in any way be diminished.

More crucial are those questions of role as they affect interpersonal relationships in the class and the growing threat of anonymity and impersonality if machine-oriented teaching means restricting the occasion and incidence of teacher-pupil and pupil-teacher interaction. Programmed learning must insure and enable more and deeper relationships between teacher and learner by releasing the instructor from time-consuming routines. In fact, the introduction of auto-instructional devices should be justified on this basis as well as on that of learning increment.

Harold L. Cohen, educational director of the Institute for Behavioral Research, in a small but promising pilot study with twenty youngsters at the National Training School has reported spectacular educational gains through the use of programmed instruction tied to "points" gained for making academic progress. The points are used to "buy" free time in a lounge, to purchase clothing, to play a pinball machine, or even to take another course. The experiment involves the establishment of real and significant consequences for basic learning that are so lacking in the regular classroom for many deprived and delinquent youngsters. The "pay-off" attached to academic growth via automated instruction insures learning. What it might do to improve human relationships, what effect it might have on the youngster's value system, and how it might be related to causative factors in the delinquent's background and history will need to be explored.

Many of the current experimental studies of the use of self-teaching tools and techniques report that students "enjoy the experience of learning with auto-instructional devices." The teaching personality must be pale indeed if students prefer to relate to a machine. Perhaps these devices have something in their favor. Unlike some mentors, the machines are infinitely patient and always rewarding via "positive reinforcements." They will never "take it personally" or "take it out on the learner" if at first he does not succeed. Machines may have the psychological advantage of not getting psychically involved. Few learners will be afraid to admit to the mechanized teacher "I don't understand" or "I don't know"—phrases that bounce harshly off the sensitive ears of many human teachers. And in those classrooms where the climate is hardly safe or sanitary from a mental hygiene point of view, introduction of self-teaching devices may even help to neutralize the atmosphere. But again, who wants to relate to a machine, especially as it does not care?

When the novelty of levers, lights, and pushbuttons wears off, auto-instructional devices may have difficulty in attracting, interesting, and especially exciting the student to greater effort. As Anatole France once pointed out: "The whole art of teaching is only the art of awakening the natural curiosity of young minds for the purpose of satisfying it afterwards."[2] This is the "botherer" or "motivator" role of the teacher. In stimulating, if not inspiring, the reluctant and recalcitrant learners (the number two problem of the teacher according to an NEA study of working conditions in the classroom[3]), the auto-instructional machinery may fail because many nonlearners, who now refuse to open their books, may refuse to turn the gadgets on. In anticipation of this problem, any requisition for these devices should include a sizable order for the model that comes with built-in handcuffs and leg irons that will be needed to hold many pupils at their machine-desks. Of course this may eliminate the post of "truant officer," currently a very busy functionary in many neighborhoods in the larger urban-industrial centers. But that's the way it is with automation—it always means the elimination of some jobs!

Today through the intricate and intimate process of identification based upon a positive relationship between learner and teacher, many human mentors affect the lives of children and youth and bring about significant changes or modifications in their behavior when they play out their role as parent surrogates and their role as creators of a moral atmosphere by presenting themselves as attractive and inspiring character models. If we assume that few learners will identify with the machine-instructor, we cannot, at the same time assume that all learners will readily identify with their human mentors. But some youngsters do, and more could and should, identify with their teachers. It is the person, or personality, of the teacher that is a paramount factor in improving the quality of the learning process. The teacher who has not himself achieved an emotional maturity and authenticity and who is hardly excited about or interested in the teaching-learning

---

[2] Anatole France, *The Crime of Sylvestre Bonnard,* eds., S. Braun and G. Breé (New York: Holt, Rinehart, & Winston, Inc., 1958), Chap. 4.

[3] Reported by Kenneth R. Brown at the Annual Meeting of the National Education Association, St. Louis, Missouri, July 1, 1959.

drama in his field will not communicate to others the adventure, romance, and battle-heat implicit on any learning frontier. Instead of merely looking for a machine replacement, we should find for this instructor a better human replacement. The terrible reality that many youngsters face daily in the classroom confines them to close living with dull, listless, and lukewarm personalities, and the classroom becomes a place of boredom filled with never-ending and useless tasks that must be completed to keep the teacher happy or at least out of the student's hair. In contrast, perhaps the blinking and clicking machine looks exciting and contemporary to the bored learner. It is significant to note that after twelve years of association with teachers, very few high school graduates rush to fill in the ranks of the teaching profession, and that such occupational selections generally represent second or third choices.

It has already been suggested that justification for using self-teaching equipment must stem from both learning increment and the fact that these devices can free teachers and enable them to play out their human relations function in a socialized classroom. Through this desk-side function, it may be possible to make what is learned on the machine and elsewhere significant and meaningful in life situations. "Trees and fields tell me nothing," Plato once observed, "Men are my teachers."

Auto-learning devices are here to stay. They will not revolutionize the classroom nor will they eliminate nor even minimize the job and function of the human teacher. Karl Marx once expressed his concern for "intellectual desolation artificially produced by converting immature human beings into mere machines." To paraphrase him in the present situation, we should be concerned with the threat of emotional desolation that may be artificially produced by crowding the teacher out of the classroom and learning laboratory, thereby converting immature human beings into mere intellectual machines. Our vision certainly must not be "machines for making more machines."

20 Measuring the Intangibles: Yardsticks for Teacher Competencies

---

Is it possible to judge the teachers' fitness and ability to handle the non-conforming adolescent? What kind of guides for appraisal can be established in this area? How can they be put to most effective use?

In its report on *Teachers of Children Who are Socially and Emotionally Maladjusted,*[1] the U. S. Office of Education enumerates specific and distinctive competencies that tend to make up the role of the effective teacher who comes in close and continued contact with the emotionally and socially maladjusted student. This two-pronged investigation includes both the opinions of experts and testimony of experienced teachers in the field against the background of research on significant differences between delinquents and non-delinquents. Using these findings, the following guide for appraisal has been compiled to enable the classroom teacher to inventory his own readiness for working with and relating to the non-conforming behavioral deviate. This guide has been assembled under five

---

[1] Romaine F. Mackie, William C. Kvaraceus, and Harold M. Williams, *Teachers of Children Who Are Socially and Emotionally Maladjusted* (U.S. Department of Health, Education, and Welfare, Office of Education. Washington, D.C.: Superintendent of Documents, Government Printing Office, 1957), pp. 52-62.

major categories: (1) Teacher as a Person; (2) Teacher as a Guide in the Learning Process; (3) Teacher as a Team Worker; (4) Teacher as a Counselor; and (5) Teacher as an Appraiser.

This instrument or device should be used to gather *evidence* on which to base an estimate of the teacher's potential for dealing with the overt aggressive youngster; merely to check each item "yes" or "no," without first gathering the evidence on which conclusions concerning the extent of the teacher's competencies in helping the malbehaving child can be based, will yield little more than a perfunctory rating.

It has already been suggested that deviant behavior exists on a continuum and that the schools' responsibility toward the delinquent does not differ essentially from the schools' responsibility for other children. Hence, this guide for self-appraisal reflects competencies generally useful with all children in the classroom. However, no attempt has been made to present with these sixty-five items a comprehensive listing of teacher competencies other than those which are most crucial and imperative in dealing with the more difficult youngsters who rebel and who express their feelings in such a manner as to hurt themselves or others. Therefore, other items may be added to this list. All the items which have been selected from the original source[2] have been screened through the research literature on delinquency causation and treatment.

Teacher Competencies for Dealing with the Delinquent and Predelinquent: A Guide for Appraisal

Teacher as a person.

1. Has a clean bill of health physically, mentally, and emotionally.
2. Shows a strong inherent interest and liking for youth, including the disturbed and disturbing members of the class.
3. Shows a firm faith in youth and in their ability to grow and improve.
4. Illustrates in his own daily behavioral adjustments a high degree of emotional maturity, thus presenting an effective imitative example.
5. Has a keen awareness of his own limitations and idiosyncrasies.
6. Takes care not to work out his own problems (adult or childhood remnants) through the delinquencies of others.
7. Shows ability to tolerate anti-social behavior even when directed to authority.
8. Is able to absorb and accept negative and hostile behavior.

[2] *Ibid.*, pp. 52-60.

9. Is willing to follow through and maintain continuous contact with the child who is weighted down with academic, social, or emotional problems.
10. Does not react to classroom malbehavior personally but preserves an objective point of view.
11. Is able to distinguish between the child and his behavior, rejecting malbehavior without rejecting the child as a person.
12. Defines and maintains his role as a teacher.
13. Is free of any driving need to be liked by all students.
14. Works within his own limits and, without personal or professional guilt; refers more difficult problems to experts in school or community.

Teacher as a guide in the learning process.

15. Takes recognition of the different methods of rearing children in special and different cultures, with due reference to the relationship between rearing and personality formation.
16. Shows a working knowledge of the modes of living of different social and cultural groups in the community.
17. Makes effective use of his knowledge of the basic human physical and psychological needs.
18. Shows a sensitivity and awareness of the etiological factors in their complexity and views the present delinquency as a purposeful, need-filling, anxiety-avoiding behavior arising from pathological interpersonal experiences.
19. Recognizes delinquent behavior as a symptom of underlying conditions and the result of a sequence of events in the lives of children.
20. Seeks out the underlying motives behind the manifest malbehavior and refrains from merely judging unusual non-conforming behavior.
21. Shows sensitivity toward the significant positive and negative environmental factors which have contributed or may contribute to delinquency.
22. Recognizes differences between maladjustments which reflect economic deprivation and cultural dictations and those delinquencies which result from inadequate interpersonal experiences and poor mental hygiene.
23. Shows a working knowledge of special values inherent in the contemporary adolescent culture as they relate to the teacher's own instructional area.
24. Reveals an effective understanding of the significances and causes of failure to learn, and the meaning of learning disability to the child.
25. Establishes specific and meaningful goals within the range of the learner's potential.
26. Makes effective appeals to the healthy aspirations of the student while accepting him as he is.

27. Fosters the social responsibility of delinquents by promoting wholesome social participation and relations.
28. Makes effective use of the information of interaction among maladjusted pupils.
29. Adapts techniques to classroom situations for relieving tensions and prompting good mental health.
30. Establishes "limits" of social control (neither over-restrictive nor over-protective).
31. Shows a working knowledge of the legal framework within which provisions for education of the delinquents are made.
32. Develops a pupil-centered rather than a subject-centered curriculum based upon individual interests, abilities, and needs.
33. Takes advantage of flexibility of school programs and schedules to permit individual adjustment and development.
34. Tailors individual methods, materials, time schedules, space arrangements, teacher's role, and grouping in accordance with, the major needs of the delinquent child as determined by clinical study.
35. Uses effectively therapeutic tutoring with the delinquent child.
36. Provides advantageous learning experiences in which the delinquent pupil can be successful.
37. Uses a wide variety of media and finds that appropriate media which is significant to the delinquent child, allowing for a sublimation of energies and a growing sense of achievement.
38. Avoids making identical, stereotyped demands on maladjusted pupils.
39. Uses effectively remedial reading techniques.
40. Uses a broad range of community resources (people, places, things) in teaching the delinquent child.

Teacher as a team worker.

41. Establishes and maintains good working relations with other professional workers such as social workers, probation and parole officers, guidance and psychological personnel.
42. Has a working knowledge of children's physical, emotional, and mental growth and development, which will enable him to collaborate with medical, psychiatric, psychological, and social work professions.
43. Shows a working knowledge of the function and activities of the psychologist, psychiatrist, group worker, social worker, and school counselor.
44. Demonstrates a sensitivity to and a working knowledge of the many facets of the schools' organization which can serve the delinquents' needs.
45. Synthesizes and coordinates classroom practices and instruction in accordance with the general organizational structure of the school, always using the classroom as an integral part of the child's total rehabilitation program.

46. Under supervision, functions as a member of a treatment team.
47. Makes classroom interpretations from reports of the counselor, social worker, school nurse.
48. Makes perceptive observations and communicates these to other members of the school-community team.
49. Helps solve communication problems involved in integrating the various professional services.

Teacher as a counselor.

50. Presents an accepting attitude toward the nonconforming student.
51. Develops and uses cumulative educational records.
52. Has a working knowledge of the variety of roles the teacher is capable of assuming in response to study and treatment needs of nonconforming youngsters.
53. Accepts the role of the parent figure.
54. Guides the learning experiences of the delinquent child by making effective use of his knowledge of guidance, testing and measurement, interpreting case records, and diagnostic and treatment techniques.
55. Aims to develop self-imposed social controls within the pupil.
56. Counsels maladjusted pupils regarding their educational, vocational, and personal problems.
57. Identifies the delinquent-prone youngster and refers him to appropriate specialists within the school-organization.
58. Takes part in case conferences regarding the delinquent.

Teacher as an appraiser.

59. Uses information received from psychological and psychiatric reports.
60. Uses and interprets results from individual tests of mental ability.
61. Administers and uses group tests of achievement and intelligence.
62. Uses and interprets results of individual diagnostic tests of arithmetic and reading disability.
63. Makes use of anecdotal reports.
64. Uses test data from all sources as a part of individual diagnostic and teaching technique, not in terms of what he would like the child to achieve but in terms of the child's own abilities and aspiration.
65. From time to time helps the delinquent child to appraise his own growth and achievement, finding thereby a sense of security through success.

PART FIVE

The State Agencies and the Police

21 Community Resources: What Are the Responsibilities of the State Toward Its Youth?

The state does not suffer from a lack of services and agencies to offer help to youth and their families. However, lack of coordination among these agencies weakens their effectiveness. How can they be brought together on the principle of team-work? What steps can be taken toward coordination of court activities and services? What significant accomplishments can be achieved in focusing on the prevention of delinquency? How can youth be encouraged to become useful members of the community? What considerations should be given to work laws so that young people may be usefully employed? What are the research responsibilities of state agencies?

Programs and services for children and youth are maintained by both the state governments and the local communities.[1] These are premised on four implicit concepts or principles:

1. The dignity and worth of every human being.
2. The inalienable right of every individual to have the opportunity to develop and grow in accordance with his full potential.
3. A rational or scientific approach to the problem of services and to the solution of youth problems.
4. Safeguarding of the future through education and training of today's youth.

---

[1] William C. Kvaraceus, "The State's Responsibility for Its Youth," *State Government and Public Responsibility,* Papers of the 1960 Tufts Assembly on Massachusetts Government, ed., Robert R. Robbins (Lincoln Filene Center, Tufts University, 1960), pp. 81-82.

As a corollary, the state and the local communities must reject the concept of "human rubbish" and the Darwinian principle of "the survival of the fittest." At the same time, as youth programs are planned, organized, and evaluated at state and local levels, the adult leadership must operate on the basis of facts and verified data, not on subjective opinion, hearsay, casual observation, or prejudice. Finally, adults, both lay and professional, who work with youth must show strong faith, belief, and trust in young people. When they speak of "our most valuable resources," they must mean it and act accordingly. All state and local community workers whose job it is to serve and work with youth must be intrepid in their commitment to this view. Otherwise, the future cannot be insured through the optimum development of all youth. This is the great responsibility that rests with all those institutions and agencies that work with young people at the local and state levels.

There are many and varied services—local and state—that are concerned with the health, education, and welfare of children and youth. As one studies the organization and structure of state government, the following departments, divisions, commissions, and boards can be listed as having a direct, continuing, and pervasive influence on youth and children: Department of Education, Division of Youth Services, Department of Public Safety, Department of Public Health, Department of Mental Health, Department of Public Welfare, Department of Correction, Division of Employment Security and its Bureau of Public Employment Offices, State Housing Board, Commission against Discrimination, and the Judiciary. All of these units are autonomous; all are engaged in carrying out important functions that affect youth.

What is most striking in this long list of governmental units is the richness, the variety, even the proliferation, of services, based on varying needs, which are available to the individual youngster and his family. Depending upon the number and nature of the child's needs, he is, in a sense, divided up by the different agencies that offer their specialized seervices. Each of these departments or divisions may itself represent a complex network of services to youth. Each has authority and responsibility for coordinating its activities, developing standards, modifying present services or making new adaptations, relating its functions to those of other agencies at the state or local level, using the services of other agencies in the state, and stimulating leadership, program planning, and improvement in the local communities. But the fragmentation of services to youth underscores the need for seeing the youngster as a whole.

Agency isolation in state and local government cannot be countenanced. The principle of teamwork and coordination must be visible within each state department and division; it must be visible between departments and local communities. The coordination and meshing of services to youth must be both horizontal and vertical.

Strategic and effective use of the wide variety of services for youth will not occur fortuitously or by chance; it can be achieved only by the skillful and conscientious effort of all state and local workers. Consideration needs to be given at the executive level to some form of planning and coordinating body, operating on a quality-control principle, to insure practical coordination and meshing of the myriad of services now available to any youngster or his family. Such a body should check on the duplication of services to youth by these many independent agencies. It should work to reduce the number of uncoordinated units that may still be found in the current structure of the state government. And it should work to draw as many youth-serving agencies as possible under the administration of a single umbrella agency whose major concern would be children and youth. The current practice of extending medical help from one unit, financial help from another, educational guidance from another, vocational placement from another, and protective custody from still another to the same children and family can result in costly confusion and inefficiency.

The idea of an umbrella agency coordinating all services to youth may appear as a very remote possibility when one views the present structure of local and state governments. However, steps in this direction can be taken within related circles of functioning. A good example can be found in the operation of the courts as they deal with problems concerning children, youth, and families. Within the commonwealth of Massachusetts, for example, the care and protection of delinquent, wayward, and neglected are, under law, placed within the jurisdiction of 72 District Courts and one Juvenile Court. On the other hand, adoption and guardianship proceedings involving children are placed by law in the Probate Courts. At the same time, the care of dependent children is prescribed by statute to be not subject to the courts but a matter of the Departments of Public Welfare of the state and of the various cities and towns. Furthermore, depending on geography, there is much unevenness in the quality of the service rendered by many courts working with juvenile offenders. Most of the District Courts handle a very small number of children in the span of a month or even a year. With very few exceptions, juvenile sessions operate on a part-time basis and without judges selected because of special interest, knowledge, training, or ability to deal with the complicated problems of norm-violating youth. The procedure in handling these cases varies considerably, as do the nature and quality of the probation staff in the different courts. The kind of treatment and consideration that the youngster will receive in a given court will depend more on the place of his residence or the locale of his violation than on any other single factor. Much needed is a re-evaluation of the handling of problems affecting children and youth by the courts. Consideration must be given to the merits and advantages of a comprehensive family court with exclusive jurisdiction in the area of delinquency and neglect, adoption, separation and divorce, custody proceedings, and guardianship. In this way, steps toward coordination of services to youth may be taken within the orbit of a single agency.

The focus of most state and local agencies is on the provision of certain essential services to future citizens within the framework of the mental-health concept of a well-integrated and well-adjusted citizen working up to his full potential. The service rendered may be in the form of schooling, financial aid to dependent children, institutionalization of mentally retarded children, clinical diagnosis and treatment for the emotionally disturbed, special education and vocational training or counseling for the physically handicapped, or housing for the child in a low-income family. The past 25 years have witnessed an unprecedented expansion and growth of many departments in many states. The level of operation and job performance has improved considerably through upgrading of staff and through in-service training. But a continued emphasis on improving and increasing services to young people is not enough. What is sorely needed in many agencies—such as Public Health—is a shift in focus to the conditions and factors that tend to bring about the need for these services in the first place. Governmental agencies, local and state, too long have been exclusively concerned with the *consequences:* they need to focus their attention and efforts on the *antecedents*—on those family, neighborhood, and community forces that tend to weaken and disorganize personal and family living or that tend to bring about the social, emotional, economic, and moral problems of the young.

In Massachusetts a good example of a promising trend in this direction can be found in the legislative mandate to the Division of Youth Services to focus on the *prevention* of juvenile delinquency as its primary and major responsibility. The development of field-consultant services now available to local communities throughout the state to aid in local study and organization for delinquency prevention and control is a concrete and forward movement in this direction. Similarly, the establishment of adjustment-counselor services within the elementary schools in local communities, with strong financial support from the state, provides another good example of attacking the problem of delinquency closer to its roots. In spite of these efforts, the budget allocations for preventive work focusing on the antecedents of delinquency as found in home, school, neighborhood, gang, and community still represent but a minor emphasis, whereas the detention, classification, and rehabilitation of the delinquent *after the norm-violating pattern has been firmly established* still represents the dominant time-money investment of this state agency.

Every state or local agency, department, and division which maintains a close contact or relationship with youth should consider the need for establishing an Advisory Youth Council that can serve as an instrument for communicating with youth and as a means of working closely with the younger members of the community. The Purdue Youth Opinion Polls have confirmed the rueful, if not bitter, complaint of youth that adults generally underestimate their maturity and capacity for assuming adult-like responsibility. Participation on such agency and departmental youth advisory councils could constitute an apprenticeship in citizenship through helping in the understanding and solution of social and civic problems. How local and state agency workers react to this suggestion will in itself provide a measure of the official adult community's belief and trust in youth.

Opportunities for establishing Advisory Youth Councils are most evident in such state departments as Education, Juvenile Courts, Public Health, Mental Health, and the Division of Youth Services. For example, the Advisory Committee on Service to Youth within the Division of Youth Services could with profit set up a Junior Advisory Council as liaison with youth. Similarly, local community coordinating groups or councils of social agencies could improve their programs by establishing Advisory Youth Councils at the local level as an integral part of the total community organization. In this way, opportunities can be offered to young people to engage in serious and far-reaching activity in local community study, program planning, and activities aimed at prevention and control of delinquency. Youth can assist by collecting facts, by collating data relative to the interests and activities of young people, and by helping to plan and manage their own programs. Only by making young people full partners in such endeavors can the state and local agencies and units realize their full potential in helping youth to personal and social responsibility. At the same time, the self-concept of youthful members of the community and the state can thus be lifted to a mature and responsible image. To continue to ignore youth or to keep them in a state of semidependence or passivity is to run the serious risk of social, civic, and psychic isolation of the young from the adult community.

Consideration also should be given to lowering the voting age to the eighteenth birthday, enabling youth to take full part in the political and civic life of the community. Participation of youth between eighteen and twenty-one as full-fledged voters is imperative at a time when democratic ideals, concepts, and practices must face severe tests at home and abroad.

One of the most relevant points of contact that a teen-ager can make with the world and reality is in the area of unemployment. American society is dominated by a work culture. The marks of maturity as well as status are derived largely from the job which the individual performs in his daily life activities. American youth, as in the civic-political field, are locked out of the employment market. There is very little opportunity for youthful workers. The youngster 16-18 years of age who drops out of school or who graduates before his eighteenth birthday finds himself caught in a terrible employment vacuum today.

It is true that there must be effective control of child labor to prevent exploitation of children and early school leaving which may prove detrimental to child and state. At the same time, these hazards must be balanced off against the weakening of youth by limiting wholesome work opportunities that may make a strong contribution to the young person's maturation and learning process and to the development of a working career. It is at this point that the Department of Labor and Industries must work hard with the Department of Education in an effort to control illegal and harmful employment and to open up wholesome and beneficial job experiences. And employment of youth is the concern of union organizations as well as business and industry. In view of the fact that the secondary school today fails to graduate approximately 40 out of every 100 seventeen-year-olds, the state and the community need to consider the kinds of jobs that are available and that can be handled by those who leave school early. At the same time, these groups need to explore the relationship between early school leaving and youth employment in an attempt to expand high school cooperative work-study programs which child-labor laws now restrict greatly.

All professional workers in governmental agencies and departments dealing with youth must be research oriented, both as consumers of research and as participants in action research. Keeping up with research findings and implications in any field today is not an easy task. However, whether the department or agency program merely reflects the time-worn palliatives and panaceas or actually succeeds in attaining its goals will depend upon the awareness of the results of research at three levels. First, the professional operator must have a theoretical conceptualization of youth in our culture and subcultures, with particular emphasis on a theory of personality as a form of adjustment. It is presumed that this kind of knowledge is an essential part of the professional competencies of the city, town, or state employees who direct the many activities within the different departments which work with youth. This assumption raises the issue of the qualifications of all those who are hired to work with youth in positions of professional responsibility.

Second, the state and local agencies must have up-to-date knowledge of youth, youth needs, youth problems, and youth interests. In any attempt to help and work with young people, an agency needs to get the facts on those in school, those who drop out of school, those who are employed full time or part time, and those who are unemployed. Other agencies will need to know the facts on the number and kinds of delinquent youth, their home and family backgrounds, personal make-up, church affiliation, gang membership, and so on. Still other agencies may need to inquire into leisure-time interests. Lacking such information about youth at the local and state levels, any agency will find itself out of touch with reality. Working in the dark or on an impressionistic basis will result in waste and inefficiency.

A somewhat comprehensive study of Massachusetts youth was last undertaken by the Commonwealth in 1939 with the enactment of a resolution (Acts of 1939, Chapter 38) providing for a study by the Department of Education relative to educational and employment problems affecting the youth of the Commonwealth. The issuance of the *Massachusetts Youth Study*[2] in 1940 represents the state's best and last look[3] at its youth. As suggested earlier, what is needed, if the state is to understand youth needs and problems, is the establishment of a permanent Youth Study and Planning Commission at the executive level for the purpose of gathering, collating, and interpreting data as well as for the purpose of coordinating the activities of state government in so far as they relate to the educational, physical, social, emotional, and economic problems of youth. Such a planning commission

---

[2] *Massachusetts Youth Study: A Report Relating to the Education and Employment of Youth of the Commonwealth of Massachusetts.* Prepared by the Department of Education for the Great and General Court of Massachusetts. Senate No. 620 (Boston, 1940).

[3] A more recent look at youth and public education in Massachusetts has been taken by a survey team under the direction of Dr. Benjamin Willis and has been summarized in the report, *Quality Education for Massachusetts: An Investment in People of the Commonwealth* (Boston: The General Court of the Commonwealth of Massachusetts, 1964). Yet this report provides little or no background on Massachusetts youth as a meaningful base for the proposed educational program.

should include youth and adult lay-citizen representation, together with the heads of the departments, divisions, bureaus, and commissions which serve youth. This body would offer a clearinghouse for information on youth, youth needs, and youth problems.

Some agencies such as the Department of Mental Health, the Department of Education, and the Division of Youth Services, maintain units or bureaus that carry research responsibilities. For example, the Division of Youth Services formally established a Bureau of Research and Prevention in August, 1953. One of the aims of the Bureau was to gather and maintain data relative to delinquency in the Commonwealth. This includes carrying out both quantitative and qualitative research studies and reporting and evaluating the functions, services, and effectiveness of the program of the Division. Unfortunately, funds to enlarge and extend the services of the Bureau have not been adequate to the task that was set up.

Within the research commitment on the part of any state or local unit there should be built into the agency program definite provisions for continuous appraisal and evaluation. At least 4 or 5 per cent of the departmental budget should be committed annually to research, including evaluation. Where the agency's functions include a research mission as such, this budget item would loom larger. Many units in government operation confuse activities with achievement. Counting the number of youngsters seen or serviced, families visited, or clients tested does not provide any clue to the quality of service rendered. Periodically, every agency needs to review its specific goals and objectives. It should then gather pertinent data that would indicate how well it is achieving these goals.

The third level of knowledge concerns case-study data on the individual youngster who is being served. In helping an individual child through the child-guidance clinic, the detention and classification center, or an institution for the mentally retarded, the agency must operate with full knowledge of the child, his home and family background, his peer groups, his school experiences, and his neighborhood and community environment. It is at this level of knowledge that most agencies best meet their obligation.

To recapitulate briefly: in the variety and complexity of state and local services aimed at youth, the quality of service rendered will depend on the coordination and integration of inter- and intra-agency activities. This coordination must be both horizontal and vertical. State and local agencies must shift their foci to the antecedents of the problems relating to the health, education, and welfare of children and youth. It is not enough to keep adding and improving services that focus solely on consequences. Few governmental units offer youth an active partnership in serving themselves. Consideration needs to be given to the organization of Youth Advisory Councils within the framework of local and state divisions that work with and for youth. Apprenticeship through participation in the work of such divisions may prepare young people for the role of adult citizens and may also help to solve some of youth's problems. Lowering the voting age to eighteen is imperative to enable youth to participate earlier in the political and civic life of the community. School drop-outs and employment of youth need to be considered as major youth problems by those agencies that are concerned with the education as well as the protection of young people. Development of supervised work-study courses for young people in secondary schools will help to capture for them the value of work experience and will increase the holding power of the school. All departments and divisions need to check their aims and objectives periodically in a research-evaluation process. Professional workers should operate with an integrated theory and should have up-to-date knowledge of youth in the local community and the state. A portion of every department's budget—perhaps as much as 5 per cent—should be earmarked for research and evaluation. Consideration should be given at an executive level to the establishment of a permanent body in the form of a Youth Study and Planning Commission to gather, collate, and disseminate information on youth and youth problems as they relate to education, health, and welfare. Finally, any agency—public or private, local or state—if it is to remain viable, must keep in touch with the changing needs of youth and society and with the ever-increasing research concerning agency practices and adaptations. This calls for organizational patterns and for personnel that are flexible, fluid, and experimental.

22 The Police: An Active or Passive Defense Against Delinquency?

How can police and social workers join forces in directing youth? What kind of special training must police have in order to deal effectively with juveniles? What should be the functions and responsibilities of a special juvenile department in the police organization? What kind of in-service training will help the police in their work with norm-violators? In what areas are the police wasting their energies in work that does not really meet the problems?

The cop on the beat, in the cruiser, or behind the desk will always stand as one of the main cogs in every community program aimed to prevent and control juvenile delinquency. Yet, in many cities and towns today the police, as a resource, are taken for granted, belittled, or even slurred and overlooked, particularly by some professional workers who operate in close contact with children and youth.

The police make up a sizeable army of workers that are to be found in every community; they represent an agency endowed with legal responsibility for apprehending and dealing with young offenders; they have frequent and first contact with troublesome boys and girls on the brink of more serious crime; they are familiar with the breeding places of disorder and delinquency. The purpose of this discussion is to detail how the strategy of the police can best be utilized and activated; at the same time, some of the factors which frequently sap and diminish potential police effectiveness in their work with young offenders will be identified.

In most communities there exists a wide gulf between the point of view of the experience-hardened cop and the trained social worker concerning the delinquent child. This gap needs to be bridged. Each community worker regards the young offender through his own window or frame of reference. The social worker looks at the delinquent from the perspective of a child needing help. He is not so much concerned with what the youngster has done (symptoms) as with the meaning and significance (why and causes) of the misbehavior. On the other hand, the policeman, charged with maintaining law and order, regards the young vandal's behavior from the perspective of offense (symptom) and the letter of the law. Each of these workers, if he is to discharge his proper duties and functions, must view the same child from these two different vantage points. And here is the source of much community friction and misunderstanding. Here is where the "do-gooders" and the "strong-armed" often come in conflict. But the two should and could meet if each worker were to understand and appreciate the peculiar and unique function of the other. This does not mean that we should try to remake the policeman into a social worker or the social worker into a police officer. The result would be to create a bizarre "Never-Never-Land" of vacillating responsibilities. A number of communities, by mixing up these functions, have launched delinquency-prevention programs which have run afoul on the reefs and the rocks of this very same "Never-Never-Land."

The police department represents an office charged with many important functions ranging from traffic and safety to protection of property and detection of crime. Working with young offenders is *only one* important phase of the total police function. Yet, many professional youth workers regard the police force as set up to cope mainly—if not only—with the youth problem. Although dealing with the problems of youth is only one of the many of the department functions, it calls for carefully selected and highly trained police personnel who have specialized competencies for dealing with boys and girls who show slight or severe problems. Today, judging from general police practice, most police forces have departmentalized this function by assigning a special police detail to carry the major responsibility for dealing with youths in difficulty. There is a great deal of sense in such a division of responsibility and in the emphasis on added training for officers working with youthful offenders. There is some agreement in the field that a community having a police force of one hundred men should assign approximately five officers to the juvenile detail. At least one of these should be a policewoman.

It cannot be overstressed that the juvenile unit's effectiveness will depend upon the personal makeup and the professional competencies of the members of the detail. To assign the most aged or decrepit policeman, who is on the verge of retirement and whose physical infirmities make outside work difficult, to a juvenile unit, or to use these berths as sinecures for favorite sons, is to give this program the kiss of death. Only as men assigned to the juvenile job are handpicked because of their superior personal qualities and only as they develop professional skills in working with children, families, and other youth workers can the department achieve the promise that is to be found in police work with juveniles.

The increasing number of police-training programs for dealing with young offenders that can be found on a number of college campuses, and the recent appearance of helpful text materials on this subject, reflect the growing awareness that there is a great need for specialized training in this area. The pioneering and significant contributions of the Delinquency Control Institutes of the University of Southern California and the Institutes on Delinquency and Crime at St. Lawrence University (Canton, New York) in training of police personnel represent two promising approaches. Pioneer publications which concern the role of the juvenile officer and which offer specific guidance to workers engaged in this field include: *Police and Children*,[1] *Police Work with Juveniles*,[2] *The Community and the Delinquent*,[3] and *Juvenile Officer*.[4] This emphasis on specialized training acknowledges the need for pre-service as well as for in-service training of all police personnel, particularly for those officers who are assigned the special responsibility of dealing with youth in difficulty. Later publications deal with the same need.[5]

---

[1] Alfred J. Kahn, *Police and Children* (New York: Citizens Committee on Children of New York City, 1951).

[2] John P. Kenney and Dan G. Pursuit, *Police Work with Juveniles* (Springfield, Illinois: Charles C Thomas, 1954).

[3] W. C. Kvaraceus, *The Community and the Delinquent* (New York: Harcourt, Brace & World, Inc., 1954).

[4] Harold L. Staling and David Dressler, *Juvenile Officer* (New York: Crowell, 1954).

[5] More recent works include: G. Lewis Penner, "An Experiment in Police and Social Agency Cooperation," *The Annals of the American Academy of Political and Social Science*, No. 322 (March, 1959), pp. 79-88; Bernard Greenblatt, *Staff and Training for Juvenile Law Enforcement in Urban Police Departments*, No. 14. U.S. Childrens Bureau (Washington, D.C.: Department of Health, Education, and Welfare, 1960); Mary Holman, *The Police Officer and the Child* (Springfield, Illinois: Charles C Thomas, 1962); Lynn D. Swanson, "Role of the Police in the

The police force can also make a unique contribution to community understanding of the nature and extent of the local delinquency problem by maintaining a system of records showing the kinds of offenses being committed by children and adults, the backgrounds and characteristics of the offenders, and the neighborhoods and hangouts where most of the problems take root. The police should be able to identify specific community danger factors and sources of infection. Careful assignment of the patrolman and the cruiser to and around these danger zones, as well as systematic inspection of the identified volatile areas, can do much to control the situation. This type of scientific study assumes that some person is assigned to gather, collate, and study the data reported by the police in their daily contacts with youth, their families, and with other adults in the neighborhoods where delinquency abounds. In larger cities this may call for a delinquency and crime prevention unit with a trained staff. Without such help from the police, planning groups working within a framework of a council of social agencies may find themselves working in the dark or on a trial and error basis.

The police, perhaps more than any other workers, come in contact with the initial offender or with the borderline youngster who may be on the verge or actually en route to "bigger things" in delinquency or crime. It is on this strategy of early discovery and early referral that real preventive programs may be planned and carried out. Instead of warning a child or threatening to run him in "the next time," the police can deftly refer the youngster to an appropriate child-serving agency that is best set up to work with the incipient delinquent. This "other agency" may be the probation office, the church, the school, the YMCA, or the Boys Club. This police potential for prevention cannot be attained unless the officers know what resources exist, and unless they are ready and willing to play the liaison role. The police in every community know who the troublesome boys and girls are and where they live and hang out. Channels of communication must be set up by the police themselves so that any child who comes to the attention of the department may be referred to that agency which can readily and naturally extend a helping hand. Without this type of cooperation on the part of the police force, involving a systematic referral of budding or potential delinquents, there can be little real preventive effort forthcoming in the community.

Protection of Children from Neglect and Abuse," *Federal Probation* (March, 1961), pp. 43-48; Nelson A. Watson, ed., *Police and the Changing Community: Selected Readings* (Washington, D.C.: International Association of Chiefs of Police, 1965).

In too many cities the police, in their enthusiasm for prevention, have taken upon themselves certain functions which actually are outside their own ken of legal responsibility and which could better be handled by other agencies and organizations. Typical of such functions are managing recreational or sports programs and conducting unofficial "hearings" almost in the pattern of the juvenile court itself. This does not suggest that the police should never sponsor or support recreation and sports programs; it does mean that the police have little justification to organize, conduct, or supervise such extra-police programs.

In combatting juvenile delinquency, the police department does not need to remodel itself to resemble a recreation department, a child guidance clinic, or a juvenile court. The police can best attack the delinquency problem by retaining and improving their own unique functions and responsibilities. This will mean that all members of the force are ubiquitous and unrelenting in locating and apprehending offenders, young and old. At the same time, the police will understand and appreciate the peculiar functions and roles of other workers who come in contact with delinquent youth. They will always refer, in systematic fashion, to the appropriate agency all their first contact cases, if these do not receive official help and treatment through the juvenile court channels. In addition, there will be, in the organization of the police department, a system for gathering data concerning youth and adult offenses and a sharing of this information with different planning groups and agencies. In improving the work of the police department, special assignment will also be made establishing a police detail to work solely with youthful offenders. To insure the effective operation and use of this special service bureau, in-service training programs will be instituted, including all police personnel. The first or basic step in a community program of prevention and control of juvenile delinquency is not to procure psychiatric, psychological, recreational, or casework services; the basic and initial step is to bring the police services up to their full potential.

PART SIX

Delinquency Prevention in Other Countries

23 Prevention of Juvenile Delinquency: Evaluation of Different Types of Action in Nine Countries[1]

What kinds of preventive effort have been made in different countries? How have these efforts been evaluated? What modes of intervention have reduced the incidence of delinquent behavior? What are some of the major handicaps to prevention on the various levels of control? How does one define an experiment? a project? a pilot study?

The United Nations Consultative Group on Prevention of Crime and the Treatment of Offenders meeting in Geneva, December, 1961, advised that:
"The insufficient results of many efforts made in the past several decades should stimulate a re-thinking of the foundations of prevention, research into the efficacy of the preventive techniques employed, and a move to supplement and coordinate preventive measures so as to cover all possible causes of juvenile delinquency."

[1] The author wishes to acknowledge the assistance of two of his students at Tufts University, Sandra J. Farwell and Denise Rosenzweig, whose analysis of the reports from the nine countries served as a basis for this chapter.

This Consultative Group also advised that research aimed at prevention should be directed more particularly at the following objectives:

1. Pinpointing the true causes of juvenile delinquency, by the strict verification of the causal nature of certain factors which seem to be effects rather than causes (alcoholism, vagrancy, prostitution, truancy).

2. Verifying the efficacy of the means of prevention at present employed, some of which seem to do no more than scratch the surface of the problem (purely financial assistance, discipline imposed from without).

3. Establishing a distinction between the specific means of preventing juvenile delinquency and all the other methods of general crime prevention or social progress.[2]

Working in this direction, the International Union for Child Welfare (IUCW) Advisory Committee on Delinquent and Socially Maladjusted Children and Young People circulated a general questionnaire to its membership, requesting information on the results obtained by prevention programs sponsored by voluntary bodies and by official agencies.

In soliciting information regarding programs of prevention the Advisory Committee stated:

We are interested, however, for our work conference, in descriptions of *experiments* and *evaluation* of results, particularly in their success, shown in the number of children and young people who, after being seriously endangered and already on the path of juvenile delinquency, are reintegrated into normal society. We would like to have information both on individual delinquents and on members of asocial active street gangs.[3]

As is customary, returns were slow and late. In view of the delayed returns, a separate report was prepared on controlled prevention programs in the U.S.A.[4]

A total of nine countries replied to the request for information. These reports ranged from a brief two-page statement to an eighty page documentation. The following countries outlined their approaches

---

[2] MSOA. 61/SD. 11/Add 1 (U.N. report, mimeographed).

[3] "Prevention of Juvenile Delinquency—Evaluation of Different Types of Action: Introductory Report," *International Child Welfare Review* (Spring, 1965), pp. 7-23.

[4] The USA report appears as Chapter VIII, "Programs of Early Identification and Prevention of Delinquency" by William C. Kvaraceus in the Sixty-fifth Yearbook, Part I. *Social Deviancy Among Youth* (Chicago, Illinois: The National Society for the Study of Education, 1966), pp. 189-220.

and will be cited by code number throughout this chapter as follows:

Australia	(1)	(New South Wales)
Denmark	(2)	
Finland	(3)	
France	(4)	
Germany	(5)	
Great Britain	(6)	
Italy	(7)	
Netherlands	(8)	
Spain	(9)	
Supplement to Report, USA	(10)	

The nine reports were descriptive rather than statistical and most varied in their style. Hence they did not lend themselves to quantification or statistical treatment. They represented secondary sources. Lacking the primary source data, it was generally difficult to judge the effectiveness of the intervention. In some cases the author may have run the serious risk of error in interpretation or inference in going beyond the brief reports. However, one is able to discern some trends and to draw tentative implications concerning efforts by official and voluntary organizations to prevent delinquent behavior in these nine countries as well as in the USA via the Supplementary Report.

Problem of Definition of Terms

Several respondents noted that the lack of precise definitions as to meaning of *prevention* and *delinquency* created some confusion. For example:

. . . juvenile delinquency is the fact of committing actions which may be punishable or which, if committed by adults, would be punished. This concept seems to be acceptable even internationally. . . .

Thus, the prevention of juvenile delinquency means every action which is intentionally introduced into any phase of the cycle which leads to delinquency in order to prevent it from having an unfavorable development. (7)

In similar vein another reporting group commented:

The Finnish Preparatory Committee ascertained that the word 'prevention' in the letter of the IUCW and also in the distributed report has not been used in a clear and consistent way.

Most of the general child welfare services, too, can be regarded as preventive . . . it is not possible, in our opinion, to determine what special child welfare services in each case are apt to prevent a possible delinquent symptom in the later life of the individual. In the field of child welfare it should be commonly agreed that *proper child welfare services in general are apt to prevent individual children from social maladjustment in some later phase of their lives.*

. . . all those services rendered to children and young people who already are inclined to become juvenile delinquents should be called curative *treatment* services. (3)

It may well be that the conference should redefine these terms without spending too much time in semantic debate. Yet, there is a great danger in glib reference to any program as preventive merely because it provides certain treatment services. There is mounting evidence in many scientific studies (10) that prevention is not the inevitable consequence of treatment.

Prevention: A Promise or a Pretense?

Preventive action can be direct or indirect. Intervention, insofar as it is direct, is applied to the subject himself and to his immediate environment; insofar as it is indirect, it is concerned with the many and varied conditions which affect the general socio-cultural-economic evolution of a community. One of the British reports (6), for example, implicitly recognizes this distinction and places stress on the general population as well as on target youth groups that may be endangered.

A great deal of the "preventive" work is sufficiently fundamental or generally desirable not to be directed solely at "maladjustment," e.g., playground planning. Indeed, in some schemes (e.g., Outward Bound) there seems to be only reluctant acceptance or awareness of the endangered or already maladjusted element. Some work is directed toward identifying endangered groups and relieving stress before maladjustment appears or is confirmed, e.g., fatherless families, working mothers, problem families, E.S.N. [educationally subnormal] children, word-blind children. Other projects are more specific: counseling schemes, work with "unattached" young people, schemes to divert destructive activities during weekend migrations of young people to coastal towns.

The Advisory Committee of IUCW was concerned in its questionnaire with direct preventive action aimed at vulnerable or susceptible individuals and groups. At the same time the questionnaire requested evidence by way of evaluation as to the effectiveness of action programs.

The Advisory Committee noted almost prophetically that publications in the field of prevention of maladjustment are legion, but the evaluation of work done, noting the number of children or young people who become better socialized, is scarce. Returns from the various countries give evidence that this is still true. And in some cases, as in the USA Supplement (10), even the most painstakingly controlled studies when carefully evaluated are disappointing in terms of their outcomes. A study published by the Russell Sage Foundation in New York City provides a most recent example.

This three-year intervention program with potentially deviant girls in a New York City Vocational High School confirms the difficulties in attempting to prevent or modify norm-violating behavior. In this experiment of social work interventions, the team of Meyer, Borgatta, Jones, and their collaborators[5] identified four hundred potentially deviant girls. A random sample of two hundred girls was designated as a control group; the remaining two hundred were referred to a Youth Consultation Service which provided individual casework and group therapy. Teachers, social workers, psychologists, and sociologists combined their skills and their insights in a concerted attempt to prevent the delinquent behavior of the experimental sample. All the girls were followed through their high school careers, and their progress was evaluated by the research staff. This experiment, like many of its predecessors, confirms the fact that potentially delinquent youngsters could be identified and engaged in programs designed to modify or curtail their delinquent behavior, but the combined services were not effective in abating their delinquent patterns. This study raises some serious questions about the appropriateness of social case work as an exclusive approach to delinquency prevention. However, the authors do indicate that the girls were more responsive to group work techniques than to individual casework approaches. This painstaking and ambitious experiment in social work intervention should have a sobering effect on all those case and group workers who glibly claim "prevention" via their programs but who do not gather any data to check or reaffirm their claims.

Most programs that were reported are subjectively evaluated and are weak in terms of any scientific appraisal. Some of the authors acknowledged this condition in a forthright manner, as for example:

> In the Netherlands a lot of work for and with children and young people is being done . . . but as far as we know, the results of these many actions, usually characterized as preventive work, have not been evaluated in their success, shown in the number of children and young

---

[5] Henry J. Meyer, Edgar F. Borgatta, and Wyatt C. Jones, *Girls at Vocational High, An Experiment in Social Work Intervention* (New York: Russell Sage Foundation, 1965).

people who, after being seriously endangered and already on the path of juvenile delinquency, are reintegrated into normal society. (8)

However, in sharp contrast to this position another report makes the following statement:

The worth of the methods used has been tried and proven over many years and has had gratifying results. The stable rate of delinquency in a society which is becoming more complex and in a world where there is widespread alarm at the rapid increase of juvenile crime cannot just be a matter of chance.

It is emphasized that the work in the prevention of juvenile delinquency is no longer in the experimental stage in New South Wales. (1)

Much to the point of these two comments are such questions as the following: What constitutes a scientific experiment in the behavioral sciences and, more particularly, in the area of delinquent behavior? How much can we trust subjective observations of "what works" and "what does not work?" What represents the most appropriate criterion data by which preventive programs can be measured or tested? Is it appropriate to attempt the rigorous controls required in laboratory experiment to field research? These and other questions should be considered. A review of the nine reports plus the supplement indicates something about the uncertain status of our current efforts.

In scanning the nine reports, systematic notations were made concerning the target groups at which the programs had been aimed, the nature of the intervention, the evaluation with experimental controls and statistical tests for significance, as well as the auspices under which intervention was organized and administered. While this highlights-review does not attempt a comprehensive reporting, special attention will be focused on those programs that were aimed at youth who were vulnerable or susceptible to delinquent behavior and programs which had attempted more scientific and objective evaluation of their efforts via control of operating variables other than the experimental factor or through some matching of treated and untreated groups. Since there were few action programs that could meet these criteria, attention will also be given to the more subjectively appraised efforts. Finally, a list of major observations will be presented.

Selected Programs and Problems of Evaluation

Two long-term experiments of promising design have been undertaken in Denmark (2) in recent years. Although the experiments are still in progress, their outcomes should be watched with interest in view of the careful planning of and control within these studies. The first study includes Family Counseling for residents of a densely populated quarter of Copenhagen through organized Family Centers. The experiment includes two groups of seventy families matched for social status, age, living conditions, education, number of children, and other factors. Individual social workers are provided for each family in the experimental group to help solve problems and to help refer families to other resources when needed. The Family Center provides a coordinated counseling service rather than clinical assistance. This study is to present its final evaluation in 1966-67.

A second long-term study also in progress in the same country (2) is aimed at fifteen-to-twenty-year-old males who are subject to sanctions other than probation. The total group (1100 N), chosen on a geographic basis, has been divided into one experimental section with two control groups. The experimental group receives intensive sociological and psychological testing and treatment. A team from the clinic calls on the family as soon as possible after the case is reported. The case and family situation is diagnosed, treatment plans are made by the team, and follow-up meetings are held weekly. Control group 1 will receive the same psycho-social work-up but will be placed on probation and will not receive treatment. Control group 2 will receive no treatment. The purpose of this study is to evaluate the resocializing effects of an adequate, but non-institutionalized treatment via coordinated services of different specialists. The study will also attempt some analysis of group vs. individual delinquency, recidivism, and, of course, the question of which of the types of treatment is most effective in delinquency reduction. This study is financed by the Ford Foundation and will be evaluated during the period, 1970-75. These two studies are significant in their careful design that more nearly meets the requirements of scientific research.

The Advisory Group from Great Britain (6) reports a number of studies in the area of endangered groups as well as for the general youth population. These include an evaluation of services for educationally sub-normal youngsters and an evaluation of programs for fatherless families and families with working mothers. Most noteworthy, however, is the National Study of Child Development which aims to gather comprehensive data in order to study longitudinally and in depth the relationship of conditions prior to, during, and after birth, with later all-round development. The present inquiry has three main purposes:

(1) To establish whether the children who were "vulnerable" at the time of birth have progressed normally or not;

(2) To discover those children who are now showing developmental difficulties;

(3) To consider to what extent conditions at birth, both medical and social, can be related to the children's present development, i.e., at the age of about 6½ years. Behavior, school adjustment and physical growth will be studied. (6)

The report goes on to describe the sample to be studied as follows:

The children who are to be studied took part in a national perinatal enquiry by the National Birthday Trust Fund and comprise 16,377 singleton and about 400 multiple births, who were known to be alive 28 days after birth. Together they represent 98 per cent of registered births in England, Scotland and Wales between the 3rd and 9th of March 1958. A vast amount of sociological, obstetric and medical information was collected on the mother and on the course of pregnancy and labor; the medical data were amassed at the time of delivery from antenatal and labor records, and from pediatric notes of any illness in the first weeks of life. The sociological data were collected by individual interview with the mother shortly after birth.

Information will be sought on the children's earliest adjustment at school and on subsequent progress up to the time of interview. Data will also be gathered on their pre-school development. This information will be enable those who appear to be "vulnerable" groups now to be chosen for later individual study. The purpose of this will be to help in the planning of special educational facilities, with regard to both diagnosis and treatment. Information will also become available on questions such as the effect of nursery school attendance on attainment and adjustment, the effect of the size of infant schools on children's progress, and the range of reading attainment among six- and seven-year-olds.

It is hoped to mount the first intensive study when the children are eight years old, and then to repeat them at least twice, probably at the ages of twelve and sixteen years.

Probably the largest single group will be children who show serious educational backwardness, including severe reading difficulties; the next largest are likely to be those with behavior problems, including delinquency. The long-term outcome of both these groups of conditions may well be of great social significance; inadequate adults—whether among the ranks of the unemployable, the mentally unstable or ill, or the persistent petty criminal—are likely to contain a very high proportion who as children were educationally backward, maladjusted, delinquent, or possibly all three. Retrospective and clinical studies on selected populations provide some evidence that this may be the case. But such retrospective evidence is held to be suspect on a number of counts; moreover, these studies inevitably lack suitable "controls."

Physical growth will be assessed in terms of height, weight, and other measurements. The result of a medical examination will enable us to discover whether any difficulties or illnesses at the birth period lead to later physical handicap. Information will also be sought on the children's medical history prior to starting school.

This type of growth study data are needed as a normative base to study deviancy.

The Netherland report (8) cites the existence of playgrounds as one of the factors that diminished or reduced youth mischief rates over a three-year period, 1953-55. In one year, for example, the average number of youth mischief cases is 2.3 per day. During the holidays without "special plays" the number is 3.1 per day, but in the weeks during which special holiday plays were organized this number declined to 1.1 per day. This is a typical example of the use of data on which a plea for more playgrounds or other services as a preventative is based.

The report from the Finnish Advisory Group (3) provides a typical follow-up study with evaluation overtones. A sample of 324 first offenders were studied. Of this group 17.7 per cent required no treatment; 48 per cent required temporary guidance or a warning; 22 per cent were placed under welfare supervision; and 12 per cent were placed in custody of the city child welfare board. A five-year follow-up revealed that 68 per cent of the custodial group committed new offenses, 27 per cent of the supervised group showed repeated offenses, and 15-21 per cent of the warned group were again involved in delinquency. The study concludes, "The evaluation of the suitability of different measures in different kind of cases is a most complicated and responsible task."

A comprehensive report from France (4) shows a wide variety of effort in the preventive field including parent education, social centers, clubs and teams, youth and cultural centers, rural centers, hostels for young workers, youth camps and playgrounds, child guidance centers, and other approaches. However, little evidence was provided showing any systematic or scientific appraisal of these programs. Perhaps most notable is the work of the police, particularly in the account of "Operation Holiday" which constitutes a coherent program with specific aims centered on prevention (and sometimes repression) of delinquency in resort areas. The action of the police takes place in a specific setting in which crowds of young people gather: places of public amusement and public recreation, and places of assembly. The task of the police personnel consists essentially of supervising the entry to beaches, camping sites, and places of nocturnal amusement. The report states:

It is particularly in stations, gardens, and public places that the presence of the police has shown its full effectiveness.

A marked improvement has been observed in the behavior of young people and fewer offenses have been noted in public places, while the many controls carried out have enabled runaways or vagrant youngsters to be arrested. Similarly, disturbances at night, as well as turbulent, aggressive, or equivocal attitudes have entirely disappeared.

The problem of gangs was observed particularly in 1959, and its evolution was studied in the course of the subsequent operations. In 1960, thanks to preventive action and precise information being given to the officials responsible for the operation, it proved possible to control the activities of gangs and to prevent excesses. In 1961 the police, undertaking an intensive action at the start of the summer, made themselves respected by the "blousons noirs" and incited them to prudence, if not to wisdom. (4)

In view of similar problems faced in other countries, more information on "Operation Holiday" might be sought.

The Australian report from New South Wales (1) points out:

Although it is difficult to make valid comparisons between the delinquency rates of different countries, from available statistical material it seems that the rate in New South Wales is less than half that in England and a third that of certain states in the United States of America.

Most industralized countries report a steady increase in juvenile delinquency rates. However, this is not so in New South Wales, where the rates have not varied significantly for the past six years at least. During the year ending June 30, 1964, there was a slight decline in delinquency rates among boys—*14.5 per 1000 to 13.8 per 1000.*

What, then, are the reasons for the comparatively low and stable delinquency rate in New South Wales? It is felt that the family casework service and intensive preventive work carried out by the Department of Child Welfare and Social Welfare in this State play a substantial part keeping juvenile delinquency within reasonable bounds. (1)

The Australian report describes the activities of the Department and the voluntary bodies in detail. There are some dangers in attempting such cross-boundary if not cross-cultural comparisons. The use of delinquency rates as a measure of program effectiveness and the problems of using comparative data drawn from different countries need to be considered.

The great variety of interventions of direct and indirect nature that can be used in helping youngsters and their families is best illustrated in the report from Great Britain (6). Preventive work has been attempted in all areas and with all age groups. These programs include: educational remediation, family counseling and planning, parent edu-

cation, youth clubs, job placement, special care immediately following prison release, playground activities and police familiarization.
However, few statistical tests have been applied to the results of these
interventions.

One of the most popular prevention methods of Great Britain centers around the youth club. Many of Great Britain's teenagers become
members of some organization. They join, initially, on their own or
someone else's initiative, or they are declared "unattached" and special
clubs are organized to handle the unattached of each area. Youth clubs
are financed by both public and private organizations and staffed by
paid volunteers trained and experienced in social and welfare work.
They are often young married adults, and occasionally one couple
resides at the club headquarters. Psychiatrists, psychologists, physicians
and other professional personnel are affiliated with some of the centers.
Programs are the choice of club members and vary in length with the
club—some running just weekday evenings, some all evenings, some
throughout the day (particularly to care for the great number of shift
workers), some spanning just nine months of the year, some with
extension programs for summer resorts. Program selections of the
youth range from social entertainment (dancing) to technical (camera
clubs). Summer programs include sailing, swimming, games and some
of the winter activities.

One of the greatest problems of these organizations is finding suitable quarters with available funds. Often they are given old office
space or a waiting room in an unused railway station. Once the purchase price is settled, they start from scratch to remodel. Generally
they serve some type of refreshment, usually hot and cold drinks and
cold snack foods. Juke boxes or record players, billiard tables, dart
boards, and other equipment are installed.

A frequent problem is membership. Often older teens will not participate if young and pre-teens "invade" the premises, reducing the
activities to "kid-stuff"; many of the delinquent youths served are status
seekers, and having youngsters around is not within their tolerance
limits. Clubs are now being organized to handle the younger children.
Another disturbing influence has been found to be the presence of
known delinquents, particularly if they are members of a gang. At one
club, the leaders' elation at bringing in a fairly rough group of boys
was swiftly deflated when many of the regular members refused to
associate with them. Members are referred to the clubs by police,
social workers, parents, friends, and teachers.

Of the remainder of the studies done, many show seemingly good
results, but again, the lack of statistical information and control groups
prevents any "sure" conclusion.

The report from Germany (5) describes three kinds of actions aimed at reintegrating children and young people who have become seriously endangered and are already on the path of juvenile delinquency. These include (1) the rapid development of an independent organization composed of an increasing number of clubs called the Hanseatic Youth League for children and young people who have been in some kind of trouble; (2) a program of social group work for boys and girls aged eight to twenty-one which enrolls approximately 660 children in 45 homogeneous age groups; (3) a "school help" department providing psychological service to endangered children and adolescents. Although the rapid growth programs may be taken as subjective evidence of their worth, the authors indicate, "Until now it has not been possible, due to lack of time, to establish overall statistics concerning the results of the HYL." Concerning the social group work program the authors state:

"Global investigation into the results are not yet available. It is certain, however, that essential help is given here to young people in their lives and that in the vast majority of cases the various symptoms of maladjustment are reduced. The number of cases for which admission to a residential home for children and young people proves necessary is lower in districts where social group work is carried out than in others." (5)

Concerning the "school help" program and psychological service the authors conclude:

The results of this experiment, too, have not yet been evaluated statistically. On the basis of the course taken by *countless* individual cases of which the issue has sometimes been unexpectedly favorable, the considerable significance of the action in prevention can, however, be proved. In the case of most of the children and young people treated, the symptom disappeared and socially positive behavior was achieved. (5)

This last example is typical of the evaluative comment that can be found in the large bulk of the programs that have been reported. The subjective nature of the appraisals needs careful scrutiny. Or is the value of such programs so self-evident as to make the question of more scientific or objective evaluation superfluous?

The attempt has been made to present the most promising (meaning most scientifically evaluated) programs as well as to illustrate the whole range of programs from the most objective to the very subjective (and in some cases unevaluated) through the selection of "typical examples" culled from the various reports. The length of this document did not permit an exhaustive presentation of all the programs reported by all advisory groups.

Some Major Observations and Some Issues for Consideration

The following list of observations and issues has been noted in the reading of the nine reports and may provide an outline or a starting point for consideration:

1. The wide assortment of programs aimed at various age levels and at the general and endangered youth groups requires the development of some classification or cataloguing schema. There is a need to establish meaningful categories in which to discuss various preventive approaches. One of the reports (6) arranged its program under the following nine headings:

1. Pre-School
2. School
3. Special Institutional Work
4. Community Treatment and Counseling
5. Leisure I: Sport and Play
6. Leisure II: Clubs, Spontaneous Groups and
   Detached Workers
7. Employment and Rehabilitation
8. "Problem" Families
9. Endangered Groups

These rubrics may be further refined or delineated and meaningful taxonomy night be established.

2. Special problems of assessment of the efficiency of prevention projects were considered at length in the summary from the Italian Advisory group (7). This report suggests that statistical assessment appears indispensable; it points out the difficulties that are to be found in the use of delinquency rates; it calls for the need to check the validity of cause and effect even in controlled studies; it suggests the use of multi-variate and factor analysis and calls for a clinical-statistical balance. Not only research design and statistical methods but also the all-important question concerning the adequacy of various criteria against which to test hypotheses concerning effectiveness of different types of prevention programs must be considered. This report (7) concedes, "It is very difficult to evaluate the efficiency of the system in a scientific manner," but it also makes a number of helpful theoretical observations.

3. In commenting on the evaluation problem another report (6) states:

> In gathering together and presenting these examples a far greater awareness of the need for evaluation has been found, even among promoters of rather individualistic efforts, than would probably have been the case a few years ago, but evaluation is often postponed or

carried out rather inadequately because of lack of know-how or the belief that considerable financial resources are required. (6)

What is the real reason for the lack of attention to program evaluation? Is it money? Does each program require a grant from the Ford Foundation? Do program directors have the skill and knowledge to employ effectively evaluation techniques?

4. The need for the maintenance of certain "housekeeping statistics" as a continuous evaluation to note effects of any new interventions should be considered by every community. Most action programs make of the evaluation process a very special occasion or a once-in-a-lifetime event. The community that keeps annual records on such items as school leavers, unemployment, delinquency, police contacts, truants, accidents, unwed mothers, and school failures can plot, through time series studies, rates for all these variables which can reflect the impact that new programs may or may not have in these important areas.

5. When experimental programs have been carefully designed, carried out, and evaluated as reported in the USA Supplement (10), the results have generally been on the disappointing side. Reasons for such negative results need to be explored. The prerequisites for prevention listed in the USA document (10) might be discussed and checked out for different countries.

6. Many of the reports on prevention programs for younger children seem to imply greater effect than do prevention programs for older youth. Yet more programs are available closer to the adolescent level than the pre-school period. Would not the more economical and efficient strategy be to concentrate time, money, and energies on the youngest who are endangered?

7. Most prevention programs describe single agency thrusts. It is true that there is some interdisciplinary programming visible in some countries and many reports of interagency cooperation. But what is not visible in any of the countries is a grand design or a mosaic of meaningful effort in which the social systems of the school, the police, the courts, the recreation and sports agency, the clinic, and the welfare agency mesh smoothly in a network of service to vulnerable youth and endangered family. How maximum community coordination can be brought from the verbal level to an action level represents perhaps the greatest challenge to those interested in the problem.

8. There is much confusion and loose use of the word "experiment." Too often it is used as a synonym for such terms as: new project, pilot study, survey, demonstration project. These terms are not interchangeable. The essential elements of an experimental design must be defined.

9. With one or two exceptions most of the reports described their programs with little or no discussion of the theoretical basis for their

action programs. If theoretical conceptualization is to be found, it is more implicit rather than explicit. The discussants who describe their prevention programs should be called upon to expound their major premises and their theoretical positions.

10. The changing and expanding role of the police agency in preventive work can be seen in many of the reports (1, 2, 4, 9). The shift in police activities and the greater preoccupation with the young offenders calls for a clarification of their exact role and function. Job descriptions need to be rewritten, and police need to be trained for their new and changing role in the sphere of prevention. And there is always the danger of confusion when functions overlap in child welfare programs.

11. Many of the prevention programs appear dominated by the professionals. There is always the strong smell of slick professionalism in many of the projects. It becomes obvious that the professionals cannot solve the delinquency problem by themselves. They all need the help of parents, lay leaders and youth themselves. The effective involvement of lay personnel and youth in prevention programs should merit attention.

12. The reports reveal stronger emphasis on group approaches to and group methods of delinquency prevention than upon individual counseling or one-to-one relationships. Apart from the problem of numbers of youngsters that must be served, consideration should be given to group and individual strategies as they relate to different kinds of delinquency. Each program should be clear as to what kinds of potential delinquents it is trying to help, i.e., the socialized delinquent whose problems may be embedded in the value system of the gang or the emotionally disturbed delinquent whose problems may stem from internal conflicts due to interpersonal relationships within the family, or other types.

There exists a very wide variety of prevention programs that have been developed to help the potential offender and his family. All these programs represent the helping hand of the community rather than the back of the hand. But many of these interventions are operated more on a professional hope and prayer than on any demonstrated or proven principles of operation. Some approaches are undoubtedly more efficient than others; some may be irrelevant and have little to do with the true antecedents of delinquent behavior; a few may even be harmful. As the review of the nine reports and the USA experiments (10) indicates, it is imperative that the directors of these programs concern themselves more and more with the key question: Does my program actually diminish the possibilities of delinquent behavior? This is a hard question that will call for hard data—data that are infrequently available as the nine reports testify.

24 Report of an International Conference[1]

What are some of the basic concepts and definitions in prevention and control of juvenile delinquency? How can any one program effectively insure prevention? What are some of the problems and promising practices in appraising prevention programs? What are some of the major issues concerning action and research in prevention and control?

The main task of the Eleventh Session of the Advisory Committee on Delinquent and Socially Maladjusted Children and Young People, International Union of Child Welfare, was carried through four discussion groups, led by chairmen and rapporteurs,[2] and was based on the reports summarized in Chapter 23.

This general report stems mainly from the summaries prepared by the rapporteurs. It is presented in four major segments: (1) basic concepts and definitions; (2) programming for prevention; (3) problems and practices in evaluation; and (4) issues and recommendations concerning action and research.

[1] William C. Kvaraceus, "Prevention of Juvenile Delinquency—Evaluation of Different Types of Action: General Report," *International Child Welfare Review* (Spring, 1965), pp. 23-39.

[2] Group I, Chairman: Mlle. S. Huynen, Directeur général Ministère de la Justice, Office de la Protection de l'Enfance, Bruxelles, Belgium; Rapporteur: Mr. C. Schaefer, Hospice général, Geneva, Switzerland. Group II, Chairman: Mr. K. Gilhus, Child Welfare Director, Oslo, Norway; Rapporteur: Mme T. Rividi, Secrétaire administrative, UMOSEA, Paris, France. Group III, Chairman: Mr. Holger Horsten, Director, Directorate of Child and Youth Welfare Services, Copenhagen, Denmark; Rapporteur: Mr. A. Leissner, B.A., M.S.W., Project Director, Tel-Aviv, Israel. Group IV, Chairman: Mr. P. Lutz, Issy-les-Moulineaux, France; Rapporteur: Dr. S. Jaime, Child Psychiatrist, Guadalajara, Mexico.

Basic Concepts and Definitions

All groups wrestled with various concepts and definitions, and rightly so. Without some agreement on terminology and concepts, a profitable discussion is not possible. The groups asked such questions as follow: What do we mean by normal behavior and abnormal behavior? What is prevention? How does it differ from treatment? What is meant by "different forms of preventive action?" What is delinquent behavior?

In answering these questions, the working groups reported:

Juvenile delinquency was regarded as symptomatic behavior that had a wide variety of causes which varied with each individual. The behavior was seen as violating the norms or values of the dominant community. The behavior was recognized to be on a continuum rather than in categories. The need to differentiate the delinquent and to plan prevention and treatment programs according to differentiated types was recommended with due recognition to sex and age. After research, the following typology was suggested: the gang delinquent, the solitary and isolated delinquent, the aggressive and attacking delinquent and the occasional or pseudo-delinquent. The question of mixed types was recognized, but dominant strains were said to fall in these four kinds. Some groups did not delimit themselves to a discussion of the delinquent but included the wider group of emotionally disturbed and or socially maladjusted.

A distinction was drawn between prevention and treatment in most groups. Treatment was perceived in terms of services rendered in the rehabilitation of a child already showing delinquent behavior. Prevention was regarded as early intervention aimed at an endangered child or his family or neighborhood setting. Prevention is action developed either with a view to avoiding the birth of an unfavorable determinism or to attenuating its effects. "Different forms of preventive action" was employed in two ways:

1. In terms of levels of action: primary, secondary, and tertiary.
2. Methods of approach used in intervention (case work, counselling, group work, recreation, foster placement, institutional placement, etc.).

Thus the idea of a preventive policy can be viewed at three levels following the definitions presented in the report of the Belgian delegation:

1. *Primary prevention* (general prophylaxis): this means the whole of social, medical and educative provisions which cover the juvenile population in general or one of several social groups. These measures

aim at organizing society in such a way as to guarantee the satisfaction of the basic needs of its young members and to insure their protection from the dangers to which they are in general exposed.

2. *Secondary prevention:* This aims at detecting and treating as early as possible minors whose health, security, morality, or education are jeopardized. These are not general measures, but those providing individual help (or protection).

3. *Tertiary prevention:* This seeks to prevent complications and after-effects of juvenile behavior disturbances and to prevent contagion (prevention of recidivism).

It would be naive to think that secondary and tertiary prevention will see their clientele disappear as *primary prevention* develops its social welfare policy. Each form of prevention has its own objectives and methods and one should not underestimate the importance of individual prophylaxis in relation to general prophylaxis. The relative failure of general social prophylaxis in the field of the prevention of juvenile delinquency can be explained perhaps by the over-simplified notion that what is beneficial to the members of a society as a whole (measures against poverty, sickness, ignorance, immorality, unemployment) are *sufficient* arms in the fight against juvenile delinquency.

The several groups indicated that there is need to study the normal in order to know what the deviant is deviating from. Three aspects of what is normal were considered:

1. As defined in the moral and legal code.
2. Normative or model behavior in regard to sexual deviancy.
3. Normalcy in the physical sense of well-being and growth (bad teeth, crippled).

Defining what is normal remains still an indispensable and continuous task in order to arrive at a valid perspective of delinquent or deviating behavior as well as valid goals and methods. The term has a moral as well as scientific connotation. Difficulties were seen in the middle ranges, where the lines are hazy between normal and abnormal, sick and healthy, adjusted and maladjusted, permitted and prohibited, etc.

Programs for Prevention

A wide variety of programs for the various age groups were discussed. Priority was given to no one program and to no one technique or approach. Both individual approaches and group approaches received their share of attention. If there was an imbalance, it was, rightly, in the direction of group and club-work approaches reflecting the large category of gang delinquents reported in many countries. No one seemed to hold out a magic method or a sure prescription.

Two topics received the large bulk of the groups' attention: early identification of endangered groups at various age levels, and the necessity of coordination and cooperation between agencies and institutions.

On what age groups should the state and community focus?

Group opinion crystallized into two divergent views, with some points of agreement:

1. One extreme is represented by the view that character traits, personality syndromes, and behavior patterns are firmly established during the first six years of life.
2. The other view is that there are sensitive or crisis phases throughout life, especially during puberty, adolescence, and the first adult-adjustment period (ages 18-20), which offer opportunities for personality rebuilding, our cues for intervention.

Early-Childhood Emphasis View holds that prevention should start as early as possible in order to avoid the need for later patchwork. The cooperation of the parents is essential and often dependent upon the professional image perceived. This necessitates more public relations work by the profession. Primary prevention must be the focus of professional approach and research.

Continuum of Sensitive Phases View stresses the necessity to extend Freudian psychology in accordance with the requirements of a modern dynamic society. Peter Blos is cited as a clinical authority who sees puberty and adolescence as decisive developmental phases which offer continued opportunities for character formation.

Emphasis on intervention was related to the problem of priorities, in that large poverty groups confront us with a great number of youngsters who have been exposed to destructive influences in early childhood and who must be reached during adolescence.

Gang-work experience was cited as showing need for support during adulthood-adjustment phase around the age of eighteen. This is especially important where society does or does not provide rites of passage at this period. Example of lack of rites of passage is the lack of marriage opportunities in United States Negro slums, resulting in large numbers of illegitimate births. Israel provides rites of passage through universal military service, and youngsters who are excluded show the effects of severe crisis.

General agreement.

We need early preventive work wherever possible, as well as intervention during sensitive phases of puberty and adolescence.

The doubtful validity of much of our research and lack of sufficient longitudinal studies do not offer enough evidence to state with certainty that preventive work is more effective with one or the other age group.

It is likely that we need continuous preventive work throughout all phases of childhood and youth in order to assure adequate adult adjustments.

Vulnerability to delinquent behavior was discussed in all groups. While no specific set of factors was spelled out in a delinquency-proneness scale, recurring emphasis on such predictive variables as the following could be found: deprivation of normal home life, lack of academic aptitude, contradictory and confusing value systems (double standard), school failure and lack of success, mobility, low self-concept, poverty. It must be pointed out that the predictive power of these separate variables needs to be validated.

Emphasis was placed on the need to utilize all community workers in the early detection of vulnerable youngsters in lower socio-economic levels as well as in higher socio-economic milieux. This will call for the cooperation of all elements in society (schools, parents, social workers, police, etc.).

Apprehension was also expressed concerning early identification of the so-called predelinquent. The self-fulfilling prophecy of declaring a youngster a pre-delinquent might be followed by his living up to the label.

The need for validating prediction measures was repeated.

Concern was expressed in several groups for the twelve to fourteen age category which contributes a large share to the delinquent population. A crucial problem of this age group is that of the organization of leisure time. It was pointed out that those children who take part in organized leisure-time activities are not, in general, those children whose need to be helped in this way is the greatest or most pressing. Various measures were suggested to get at these youngsters, including playgrounds with special wardens or leaders, special after-school club programs, early identification and referral of these youngsters, use of child guidance services.

Coordination and cooperation represent a common bedrock theme that appears in every report. What is found here is more than lip service to a platitudinous principle. Coordination and cooperation were discussed at various levels and in a variety of contexts: between agencies, disciplines, theorists, and practitioners, between administrators and service personnel, between parents, lay and professional, volunteers and professional workers, between ministries at the national level. While most agreed to the need in principle, with few exceptions most participants also agreed that we have a long way to go to achieve optimum interaction so that the right youngster gets the right service at the right time. Various reasons were given why we have been slow. These range from sibling rivalries between agencies to petty bureaucratic inefficiency.

Preventive programs for preschool age children.

After having stressed the primary role of kindergartens, nursery schools, etc. in preventive programs, the question was asked whether research had been done to establish whether children having benefited from such measures showed better adjusted behavior subsequently. It was mentioned that thanks to the early detection of character problems, language disturbances, etc., certain specialized services have been established in different countries at preschool age (Denmark, Belgium, Germany). This preventive work deserves to be undertaken more systematically.

Preventive programs for school children.

It seems that there are few studies on the child aged from six to thirteen (with the exception of those done by Piaget). If this is so, on what psychological elements should preventive work be based?

It is also found that the children who participate in organized leisure-time activities are not generally those who have problems. How can one reach this category of children?

Interdisciplinary programming and interagency cooperation.

Regarding the passage from theory to action and practical achievement, the following problem was posed. Does the difficulty in implementation stem from a lack of coordination of the services concerned, from rivalry between the different categories of technicians, from certain religious or national traditions?

Lack of coordination, both at local and at national level, and a certain rivalry between the services concerned and also between the different categories of specialists were all considered as possible reasons for the failure of action.

Youth clubs.

The club programs of certain countries (Denmark, Norway, Poland) were described. It was, however, pointed out that this was no more than a simple inventory and that the problem of evaluating the action of the clubs still remains. One would need, of course, to be able to ascertain whether youth clubs have a positive effect on juvenile delinquents. How can such studies be carried out?

Some research carried out in France concerning the technical problems of evaluating preventive action were quoted. A large number of factors intervene: how can one isolate them and study their effects? There was discussion on types of secondary and tertiary prevention, and arising out of this, the problem of the training of personnel was raised. Should one use voluntary, non-qualified personnel, or only trained personnel?

The problem can be put in this way: Do scientific criteria enable the conditions to be determined in which one can associate voluntary work with preventive action, and does this voluntary work pay?

There was a strong feeling that to say that more prevention programs should be concentrated on the youngest group of children should not mean that we have to reduce the energy and interest we devote to working out problems with the adolescents. There was discussion of whether the so-called "endangered groups" will develop into normal individuals without assistance, recognizing how limited we can be when we venture into prognosis concerning these youngsters.

It was agreed that we must work positively with parents and must increase the establishment of family services. In this connection, consideration was given to the extent to which the prenatal and postnatal education for younger parents in Belgium (the example suggested to the group) will contribute in the long run to the prevention of juvenile delinquency. Through such education, the parents can learn what the family means and can become aware of the urgency of individual needs, emotional and educational, and adjustment to society by family members.

The group found imbalance between the real situation and the individual needs, not only in the home but in the whole environment. Often schools do not do their part in the prevention of delinquency because teachers sometimes do not have adequate psychopedagogical training and knowledge which will make them quick to detect abnormal behavior. The school is not always able to cooperate with child guidance centers or vice versa because of a lack of communication.

On this point, there was discussion and agreement on the importance of realizing that an increase in juvenile delinquency is related closely to the increase in population. When society becomes more industrialized, this affects the family environment and brings confusion to the youngster in his identification as a member of his family unit, and the pressure of the society's standards upon the individual is lessened.

Finally, in discussing the vulnerable kinds of children and the vital importance of early detection, the group stressed the following point: taking into account that the deprivation of a normal home life plays an important part in the causes of delinquency, the services and institutions helping children who are suffering from partial or total deficiencies in family care should be seen as an integral part of preventive measures and should have at their disposal adequate medical, psychological, and educational facilities to enable these children to reach adulthood on a healthy basis, ready to bear individual and family responsibilities and to exhibit socially approved behavior.

Coordination between agencies and personnel seems to have two aspects:

1. Bureaucracy and overemphasis on professional status as an obstacle to the best use of professional approaches.
2. Overdefensiveness and reluctance of professionals to delegate functions to untrained staff resulting in wasteful use of skilled personnel and failure to make full use of the potential of the lay community.

Program leadership, professional and voluntary.

Attempting to care for all social needs through professional intervention alone endangers the social solidarity of the population and runs counter to the generic principle of helping a client to help himself. We need better criteria for the best application of professional functions and suitable opportunities for using an untrained staff. This is an important task for research.

The historical struggle in the social welfare field for professional recognition and status has led to the danger of professionalism for its own sake in some areas. The professional worker has a responsibility to use his skills and professional judgment for careful selection and suitable assignment of functions to the untrained staff. Voluntary leaders are often selected according to the values of professionals, rather than in accordance with the actual power structure of the population. We must be ready to seek the cooperation of leaders, even if their norms and behavior do not suit our value-conditioned expectations.

A world shortage of professionals makes the use of untrained workers imperative. Professionals will have to accept supervisory, directing responsibilities more and more often, rather than providing direct services themselves. Israel offers an example of this situation. Professionals have to take over leadership functions often right after termination of their own training. Britain offers an example of an upsurge of readiness to volunteer among British teenagers which meets with reluctance by the professionals to use this resource fully.

The following additional questions were raised:

Are we aware of, or do we make a correct evaluation of, what delinquent behavior means?

Do we have in each community the resources to meet the individual needs?

Are we aware of looking at a society of rebels and conformists?

Is juvenile delinquency a social phenomenon of our developed societies?

What kind of juvenile delinquency do we mean by "positive"?

It was agreed that we cannot generalize symptoms. We must understand the causes of the symptoms, and in this way we can find a positive aspect of the problem. In saying this, we do not mean that juvenile delinquency is necessary; but to talk about the elimination of juvenile delinquency, we have to consider first what life means, what moral norms mean, who is establishing these norms, and how we interpret the norms. These points are crucial especially for the parents, for the family as a unit, and for professionals.

Youth participation in delinquency prevention.

It was agreed that youth participation in delinquency prevention and control should be maximized. But the principal problem remains: How is this to be done? For example, youth-club leaders may provide a good hero model according to the norms of the society in which he lives and his success in achieving the society's goals. On the other hand, these measures, too, must be evaluated. We are familiar with the delinquent gang structure. The therapist who has experience in this line must have a complete understanding of the structure of the individual personality, the delinquent-group personality, and how to give help to each individual and to his group. It is necessary not only to obtain the participation of the youth, but also to find motivation for him and to give him the help to which he is entitled. He needs to "find" himself within his own self and within his society. The value of group work in this connection was stressed throughout the discussion.

The reports also consider the use of mass media in informing the community and the parents, the training of personnel—professional and volunteer—and the involvement of organized parent groups in program planning and operation.

Problems and Practices in Evaluation

Certain impeding factors were identified that limit evaluation of prevention programs:

1. Lack of valid criteria for evaluation, and inadequate measures for evaluation.
2. Personnel attempting research are often practitioners who are lacking in skills and who are involved in the operation. They confuse inventory for evaluation.
3. Not enough qualified, specialized researchers on staff.
4. Studies start too late and are short term, thus do not give a valid picture.
5. General reluctance to engage in research is widespread and is rationalized in many ways.
6. Little or no budget available for research and development. Considered as fluff or as a fad.
7. Practitioners are illiterate and cannot read nor interpret research reports.

Reports point out a number of gaps between researcher-practitioner:

1. Not using the research that exists: gap between research and implementation.
2. Research takes time: action-oriented people must make decisions now, cannot wait two years for a decision.
3. Theoretical and practical research are needed.
4. Feedback: practitioner cannot understand the statistical research report.
5. Factors that impede the immediate implementation of research findings were explored and a finger was pointed at administrators.

We must see our effort as one of continuous and systematic collection of significant data on relevant items of information which enable us to make judgments and decisions.

The evaluation process was described in the following steps:

1. Determination of specific goals and objectives;
2. Selection of appropriate or most promising tests and techniques for gathering data;
3. Validation and reliability check of data-gathering techniques;
4. Careful and continuous collections of information;
5. Noting differences and testing for significance in change or improvement.

Historical factors, such as the competition with the natural sciences for scientific status, have resulted in a certain reluctance to acknowledge the value of social research and to test results by repeating experiments. We know more than we think, but we do not have enough feedback of our findings to the practitioners. There are no absolute results in social research, only insights and indicators for practice. We should be ready to repeat experiments and regard the results, whether they are similar to the original findings or seemingly contradictory, as indicators of social change and as experimental pointers.

British experience with "cohort" studies which focus on a population group born in a certain time period and carried over a period of fifteen to twenty years offers a model for longitudinal, multifaceted research which promises best results in the long run, while offering periodic interim findings for practical application.

Research should strike a balance between longitudinal, inclusive studies and more limited, short-term studies centered on specific issues.

Studies of well-adjusted as well as maladjusted behavior are needed in order to arrive at valid conclusions.

Case studies should not be neglected, but should be related to or built into area and population studies that deal with problems in their social context.

While research should be concerned with the adjusted population, as well as with the continuous collection of data and records, ongoing study with periodic evaluations of the program was considered as highly desirable by all groups. Distinctions must be made in the use of this method for (a) accountability, (b) supervision, (c) evaluation. Data can be used for (a) and (b), then channelled to research.

Descriptive studies should not be neglected in favor of quantitative studies. Both have their function in research.

Results of evaluations may be statistically significant, but unless pointed to productive goals and problems do not offer guidelines for practice or insight, thereby engendering distrust for further research among practitioners.

Historically, universities have emphasized pure research, causing applied research to be regarded as second-class. University research for purely academic purposes, often carried out in superficial manner by students, has caused resentment among practitioners.

Research must become the object of educational, public relations effort in order to convince practitioners that it is worth doing and meaningful, and in order to educate staff and sponsors regarding its function. Sponsors (boards) often regard research as a form of magic which will effect immediate changes.

Three kinds of research sponsorship were found to predominate:

1. University research, usually pure research, often self-serving rather than directed toward needs of agencies or profession;
2. Government-sponsored research, often self-justifying, inventory-evaluation based upon vested interest to prove something, therefore suspect;
3. Independent research bodies. These seem to have done most useful and objective work.

Countries ruled by dominant ideologies pose special problems to social research, as direction and results are often severely limited by ideological precepts and, in some cases, by the feeling that certain disclosures may threaten national security. Increased opportunities for international contacts and discussion would help the professionals of those countries to liberalize national policies regarding research.

The group discussed whether the agencies, as well as their workers, must pause and define their functions and specific roles. Social workers came into focus here. Again, we noted the lack of supervision of the work on an individual basis; not only in relation to this specialized element of the social worker but to each and all elements in the group. Despite the need for definition of roles of each practitioner, we realized that each member has to have the possibility of flexibility, some freedom, and to use his own judgment; and we looked at the different situations which each one of us can encounter. In addition to the definition of roles of the different agencies and worker, there must be coordination and a continuous evaluation of the personnel of each agency, stressing the need to understand that our work is on a team-work basis, with a periodical revision and evaluation of its own characteristics. The constant reviews of the aims planned, the failures obtained, should be visualized within the whole scope of rehabilitation, from both main aspects: the economic and the therapeutic. It is known to all of us that the administrator of institutions and agencies visualizes the problems from an economic-productive approach, and the therapist or educator from his own approach, so a dialogue must be established between therapists and administrators, with a constant evaluation of our work and the results obtained. It is obvious that definition of roles does not mean identification with our role, and the diversity of attitudes encountered in each one of us and what the human being means was brought into the discussion.

In this connection, it was emphasized that "youth" are individuals and that we must learn how to deal with and communicate with each one of them. We referred to the evolution of the ways of dealing with juvenile delinquency, in the past with a more punitive attitude and now oriented in a therapeutic manner, and to the need to increase our energy in order to achieve it. At this point the group stressed the necessity of being able in our daily work to engage in self-criticism, to be able to evaluate ourselves, to make time to reflect upon our mistakes, successes, and responsibilities, to accept failures and use them as well as our total experience. We realized that all our training and "skill" can be distorted when we do not understand, when we do not realize, what communication means between adults and youth.

Issues and Recommendations Concerning Action and Research

We need complex research designs in order to match the complexity of modern society. A double standard of explicit and implicit values poses problems for definitions of a normative nature. Rapid historical changes in mores and expectations and the state of flux of modern society pose problems to longitudinal studies.

The researcher is part of the society he studies, in some ways part of the situation he seeks to analyze. He can contaminate his own research.

We do not deal with categories, but with a continuum of behavioral patterns. Research runs into most difficulties in the middle ranges, where the border lines between the normal and the abnormal, the sick and the healthy, the adjusted and the maladjusted, the permitted and the prohibited, remain vague and fluctuating.

A research sequence should be maintained consisting of the following three stages:

1. Orientation (survey studies of a comparative nature);
2. Exploration (consisting of two to three years of preliminary research aimed at arriving at an hypothesis based upon empirical evidence);
3. Intensive research on specific aspects of an hypothesis.

Independent research organizations should be encouraged in all countries.

The International Union for Child Welfare (I.U.C.W.) should be more aggressive in reaching out for participants from the many countries not represented at this conference, especially the new developing countries and those countries which are ruled by clearly defined social and political ideologies.

Each program evaluation requires basically trained personnel who will appraise the program effectively and specifically, providing enough time for adequate supervision, in addition to an understanding of what evaluation means and the advantage of undertaking it. A further necessity is to educate authorities in this area and to enlist their cooperation.

More work should be done in public relations in order to get the cooperation of parents for early preventive work.

Each country should form an interdisciplinary body in order to establish priorities of service in accordance with the available professional resources and the needs of the population.

Administrators should not have a narrow, specialized view conditioned by their own professional identification, but should gain over-all perspective in order to avoid narrowing of emphasis on the policy-making level. They should be given sufficient time to gain and use a broad understanding of issues. (Negative example: Rapid turnover of top-level civil servants in Britain.)

The profession must devise suitable supervisory techniques and training methods to assure the best use of a wide range of trained leaders, untrained staff, and volunteers.

A policy of a wide range of specializations combined with good central planning and local coordination agencies is recommended.

The I.U.C.W. should initiate international surveys with periodic reports in order to encourage cross-cultural studies. The purpose is not to change national social structures, but to aid professionals to adapt methods to regional and cultural needs. I.U.C.W. reports should be readable, short, and void of destructive criticism. Researchers cannot rely solely on official government informants, but must seek information from reliable independent sources within the surveyed countries.

An international conference on coordination and planning was recommended.

In early identification of the "predelinquent" and socially maladjusted, there is danger of stimulating criminal tendencies as well as stigmatizing client groups. There is some evidence that early-detection research resulted in stigmatization which may have led to higher vulnerability of members of target groups.

The group nevertheless considers it very important that the detection of children in danger should take place as early as possible.

Establish a list of *ways and means of early detection* of individual cases of child victims of social maladjustment;

Study methods of preventive intervention in individual cases and assess to what extent their evaluation is possible;

See to what extent it would be possible to establish a list of some key words, rigorously defined to enable clarification of all discussions or studies seeking to evaluate preventive programs, and, if necessary, evaluation of one of its effects, delinquency.

Comparison of a series of attempts at detection carried out in France, Belgium, Holland, and Denmark showed:

Detection comes on at different levels;

Probably in most regions, the attempts at detection only partially cover the population which should be detected;

Detection through the channel of the juridical machinery is inadequate, even when juridical personnel consider themselves responsible for preventive work.

The group agreed that in most countries there was still a chasm between the verbal level of coordination and implementation in practice.

How can the youngsters themselves be interested in the prevention of juvenile maladjustment? Are there criteria valid for all countries relating to the involvement of young people in this action? The socio-economic and political context is often the determining factor. In some countries, maladjusted young people with behavior problems and endangered youngsters are integrated in youth camps linked with national ideals (e.g., youth camps in Yugoslavia, Komsomol in Russia, citizens' camps in Ghana).

Another point discussed was the way in which the "sensational" press exploited happenings in institutions. The general public is ill-informed about the work done in the field of resocialization by these institutions and the various specialists concerned. There is need for better information in order to achieve a better awareness on the part of the public.

Delinquency is only *one* of the effects of *social maladjustment,* and the latter can also take the form of simple mental disease.

Scientific research in the field of social maladjustment should no longer content itself with quantifying and categorizing the disturbances, but should resolutely trace them back to their psychological or social causes.

The question of the training of personnel was raised. Should untrained voluntary workers be used, or should only trained workers be used? Experience in different countries showed that although there are varying proportions, voluntary workers as well as trained personnel participate in preventive action. There do not appear to be studies available on the results obtained by trained workers and those obtained by voluntary workers. This problem can perhaps be put in this form: do scientific criteria enable the determination of conditions in which voluntary action can be associated with preventive action, and whether such voluntary action is productive?

It appears that there are relatively fewer studies made on children of the age group six to thirteen years old, and particularly for the twelve to fourteen age group, than on the younger children. If this is so, what psychological, pedagogical, and sociological factors should be used as bases for preventive work?

The crucial problem in regard to this age group is that of the organization of leisure time. Those children who take part in organized leisure-time activities are not, in general, those children whose need to be helped in this way is greatest; i.e., children with problems who are in special need of supervision, "key children." How can such activities be organized in order to attract this type of child? It appears that many fail to make the maximum use of leisure time; daily leisure time and activities should be made more worth while; i.e. playgrounds, supervised by wardens or "leaders" seem to be a good formula; within the school itself, it seems desirable that:

The total number of children in a primary school should not exceed 500;

There should be a service responsible for early detection within the school service: child-guidance service.

The importance of controlling and coordinating the function of state financing was noted. However, too much emphasis on state subsidies and controls may stifle local initiative. In some cases, coordination and implementation of research may be safer in the hands of a central authority or independent agencies, as local authorities may be too subjective and have a vested interest in maintaining the *status quo.*

Assignment of priorities is influenced by public opinion and the mass communication media. This necessitates emphasis on public relations work. Secrecy is detrimental to good planning. The political vested interests of the mass communication media must be taken into account by central bodies.

Defining what is "normal" remains an indispensable, continuous task in order to arrive at valid research methods and goals. The term has a moral, as well as a quantitative, scientific connotation. Both must be considered; neither one alone offers satisfactory answers.

Regional surveys are needed to establish areas of need and priorities. Unnecessary work is often done because it is comfortable, while necessary work is neglected because it is difficult. Evidence is available that expenditure is not necessarily related to need in many areas. Case studies and life histories of delinquents can be useful in establishing where services are lacking, complement each other, or overlap.

A dearth of references to the field of community organization in the discussions reflects a lack of this important service. Community organization leadership is essential for adequate planning which takes social structure, regional, and class differences into account.

The problem of bureaucracy appears to be an obstacle to coordination, program planning, implementation, and evaluation everywhere. A balance between top-level people with over-all perspective and local people with specific local experience is needed in order to avoid isolation of tho two levels; also a distinction must be made between coordination and cooperation—local-level interservice cooperation. One important coordinating function of educational activities can be the dissemination of information.

PART SEVEN

Tomorrow's Youth

25 What Lies Ahead for Tomorrow's Youth and Tomorrow's Citizens

In summarizing the points raised in the preceding chapters, can we draw any conclusions about norm-violating behavior and its causes? Can we look to any positive guides for action? How does a youth's awareness of his disenfranchised status increase his tensions and problems? What attitudes toward marriage and family life are being established in his high school years? What can adults do to create an atmosphere of communication and understanding between themselves and adolescents? Can the schools direct the youngster away from group-dominated activities to independent, self-disciplined behavior? How strong is the influence of example; can the adult world offer models of good citizenship that will show the youngster behavior worthy of being imitated? As fast, easy transportation makes the individual a "citizen of the world" what are the new requirements for living on this basis?

The role of women in the changing society must be considered. How can the prejudices against women in politics and business be removed? What special problems of the working mother are apparent, and is there a solution for them?

In facing up to these many questions, what is the challenge that now awaits the thoughtful planners and citizens of today's society?

There are many varied and complex citizenship-forming influences in the growth and development of the young adult. These include knowledge (as well as misinformation), attitudes, habits and behavioral sets, and the socio-economic-cultural forces that form the youngster's effective milieu of his primary frame of reference. From the interaction of all these inner and outer forces emanates all behavior, which may be studied against the current criteria of what constitutes the "good citizen" within a given society.

As a transitional period of adulthood, the teen-age years, especially in our civilization, are accompanied by many pressures which make them turbulent and anxious years. Living through this period, the maturing child may undergo learning experiences that will help steer him in the direction of worthy and effective citizenship or in the opposite direction of the adult who flees from or denies his civic and social responsibilities. The school agency has been given the mandate to see that sufficient forces can be controlled and marshalled so that the goals of effective citizenship in our society are achieved by all youth.

In this discussion, we shall first consider those factors and forces within the adolescent character of American youth which have strong bearing on and implications for future adult citizenship. Next we shall examine some of the stronger currents, already being felt in the cultural stress, which merit the concern of those curriculum planners whose purpose it is to assist the young to more effective self-direction and social-civic participation in local, state, national, and international affairs.

The American Adolescent and His Subculture

The literature on the American adolescent is replete with bio-psycho-social research studies. The adult American preoccupation with the adolescent has done much to shape the emerging teen-age subculture in this country. The more relevant and crucial trends of the adolescent subculture for future citizenship education will be cited in this section without attempting a comprehensive coverage of all the available literature on "the adolescent."

The early mating pattern.

Adolescence represents a period of physical maturation. During this growth process the American boy and girl show one major dominating concern: to meet and to fix on an appropriate future life-partner. This focal concern of American Youth frequently annoys and even scares parent and teacher. They bemoan the "boy-crazy" and "girl-crazy" antics of the teen-agers. At the same time, home, school, and community provide many programs and opportunities for activities in all aspects of daily living which engender a free and easy boy-girl relationship. The worst fate that can befall a high school youngster is to be left sitting at home, undated, on the night of the junior prom. Problems relating to the emerging sexual-social roles, and questions concerning petting and dating (as reported in the Purdue Survey[1]), reveal a strong concern with the process of finding a suitable life partner.

In a sense, school and community offer a rich practicum in living with, working with, and playing with members of the other sex with little or no didactics. The husband-wife and mother-father roles of the future citizen are carefully skirted by the school. The current trend toward earlier marriage (average age now eighteen), with the appearance of married students in the high school, and the higher reported incidence of divorce and separation among the early marriage categories argue for the necessity of giving earlier priority to the mating concerns of the adolescent within a family-life education program forming an integral part of the school's citizenship training experience. At the same time, the steady increase of unwed teen-age mothers and the widespread adoption of the female-based household as a prevalent type of family unit, particularly in certain neighborhoods in which the male, acting in the "father" role, is absent from the home, only sporadically present, or, if present, only minimally or inconsistently involved in the support and raising of children, also testify to the need for citizenship training in mating and marriage experience. Effective parenthood in the family circle must be seen as prerequisite and part of citizenship in the community.

The exploited and exiled adolescent minority.

Except for the real and difficult task of finding an appropriate mate, adolescents generally find themselves disenfranchised from the adult community. They have no vote; their opportunity for work is circumscribed by labor laws and by union regulation; their extended education requirements for entering many occupations prolongs their dependency period; and the opportunities extended to them for practicing and participating in the adult citizen role are kept at a minimum. The resulting self-image does not build self-respect, nor does it establish any feeling of personal worth. Much of the norm-violating behavior of youth that borders on adult precociousness—driving a car illegally or recklessly, engaging in early sex experiences, drinking—can often be interpreted as something more than adolescent protest. More frequently such expressions may be used to fill a void or vacuum between late childhood and adulthood and represent a reaching in the direction of adult responsibility or a tryout of the adult roles.

---

[1] H. H. Remmers and D. H. Radler, *The American Teen-ager* (Indianapolis: Bobbs-Merrill Co. Inc., 1957).

As in the past, the American adolescent will continue to be the delight and despair of the adult community. The teen-age subculture will always remain highly functional for the elders, albeit the function may fall in the area of the negative stereotype of the scapegoat. The following question must be raised in every citizenship training program: "How can the negative stereotype be dissolved and a positive functional value be assigned to the fast-maturing students in school and in community by including them as worthy partners in social and civic enterprise?"

To improve citizenship training programs in school and community, it will first be necessary for teachers, parents, and other adults to formulate and sell a more positive and constructive image of the teenager as a law-abiding and useful citizen. It may not be easy for many adults, including teachers, to discard or divorce this negative stereotype of youth, since youth have always served as a convenient scapegoat for the adult community. The adult need for a comfortable and convenient institutional hate object has often been too easily satisfied by precocious and irritating youth. Many parents and teachers who are pressured and bothered daily by many family, municipal, state, national, and international problems involving such factors as the high cost of living, taxes, depression-recession, hot and cold war, threat of atomic warfare, tend to express their frustrations via complaint and attack on youth. Bitter laments concerning useless, ungrateful, spoiled, lazy, shiftless, incorrigible, pleasure-seeking, undisciplined, and egocentric youth reappear perennially in adult conversation and writing. The cumulative effect such complaints have on the formulation of the authority-image on the part of youth should not be overlooked. Jenkins and Lippet[2] have reported significantly that students see teachers generally as operating in a power situation; nor do the students perceive "friendly relationship" as desired on the part of the teaching staff. School-community citizenship programs for youth must consider ways and means for providing true co-worker experiences in which the power struggle between youth and adults is minimized and gives way to cooperative and participatory endeavor. Instead of priding themselves on what they do *for* youth, *adults* must concern themselves with what they do *with* youth particularly in programs for social and civic betterment.

Since youth represent a disenfranchised non-voting minority group, they are not organized to make their voice heard above the adult lobby

<hr>

[2] David Jenkins and Ronald Lippitt, "Interpersonal Perceptions in the Classroom" in *The Adolescent, A Book of Reading*, ed., J. Seidman (New York: The Dryden Press, Inc., 1957), pp. 583-599.

except perhaps through the street-corner gangs and even through the delinquency protest. Lacking legitimate means to achieve status in American society, many youth follow illegitimate methods to gain attention, prestige, and status via practice in poor citizenship behavior. A citizenship program for young people must be set on the bedrock of wholesome practice and experience in good citizenship via home, school, and community programs. It is pertinent to note that a typical study[3] reports that 79 per cent of the Nation's youth complained that their elders usually or sometimes underestimate their true maturity.

Too often and too long American youth have been limited in their participation in important and worthwhile adult-like activities by law, by sentiment, and by overzealous adult-planning for youth. As a result, youth are too often relegated to passive participation roles or to the role of recipients of services rendered by adults in such areas as recreation, social and civic activity, religion, and schooling. The Boy Scout and Girl Scout studies[4] have reported that approximately two-thirds of the youth in many communities do belong to some kind of organization. Hence, there are many opportunities for youth to experience various citizenship roles. School-community citizenship programs should exploit the practicum possibilities in all youth activities and organizations by enabling youth to serve themselves and the community. Only in this way can lessons of self-direction, responsibility, and social participation—three important cornerstones of effective citizenship—be learned and applied.

The threat to future youth (and future adults) will stem from the continued exile and disenfranchisement of the young. Adolescents, like nature, abhor a vacuum. Locked out of meaningful and worthwhile adult-like tasks and activities, youth will try to fill in this waiting period with some kinds of maturing activities even though these may be along disapproved and delinquent routes. The emerging independence-seeking concerns of youth would tend to indicate that high school students are more ready to accept responsibility for adult-like tasks than are the grown-ups ready to provide opportunities for such experiences.

The self-concept thus engendered is not one of high prestige or personal worth. Youth, like adults, must find fulfillment in being good at something or for something. Pitkin and others have asked youths of varied ages the question: "What is the most important honor you

---

[3] Remmers and Radler, *op. cit.*

[4] Boy Scouts of America, *Study of Adolescent Boys.* (New Brunswick, New Jersey; Boy Scouts of America, 1955); Girl Scouts of America, *Study of Adolescent Girls* (New York: Girl Scouts, Inc., 1956).

have ever had?" While many youngsters are able to cite one or more positive experiences of recognition, there is a substantial group that is unable to think of anything approaching an honor. "I have never had an honor," they say. For example, in one group of 60 pupils in the lower academic third of the class, Pitkin[5] reported only three pupils who claimed having received an honor of any kind in school or out.

In establishing a practicum in citizenship for young adults, the problem in communication between adults and adolescents will need to be solved. The lack of communication in face to face relationships between the young and their elders, and the problems arising out of differential perceptions, need to be anticipated by parents, group leaders and teachers. Various researchers have reported that an invisible screen exists between adults and youths in most schools and communities. By working face-to-face on mutual problems involving civic and social issues it may be possible to penetrate the psychic insulation that now separates the maturing student from his parents and teachers.

Group anchored values and decisions.

Many studies[6] report that the adolescent would prefer to be wrong with his gang or his peers than right with his parents and the adult world from which he has been detached. The Purdue Opinion Polls confirm that teen-agers are consistently more sensitive to the feelings and opinions of other teen-agers and even of adults than to a "voice from within." They are, in the Riesman terminology, "outer-directed." If the "good citizen" ideal calls for the essential ingredient of self-determination, which includes personalized and individualized critical thinking and decision-making as opposed to sheep-like following of the crowd, clique, gang, minority pressure group, or even the mob, then the school must concern itself early in its citizenship education program with this threat to the democratic process. There is a great danger of a future citizen (the signs are already visible in adult citizenship behavior) who will base important decisions more on the pressure-group demands than on the issues per se, or who will react to proposed legislation more out of fear of group opinion than in terms of the meaning and implications of the proposed legislation for local, national, or international benefit. There is strong evidence that the pres-

---

[5] Victor E. Pitkin, "Youth Development and Democratic Citizenship Education," *Citizenship and a Free Society,: Education for the Future,* 30th Yearbook of the National Council for the Social Studies, Franklin Patterson, Editor (Washington, D.C., 1960), pp. 33-63.

[6] Remmers and Radler. *op. cit; Study of Adolescent Boys, op. cit.; Study of Adolescent Girls, op. cit.*

ent adolescent subculture is fostering a dependent, group-oriented, nonthinking, and much too emotionalized personality. How much of this is a reflection of the adult culture rather than a unique and transitory subcultural adolescent pattern is difficult to ascertain. In any case, the implications for the school's responsibility and opportunity to groom a more effective future adult-citizen become obvious.

Uninformed and unthinking youth.

One of the most ominous and disconcerting findings of the Remmers' Purdue Polls[7] was in the reports of high school students' knowledge, beliefs, and attitudes on important economic, political, and social issues. The political and economic naiveté, the strong tendency toward group conformity and authoritarianism and toward repression of civil liberties, the sex prejudice expressed toward women's wider participation in the civic and social life of the community—these should be of concern to those who wish to improve the present and future programming in citizen education. Of course, the fact that some of this may reflect adult opinion, prejudice, ignorance and misinformation should not be overlooked.

Adult civic models for imitation.

Youth polls have shown that teen-agers tend to mirror adult attitudes and adult behavior. The fact that youngsters reflect so strongly their family and parental attitudes and opinions must force a consideration of expanding and continuing citizenship education at the college and adult levels. Youth's concept of the "good citizen" and the "poor citizen" as reported by Ayer and Corman[8] revealed the exemplary model to be a rather conforming individual who seldom engages in unpopular citizen activity. The frequent stoning of peace marchers by teenage youth illustrates the nature of this problem. Youth need help in setting up criteria of what constitutes a "good citizen." This will not be accomplished by precept in school alone; it will need to be reinforced and supplemented by good adult citizen example. It is doubtful that growing youngsters, even with the help of good school programs, can rise very far above the level of the watermark set by adult examples which are paraded before them daily and which serve as models for imitation. Growth and improvement in better citizenship should be pursued in school, in the home, at the factory or office, and in the

---

[7] Remmers and Radler. *op. cit.*

[8] Frederick L. Ayer and Bernard R. Corman, "High School Students Evaluate Adult Citizens," *Social Education* 15: 375-376 (November, 1951).

community. To continue a unitary approach via the school agency and to overlook other resources that may help or hinder the practice of good citizenship will diminish the potential of any school-community endeavor to upgrade the present and future adult citizen role.

Differential needs of the adolescent.

It is easy to fall into the trap of the stereotype in discussing the American adolescent character and the American adolescent subculture. Although the factors which have been stressed in this section represent communal or frequently noted traits, characteristics, and opinions of the adolescent, it is still true that one adolescent may differ from another on many of the dimensions which have been discussed. The objectives of a citizenship training program will not be achieved through the adoption of one course of study or one set of textbooks for all learners. The needs of adolescents vary according to their abilities, interests, specialized talents, home and ethnic backgrounds, class status, future goals, and acquired knowledge and experience. All these variables must be taken into consideration in planning local programs geared to local and individual needs. Citizenship education programs will need to be differentiated to meet the significant individual variations noted in the school and classroom.

Socio-Economic-Political Milieux

The adolescent learner and his parents live, work, and play in a complex and changing culture and in overlapping subcultures in the United States. The way of life in the young learners' primary reference groups will be a strong determiner of patterns for citizenship behavior as well as of the imperative needs that must be met through the school's program for maintaining and improving citizenship knowledge, attitudes, and proficiencies. In this section a number of dominant trends which are prominent in the "generalized culture" and which have implications for future citizenship in the United States will be isolated and examined.

Completion of the urbanization process.

The steady shift in population toward large urban centers will end eventually and will then find the future citizen a resident of a megalopolis stretching in unbroken chains of heavily populated cities in widely separated regions of the country. Spindler[9] has estimated that

---

[9] George D. Spindler, *Report to NEA Southwest Invitation Conference on Instruction* (Oklahoma City, Oklahoma, February, 1959), pp. 25-28.

more than 90 per cent of the nation's population will reside in tomorrow's 100-mile-lane-strip cities. Small town and rural citizenship with its face-to-face intimacy will give way to the impersonality and anonymity of the large urban clusters. The local citizen will find himself in a relationship more remote from those who carry on civic and political business. The vote he casts will appear to count for less than before. He is likely to feel less well represented in local, state, and national governments. There is real danger, as the distance between the vote-caster and the vote-getter widens, that civic lethargy and disinterest will increase. The bureaucratic organization of the city political machine, the multiplication of minority groups with specialized interests, and the manipulations of lobbying interests which breed in the larger urban communities are likely to leave the future citizen feeling both helpless and voteless. At the same time, "the grass roots approach" will become a phenomenon of the past, although synthetic counterparts of this process will be engineered using Madison Avenue techniques. How to prepare a youngster for the more difficult role of effective citizenship in the megalopolis of the future will present a major problem to those revising and rebuilding school curricula.

Mobility factors and citizenship.

There are three kinds of mobility that have implications for the future citizen. These three types of movement are already visible in the daily life of the nation and give a feeling of urgency for certain emphases in those aspects of the school curriculum which aim to improve and insure a high quality of citizenship. First, there is the mobility recorded in the frequently changed address; second, there is the mobility of the world traveler who can visit and see foreign lands and people via rapid and inexpensive transport; and, third, there is the mobility of social status. Each of these will be discussed separately.

One out of every five families in the United States today shows a "change of address" annually. Much of this mobility we have already pointed out is in the direction of residence in the big cities or the suburban areas that poke out of or fringe the large metropolitan centers.

What are the implications of mobility from neighborhood to neighborhood and from city to city for the curriculum planners? Families on the move represent, at best, transient citizens. Lacking permanent residence and roots, the transient citizen may fail to register and to vote, he may feel that long-range community concerns are not important to him, and he may convince himself that his thinking contributes little to the more permanent social, civic, and political life of the community. In short, his contribution to the life of the community may be minimal or nonexistent because, as a transient, he fails to acquire any "sense of community." Building of effective citizenship in transitory community-living, as a part of the education of future adults, must receive a high priority on the part of the curriculum planners.

Secondly, ready access to inexpensive and fast transportation will make near neighbors of children and adults living in different sections of the United States as well as those who live in formerly "remote" parts of the shrinking globe. Jet and other fast means of transportation will make the common roadmap a less useful tool and the modern highway system an expensive anachronism.

Instead of transporting a group of high school students to the nation's capital during the Spring Holidays or at the culmination of the school year, buslike jets will enable the high school class to see, first hand, the wonders of the Grand Canyon, and to learn the lessons of the Mission Trail in southern California, the Alamo in San Antonio, the Liberty Bell in Philadelphia, Fanueil Hall in Boston, and the Colonial life in Williamsburg, Virginia. All of these national shrines and resources will serve to reinforce directly classroom instruction in citizenship and the American Heritage.

Already thousands of U.S. citizens, young and old, can be found visiting, studying, and working in many foreign countries. It has been estimated that over a million American tourists go abroad annually. In addition to this annual crop of tourists, William H. Hale[10] has enumerated over 200,000 service men, more than 35,000 government officials of various types, another 30,000 citizens on short-term business or government assignments, 28,000 religious missionaries, more than 24,000 business representatives, over 10,000 students, in addition to 5,500 teachers and scholars abroad. This number will increase. Visiting and working in foreign countries can result in an effective travel-diplomacy as it engenders better understanding of other peoples and at the same time erases the negative stereotype of the U.S. Citizen that permeates many lands. The U.S. traveler will need to know much more than the geography of other countries. He will need language competency as well as understanding and appreciation of the history, culture, and political systems of other peoples. He will need to turn his focus from "standards of living" to "standards of life" as found in his own country as well as in all the other nations of the world.

---

[10] William H. Hale, "Millions of Ambassadors," *Saturday Review*, XLII (January 10, 1959), 9-11+.

Still a third type of mobility—social mobility—will need to concern the curriculum planners. The hope and the fantasy of a "classless society" will give way to the realities of a more clear-cut stratified society in which vertical mobility will be less frequently observed (except for the large reservoir of vertically mobile ethnic groups such as the Negro and Puerto Rican) and in which psychic-insulation between subgroups will present major problems of communication and cooperation.

"Good" or "bad" citizen behavior and conduct often stem from the individual's subculture or special milieu and reflect, in the approved or disapproved citizen behavior, a complex interplay of cultural forces which tend to reinforce or encourage such behavior. For example: running for public office, going to the polls, keeping the streets clean, becoming informed on social and civic issues, respecting other persons' points of view and property may represent a way of life of the upper and middle class and may reflect special and unique focal concerns within the citizen's primary reference group. Likewise, failing to vote or to take an active interest in local, state, national, and international affairs may relate to a way of life followed by a large segment of the citizenry of this country whose concerns, values, and characteristic patterns of behavior are the outcomes of a well-formed cultural system.

The terms "lower class," "upper class," and "middle class" ring harshly on the American ear. We have used these terms here to refer to systems of behavior and concerns, in other words to cultural systems and not to economic groups as conventionally defined. There is a strong tendency in citizenship education to overlook or to gloss over the cultural implications and the realities of class differences with the conviction that "all men are created free and equal."

Citizenship education programs must aim to introduce and to strengthen within all subgroups of our stratified society an interested, active, and thoughtful participation of all members, lest the civic and political life of the United States become the exclusive concern of the middle and upper classes. How to encourage and enable citizens from the lower classes to show a more active concern and interest in the civic, social, and political life of city, state and nation represents a major challenge for the educators. Hitherto, the citizen, young or old, who has been born and bred in the lower-class stratum has either been ignored or exploited by the dominant middle and upper classes in the power structure of the average American community.

A classless society is not conceivable in the foreseeable future. Effective citizenship education via the great American public school system must continue to insure social mobility; at the same time, the public schools should undertake to develop a civic and social consciousness and concern in the membership of the lower-class groups. The attempt to involve the poor in the war against poverty represents a hopeful step.

Nationalism and internationalism.

As Richard I. Miller[11] formerly of the NEA's Committee on International Relations has pointed out on several occasions, nationalism represents one of the dominant political facts of the twentieth century. For example, Mr. Miller indicates that, since 1945, more than twenty new nations, containing a fourth of the world's population, have come into existence. Many of these nations, undergoing a process of self-realization and identification, have tended to establish their separateness and their exclusiveness and, at the same time, have tended to show an aggressiveness toward all out-groups. This is in contrast to another emerging twentieth-century concept of internationalism as seen in the feeling for neighbor-nations or as exemplified in the United Nations and in education for citizenship in world affairs. Citizenship education at the end of the twentieth century and at the beginning of the twenty-first century will need to focus on what Dr. Miller terms "positive nationalism" as well as on international understanding or "education for cultural empathy." Dr. Miller includes in this concept of education for adaptability: education for ideological clarity, education for respecting similarities and differences, education for patience, and education for knowledge of the world.

Growing concern that American education may be failing to prepare students to live in an international, interdependent, divided world has been voiced by Henry M. Halsted[12] of the Educational Policies Commission. Speaking at the National Association of Educational Secretaries, Mr. Halsted presented four imperatives or "musts" if American citizens are to be internationally competent: (1) they must know precisely what they believe and why they believe it; (2) they must be able to explain and discuss effectively the aims, ideals and accomplishments of American democracy; (3) they must have a clear and accurate understanding of world communism; and (4) they must revive their faith in the democratic ideal and in themselves. Citizenship education in the classroom of the future (even of the present) must equate

---

[11] Richard I. Miller, "Education for International Leadership," *School and Society* 86 (November 8, 1958), 397-98. "The World, the United Nations and You," address before the International Society for Business Education Association, Chicago, Illinois, February 12, 1959.

[12] Henry M. Halsted. Address before the National Association of Educational Secretaries, National Education Association, Atlantic City, February 15, 1959.

local responsibility with world-wide responsibility and must enable the present and future citizen to match means with desirable ends. Only through the development of a positive nationalism with due concern for the rights, privileges, and responsibilities of neighbor-nations on a shrinking and crowded globe can there be found any hope for the future.

Citizen-worker in a technological vineyard.

The future citizen will live, work, play, and vote in a scientific world dominated by the IBM machine, TV set, telephone, flying jet, atom-driven spaceship, and hydrogen bomb. Daily dependence on the mathematician, physicist, engineer, and technician will increase and will threaten to make second-class citizens of other worker-citizens.

Labor statistics compiled for the past decade reveal a striking rate of increase among professional and technical workers (60.6 per cent) and a heavy increase of clerical workers (22.8 per cent). But during the same period factory operatives have increased only slightly (4.4 per cent) while the rate of increase for laborers has been even less (4.1 per cent).

With mounting automation, plant modernization, and increased efficiency, fewer production and maintenance workers will be needed. In contrast, this shift will demand more engineers, technicians, and computer-clerks. The white-collar workers already outnumber the blue-collar labor force. This fall-off in rate among blue-collar workers with the increase in white-collar force—clerical, technical, and professional —will have significant repercussions particularly in the unionization of white-collar groups and the loss in power of the organized trade unions.

The accelerated technological revolution will place a premium on the educated citizen in the manpower pool. The ever-increasing and complicated stock of scientific knowledge that must be absorbed and which can only be mastered by a few with specialized talents will raise the threat of a ruling scientific aristocracy in the political, economic, and educational world. At the same time, there is the steady undercurrent of job-dissatisfaction within over-specialization and job fragmentation such that the worker seldom has the opportunity to create and complete a task. Performing a small and repetitive operation without the satisfaction of seeing the total product or feeling one's effort to be a meaningful and vital part of a total endeavor can have a disintegrating effect on the worker's personality. The future scientist-citizen—whether producer or consumer—will need to have special built-in skills that insure citizenship competencies which will make him an asset rather than a threat to the social, political and economic life of the local and world community.

Members of a bureaucratic and centralized society.

In an effort to benefit more individuals with better health, education, productivity, and recreation, a strong movement to combine and centralize services at the local, state, or federal level has caused individual rights and freedom to become more and more restricted. This can be seen in the regimentation that comes from joining a union, serving in the armed forces, working in a large business organization, or becoming a member of a professional group. The submergence of the individual to the group, the organization, the system, in the interest of achieving more and more "benefits" for more and more individuals, is seldom without the attendant loss or sacrifice of personal liberties. How to balance individual rights and freedoms against the increased social and economic benefits and services to be acquired within the shadow of greater regimentation will continue to force decisions calling for maximum skill and knowledge on the part of all future citizens.

Member of an organized and special interest group.

It is the exceptional citizen who does not belong to some organized group representing a union, a political club, a professional society, a commercial interest, or a social or recreational association. Many of these organizations are built to serve special interests. Examples of such associations include: American Medical Association, American Legion, U.S. Chamber of Commerce, National Education Association, AFL-CIO, Society for the Prevention of Cruelty to Children, Society for the Prevention of Cruelty to Animals, Daughters of the American Revolution, American Bar Association, United Manufacturers Association, Parent-Teacher Associations, Legion of Decency, and National Association for Retarded Children.

All these groups work through committees; all have lobbying groups; all involve their membership in group discussions and decision-making situations in which the special interests of certain other members of the community or even the community as a whole are secondary. The demands on the future citizen to utilize specialized skills in working as a member of a group and the need to follow parliamentary processes will increase. At the same time, the future citizen will need help in rechecking his value system lest, in his group membership and allegiance, there lurks the constant threat of the narrow and selfish interests of the organized minority group acting without due regard for society as a whole.

A citizen of wealth and leisure.

The future citizen dwelling in the wealthiest country in the world, with the highest standard of living and the shortest work-week, will need to shoulder many responsibilities of the "over-privileged" as the gap widens between the United States and the "under-privileged" or less-developed countries of the world. Deciding what action can be taken and should be taken in programs of foreign economic and technical assistance on a long-term basis of mutual help and aid will demand prudent and discreet action on the part of world-oriented citizens. Whether the frightening gap between the "have" and the "have-not" nations can be bridged and eventually closed will present the major challenge to the future citizens who now live and enjoy, as youngsters, the highest standard of living in the most affluent society. Unless the citizenship education programs and experiences continuously reaffirm, re-emphasize and implement an adherence to the democratic ideals by raising the concept of the role of the United States citizen imbued with a high standard of social responsibility beyond the immediate family and neighborhood, this country may fail to match privilege with obligation. In this failure, it may suffer the loss of the democratic ideal for the whole world.

In the world of tomorrow, as seen through the crystal ball of today's experience, making positive or negative use of leisure will present a major opportunity or a major hazard to living the life of a "good" citizen. Children, youth, and adults, all freed from farm and home chores and with more money to spend in their mounting "free hours," will either try "to kill" time or "to make time live." The measure of good citizenship will be based more and more on what young and old do in these leisure hours. Recreation—all the school critics notwithstanding—will need to be considered as the fourth "R" on which good citizenship programs will be based. Recreation cannot any longer be considered a frill or a luxury. Like our daily bread, it is already an integral part of daily life. It can be the bane or boon of the future. As anthropologist Spindler[13] has warned: "Education cannot afford to become solely technological or solely scientific. A mass of people, loosed on itself, with the tremendous amount of leisure time which automation will bring, and no real wants that can be satisfied within it, can

---

[13] George D. Spindler, *op. cit.*

be a dangerous force in our society." It is incumbent on the curriculum planners to consider the leisure-time habits, skills, and attitudes as an integral part of the total preparation for future citizenship role. The continuance and the flowering of American society will depend as much (if not more) on what the citizen does with his leisure time as it does on how well he is able to perform on his job during his shortening work-week.

User of mental and emotional aids.

The mounting juvenile and adult crime rates, the increase in divorces and plural marriages, the growing incidence of alcoholism, and the steady rise in mental and emotional illness as seen in the current need for clinics and hospital beds, all forebode a citizenry in want of preventive and remedial mental health measures. In sharp contrast to the deep inroads that have been made against physical illness and disease, the future citizen's mental and emotional well-being appears to be in jeopardy.

Effective citizenship must be viewed on the reciprocal base of the well-integrated and socially adjustable individual. Lacking emotional and social well-being, it is doubtful that the United States citizen of the future will be able to assume full responsibility for the consequence of all his personal-social-civic behavior, whether this be in the home or in municipal, state, federal, or international affairs. Citizenship, education, and training must be set on the firm foundation of mental and emotional health.

Sex-equated social-civic opportunity and responsibility.

Only in the society of the United States have women emerged from sex-bondage and overcome the sex-prejudices that have kept other women of the world in the status of second-class citizens. The democratic belief in the uniqueness, the indispensability, and the worth of each individual now includes all females. Women will continue to play an even more vital role in the United States of the future; this will be especially true in the civic and political sphere, as well as in the world of work.

Women now make up a third of the country's labor force. An increasing number—two million today—are found working in the professional and technical fields and almost a million are employed as managers, officials, or proprietors. Full career opportunities have blossomed for women in the labor force of this country. However, their complete emancipation still awaits their unreserved acceptance in the political arena. This is not to discount the tremendous political force of women at the voting booth or the promise in the perennial feature story: "Can we elect a woman president?" Although sex-prejudices have been overcome in most occupations, there is still a strong negative stereotype visible in this country against nomination and election of women to public office. The minute number of females that can be found in legislative bodies at the municipal, state, and federal levels stands in sharp contrast to the sex-crossed activities visible in all other daily-life activities. There is little doubt that the United States has a rich and untapped reservoir of political talent in the womanpower of the country. With only a rare female sitting in the Congress of the United States, the conclusion concerning sex-prejudice against equality of political opportunity cannot be overlooked. Fuller opportunities for women in politics must be opened up. Here is a much needed focus in the citizenship education programs in the schools of the nation.

Special attention must be given to the working mother as an American citizen playing two important roles. There were seven million working mothers in the United States in the last decade.[14] This meant that 28 of every 100 women with one or more children under eighteen years of age carried two important jobs; bringing up children and satisfying an employer. In less than ten years, from 1948 to 1957, the number of mothers in the labor force increased by two-thirds or more than 2.8 million. This represents an increase of 1.8 million among mothers of school-age children and one million among mothers of smaller children. The working woman and the working mother will not disappear from the American scene. It is more likely that the female labor force will increase rather than decrease. A citizenship-training program facing the future must acquaint the female students of their potential dual role in our society. It should also aim to combat existing prejudice against female office-holders and try to tap the large reservoir of talent that exists in the womanpower pool. Just as every woman has been given the opportunity and privilege to vote and to work, she should also be given the equal opportunity to run for and hold public office.

Conclusion

Citizenship behavior and delinquency—like all behavior—should be viewed as an interaction between inner and outer forces or as an interaction between the individual and his culture. In looking ahead to the future via the current trends and experiences of the adolescent,

---

14 U.S. Department of Health, Education, and Welfare. Social Security Agency, Division of Program Research. "Working Mothers in the United States", *Research and Statistics*, Note No. 32 (October 1, 1958), p. 1.

his adolescent subculture, and the "generalized" culture of society in the United States, attention has been drawn to certain needs, opportunities, and obligations that even now face the curriculum planners in school and the youth workers in the community whose aim is to prepare the youth of the nation for effective and responsible citizenship in the local community, in the state, in the nation, and especially in the world. Local citizenship in the United States has already come to mean world citizenship.

In looking ahead it becomes apparent that anxious youth, who are now standing in great danger, will in the future live under even more hazardous conditions. There will be more and more to learn; youth will need to learn faster and faster, and it will be harder and harder. Seemingly "minor" decisions—to elect a certain mathematics course in the 9th grade, to date steady in the high school, to leave school—will tend to have major and, sometimes, irrevocable consequences. The peer-group pressures will mount; the strong and exclusive commitment to each other will drive many youth to drink, to drugs, and to disengagement from the adult world. Communication between youth and adults will become more and more difficult and will be accomplished mainly through long distance calls, station to station. The open and competitive market place of the masses will topple the ivory tower and there will be no place left for private retreat and meditation. And any single and simple pressure applied at any point will affect the total life pattern of the young individual. This is the reality that will need to be faced and herein will lie the fears and frustrations of an even more anxious youth.

Thus it is becoming more and more important that today's and tomorrow's youth be adequately prepared to face their reality and to meet and fill the expanded role of citizen, with all that it encompasses, in tomorrow's world. Herein lies the mandate to today's adults. For the choice cannot be left to youth alone. The choice between youthful destroyer and builder will be in response to the kinds of pressure and promise that will be made by adults. The vital role of adults is to channel youthful energies toward building rather than toward destroying. The adults must accept this mandate, and they must fulfill it by finding new and better means both of preparing their young people and of helping them to prepare themselves.

In doing so adults may close the widening gap between the generations. Even now, as Leslie Paul so astutely pointed out in *Angry Young Men*, the relations between the generations is rapidly becoming the central social issue that will dominate the next fifty years just as the relations between the classes was the central social problem of the last half century.

Bibliography*

Ackerman, Nathan W., M.D. "Family Study and Treatment," *Children,* VIII (July–August, 1961), 130–34.

Suggests that therapy which includes the child and his family would throw light on the influence of the family on role adaptation, on mental illness, and on treatment.

Adamson, LaMay, and Dunham, H. Warren. "Clinical Treatment of Male Delinquents: A Case Study in Effort and Results," *American Sociological Review,* XXI (June, 1956), 312–20.

An evaluative study of a court-affiliated clinic in Detroit, Michigan.

Alexander, Paul W. "The Fable of the Fantastic Delinquent," *Federal Probation,* XXIV (March, 1960), 13–18.

Considers legal aspects of the juvenile court; asserts that constitutional rights of children and adults do differ; and emphasizes that the child is rightfully deprived of many of the freedoms extended to adults.

Andry, R. G. "Faulty Paternal and Maternal-Child Relationships, Affection, and Delinquency," *British Journal of Delinquency,* VIII (July, 1957), 34–48.

A comparative study of the father role and the mother role based on an interview questionnaire used with parents of delinquents and non-delinquents.

Barron, Milton Leon. *Juvenile in Delinquent Society.* New York: Alfred A. Knopf, Inc., 1954.

Views the problem of juvenile delinquency in a comprehensive, societal frame of reference and calls for orderly modification of the American social structure and of some of the values and functions of American society.

Bechthold, Mary Lee. "Validation of K. D. Scale and Check List as Predictors of Delinquency Proneness," *Journal of Experimental Education,* XXXII (Summer, 1964), 413–16.

Used two instruments to identify delinquency-prone groups. Reports statistically significant results on identification. Also notes a high correlation between the two instruments.

---

* All the items in this bibliography were prepared for the *Elementary School Journal* and appeared in the annual listing of "Selected References from the Literature on Exceptional Children." They have been assembled and reprinted with permission of the *Elementary School Journal.*

Beck, Bertram M. "Delinquents in the Classroom," *NEA Journal,* XLV (November, 1956), 485–87.

Discusses and illustrates various types of delinquents: social, asocial, neurotic, organic, and accidental.

———. "The Exiled Delinquent," *Children,* II (November–December, 1955), 208–12.

Points out the conflicting value system in our modern culture as a prime factor in the causation of juvenile delinquency. Decries the punitive attitude and practices of society toward these "exiled" youngsters and stresses the need for love and understanding.

———. "The Young in Conflict: Blueprint for the Future," *Federal Probation,* XXIV (June, 1960), 35–40.

Proposes a three-pronged attack for delinquency prevention and control. Suggests what needs to be done in areas of prevention, law enforcement, court services, institutional treatment, and federal legislation.

Berman, Betty. "Juvenile Delinquents Go to School," *High Points in the Work of the High Schools of New York City,* XXXVI (November, 1954), 54–62.

A progress report of the New York City School Court Liaison Program, using a school-court liaison teacher, who integrates the findings of court and other community workers and knowledge of the New York City school resources to secure optimum school adjustments.

Bettelheim, Bruno. *Truants from Life: The Rehabilitation of Emotionally Disturbed Children.* Glencoe, Illinois: Free Press, 1955.

Gives four case histories of emotionally disturbed children—a delinquent, a psychosomatic problem, an institutional psychotic, and a schizophrenic child. Therapeutic treatment is described, together with a follow-up study of each case.

Blackburn, Donald G. (compiler). *Directory of Public Training Schools for Delinquent Children.* Washington: Children's Bureau, U.S. Department of Health, Education, and Welfare, 1958.

Lists 193 institutions in forty-eight states, the District of Columbia, and territories.

Blake, Mary E. "Youth Workers and the Police," *Children,* VIII (September–October, 1961), 170–74.

Describes the problems that result from a misunderstanding of the function of youth workers and police in their work with juveniles.

Blank, Leonard. "The Intellectual Functioning of Delinquents," *Journal of Social Psychology,* XLVII (February, 1958), 9–14.

Reports results of Wechsler-Bellevue test given to a sample of delinquents.

Bloch, Herbert A., and Flynn, Frank T. *Delinquency: The Juvenile Offender in America Today.* New York: Random House, Inc., 1956.

A comprehensive and critical review of significant research related to causation, diagnosis, and treatment of delinquency.

Bobo, James H. "Juvenile Delinquency in the United States," *Federal Probation,* XX (June, 1956), 32–38.

A report of progress of the work of the Senate Subcommittee to Investigate Juvenile Delinquency, with a note concerning next steps and suggested legislation.

Bond, Richard J. "Work as a Therapeutic Medium in the Treatment of Delinquents," *American Journal of Orthopsychiatry,* XXXII (October, 1962), 846–50.

Lists basic premises for use of work as one means of accomplishing treatment.

Boodish, Hyman M. "In the Hands of the Teacher," *Social Studies,* L (April, 1959), 150–54.

Delineates the teacher's role in helping the delinquent within the limits of the unique function of the school.

Brewer, Edgar W., and Sheridan, William H. "The Family Court," *Children,* IV (March–April, 1957), 67–73.

Delineates the factors which distinguish the family court from other courts and the legal and social reasons that called for its establishment.

Briggs, Peter F., and Others. "Application of Prediction Tables to the Study of Delinquency," *Journal of Consulting Psychology,* XXV (February, 1961), 46–50.

Studied random sample of thirteen-year-old boys from an urban area to isolate factors related to the development of delinquent behavior. Suggests that the development of a methodology for selecting a homogeneous group of delinquents may pave the way for precise recommendation for treatment.

Brockman, Jim. "Who Is Delinquent?" *School and Community,* XLIII (February, 1957), 23–24.

Calls for a distinction between individuals and groups. Supports temporary institutionalization of juvenile delinquents. Warns against the too early labeling of individuals as delinquents.

Brundage, Erven. "Helping Institutionalized Students Re-enter Public Schools," *Federal Probation,* XXVII (September, 1963), 55–57.

Explains the "liaison procedural plan" used in San Diego County, California, to insure a smooth transfer of students from institutions back into the school and the community.

Carpenter, Kenneth S. "Halfway Houses for Delinquent Youth," *Children*, X (November–December, 1963), 224–29.

Relates the experience and programs of several agencies in establishing halfway houses. Offers guiding principles for closing a serious gap in programs for rehabilitation.

Cassel, Russell N. "Phoenix Youth Study Proposal for Delinquency Reduction," *Journal of Educational Sociology*, XXXIII (October, 1959), 67–72.

Outlines an experimental school-community action program for delinquent and non-delinquent youth. Program designed to minimize characteristics most significant of atypical individuals.

Chein, Isidor, and Others. *The Road to H: Narcotics, Delinquency and Social Policy*. New York: Basic Books, 1964.

A wide-ranging series of studies that shed new light on drug addiction. Studies challenge the basic premises that underlie current public misunderstanding and public policy.

Chilton, Roland J. "Continuity in Delinquency Area Research: A Comparison of Studies for Baltimore, Detroit, and Indianapolis," *American Sociological Review*, XXIX (February, 1964), 71–83.

Study of delinquency in three cities. Investigated relationship among variables.

"The Church and Juvenile Delinquency," *Pastoral Psychology*, VI (October, 1955), 7–42.

Presents seven articles dealing with various phases of the delinquency problem as seen generally from the orientation of the church's potential for helping the delinquent.

Chwast, Jacob, and Others. "Experimental Techniques in Group Psychotherapy with Delinquents," *Journal of Criminal Law, Criminology and Police Science*, LII (July–August, 1961), 156–57.

Discusses the use of tutorial group therapy, co-therapists, and individual therapy in the treatment of delinquency.

Claytor, Mae Pullins. "Juvenile Offenders Defined by Law," *Exceptional Children*, XXV (January, 1959), 205–16.

A survey of definitions of *juvenile offender* as defined by various codes and statutes in the United States.

Cloward, Richard A. "Illegitimate Means, Anomie and Deviant Behavior," *American Sociological Review*, XXIV (April, 1959), 147–64.

An interpretation of delinquency that takes frustration into account.

———, and Ohlin, Lloyd E. *Delinquency and Opportunity: A Theory of Delinquent Gangs*. Glencoe, Illinois: Free Press, 1960.

Discusses three subcultural patterns among delinquents: criminal, conflict, and retreatist. Asserts that when goals are inaccessible by legitimate means, delinquency or conflict patterns tend to emerge.

Cohen, Albert K. *Delinquent Boys: The Culture of the Gang*. Glencoe, Illinois: Free Press, 1955.

Considers the social origins of juvenile behavior and shows how juveniles who share similar problems draw together by forming a delinquent subculture for social reinforcement.

Cohen, Eli E., and Rosenblum, Lila. "Are Jobs the Answer to Delinquency?" *School and Society*, LXXXVI (May 10, 1958), 215–16.

Authors discuss the implications of compulsory education for those who show no aptitude for study. Report evidence that labor market cannot absorb younger workers.

Cohen, Frank J. *Youth and Crime*. New York: International Universities Press, Inc., 1957.

A report of the proceedings of the Law Enforcement Institute on Youth and Crime held at New York University in July, 1955. Covers topics relating to concepts and methods for reducing juvenile delinquency.

The Control and Treatment of Juvenile Delinquency in the United States. Washington, D. C.: Children's Bureau, U. S. Department of Health, Education, and Welfare, 1965.

Prepared by the Division of Juvenile Delinquency Service of the Children's Bureau for the Third United Nations Congress on the Prevention of Crime and Treatment of Offenders held at Stockholm, Sweden, on August 9–18, 1965.

Craig, Maud M. "Ten Years' Experience with the Glueck Social Prediction Table," *Crime and Delinquency* (July, 1963), 249–61.

Summarizes findings of study of ten years' experience with the Glueck Social Prediction Table and offers a revised three-factor table.

Deutscher, Irwin. "Continuity in Sociological Theory: Some Critical Comments on Cloward and Ohlin's *Delinquency and Opportunity*," *Journal of Educational Sociology*, XXXVI (March, 1963), 296–306.

Attempts to reconcile structural and cultural conceptualizations of delinquent behavior. Makes suggestions for research and offers general suggestions on what to do about delinquency.

Dinitz, Simon; Kay, Barbara; and Reckless, Walter C. "Delinquency Proneness and School Achievement," *Educational Research Bulletin*, XXXVI (April, 1957), 131–36.

Reports that non-delinquent children score consistently higher on measures of ability and achievement in reading and arithmetic than do delinquent-prone children identified by Gough California Psychological Inventory (DP) Index.

Downs, W. T. "Order in the Court," *Children*, IX (July, 1962), 139–43.

Reviews the role and the responsibility of the juvenile court as the final authority for the expression of society's disapproval and for the protection of the young offender. The latter refers to court processes.

Dresher, R. H. "Seeds of Delinquency," *Personnel and Guidance Journal,* XXXV (May, 1957), 595–98.

A study that investigated twenty factors contributing to delinquency and identified twelve that differentiated significantly between normal and antisocial groups.

Eaton, Joseph W., and Polk, Kenneth. *Measuring Delinquency: A Study of Probation Department Referrals.* Pittsburgh, Pennsylvania: University of Pittsburgh Press, 1961.

Reports results of a study made in Los Angeles by the Welfare Planning Council. Shows how public records may be used to set up a program of delinquency prevention and treatment.

"Effects on Young People of Violence and Crime Portrayed on Television," Part 10. *Hearings before the Subcommittee to Investigate Juvenile Delinquency of the Committee on the Judiciary, United States Senate, Eighty-seventh Congress Pursuant to S. Res. 48.* Washington, D. C.: U. S. Government Printing Office, 1963. pp. 1635–2592.

A compilation of testimony presented during 1961 and 1962 by witnesses from industry, Madison Avenue, subcommittee staff, and authorities representing behavioral sciences.

Eichorn, John R. "Research and Delinquency: Some Reflections," *Exceptional Children,* XXIX (April, 1963), 385–91.

An overview of research on problems of definition of delinquency, prediction, and programs of prevention and control.

Eshbaugh, Mark, and Walsh, James. "A Group Approach to Parents of Children in Trouble," *Children,* XI (May–June, 1964), 108–12.

A positive report on a project to determine whether, under court sponsorship, parents would be willing to meet and discuss their children's problems and to find out whether they can help one another.

Fine, Benjamin, *1,000,000 Delinquents.* Cleveland: World Publishing Co., 1955.

Contains anecdotal material, interviews with professional workers in the field, and references to some high spots in delinquency research and experimentation, gathered from all parts of the country.

Fooks, Gilbert, and Thomas, Ross R. "Differential Qualitative Performance of Delinquents on the Porteus Maze," *Journal of Consulting Psychology,* XXI (August, 1957), 351–53.

Reports significant differences between qualitative scores of matched groups of delinquents and non-delinquents.

Ford, Donald. *The Delinquent Child and the Community.* London: Constable Publishing Co., 1957.

Views delinquency in England in terms of the community experiences of the delinquent.

Freeman, Howard E., and Weeks, H. Ashley. "Analysis of a Program of Treatment of Delinquent Boys," *American Journal of Sociology*, LXII (July, 1956), 56–61.

An evaluation of the Highfields (New Jersey) program of treating delinquent boys. Reports a higher success rate at lower financial cost than found in most cities.

Friedenberg, E. Z. "Delinquency as Criticism," *Teachers College Record*, LXIII (March, 1962), 479–82.

Reviews current writings on delinquency. Insightful comment on status of theory on delinquency. Presents implications for research and implementation.

Fuhrman, Miriam. "School Drop-Outs and Juvenile Delinquency," *Federal Probation*, XXIV (September, 1960), 34–38.

Relates size and nature of the problem to what needs to be done about school dropouts.

Geis, Gilbert. *Juvenile Gangs*. Washington, D. C.: President's Committee on Juvenile Delinquency and Youth Crime, June, 1965.

Writing from a long interest in the subject, Dr. Geis presents a reappraisal of the problem of the gang based partly upon a review of various published studies, partly upon 15 papers delivered at annual conventions of the American Sociological Association and the Society for the Study of Social Problems in 1963.

Gillet, Myrtle Mann. "The Medical Histories of Some Delinquents," *Understanding the Child*, XXIV (June, 1955), 88–93.

Shows how physical injury can operate as a causative factor in delinquency and indicates the need for early diagnosis and treatment.

Glick, Selma J. "Spotting Potential Delinquents in the School," *Exceptional Children*, XX (May, 1954), 342–46.

Reviews the available data concerning the construction and validation of the Glueck Social Prediction Table and indicates its potential use in a school program.

Glubok, Norman. "Dealing with Delinquency: Interview with T. J. Farrell," *Nation's Schools*, LVI (September, 1955), 47–50.

Stresses the fact that the schools can be a most potent factor in combating delinquency and indicates what can be done in the schools, particularly through the use of reports on atypical pupils.

Glueck, Eleanor. "Status of Glueck Prediction Studies," *Journal of Criminal Law, Criminology and Police Science*, XLVII (May–June, 1956), 18–32.

Enumerates the existing studies concerning the validity of the Glueck tables.

Glueck, Sheldon (editor). *Problems of Delinquency*. Boston: Houghton Mifflin Co., 1959.

An encyclopedic compilation of writings by many authorities and researchers on all aspects of delinquent behavior.

————, and Glueck, Eleanor. "Early Detection of Future Delinquents," *Journal of Criminal Law, Crminology and Police Science*, XLVII (July–August, 1956), 174–82.

Compares the discriminative capacity of various combinations among the fifteen factors in the three Glueck Prediction Tables. The discriminative capacity of five social factors eliminates need for the remaining two tables.

————. *Predicting Delinquency and Crime*. Cambridge, Massachusetts: Harvard University Press, 1959.

Presents instruments that aid in forecasting anti-social behavior at various levels and ages. Highly favorable results in some samplings.

————. "Working Mothers and Delinquency," *Mental Hygiene*, XLI (July, 1957), 327–52.

A differential look at types of working mothers. The sporadically working mother appears to exert the heaviest influence toward delinquency.

Gnagey, William J. "Do Our Schools Prevent or Promote Delinquency?" *Journal of Educational Research*, L (November, 1956), 215–19.

Reviews data concerning some school factors and concludes that schools are not a factor in producing delinquent conduct.

Gordon, Robert A., Short, James F., Jr., and Others. "Values and Gang Delinquency: A Study of Street-Corner Groups," *American Journal of Sociology*, LXIX (September, 1963), 109–28.

Tested hypothesis concerning the values of gang, non-gang, lower-class, and non-gang, middle-class boys.

Grant, Marguerite Q., and Warren, Martin. "Alternates to Institutionalization," *Children*, X (July–August, 1963), 147–52.

Reports an experiment with an intensive treatment-control program in the community as a substitute for the traditional type of institutionalization.

Grosser, George H. "The Role of Informal Inmate Groups in Change of Values," *Children*, V (January–February, 1958), 25–29.

Describes how a better understanding of group dynamics in a truancy school for delinquents might help in retraining.

Halfway House Programs for Delinquent Youth. Washington, D. C.: Children's Bureau, U. S. Department of Health, Education, and Welfare, 1965.

A revision of an earlier pamphlet prepared for the Third United Nations Congress on the Prevention of Crime and Treatment of Offenders held at Stockholm, Sweden, on August 9–18, 1965.

Hamblin, Robert L., Abrahamson, Mark J., and Burgess, Robert L. "Diagnosing Delinquency," *Trans-Action,* I (March, 1964), 10–15.

A comprehensive review of definition, instigators, inhibitors, and differences noted between boy and girl, Negro and white delinquents.

Hathaway, Starke R., and Monachesi, Elio D. "The Personalities of Predelinquent Boys," *Journal of Criminal Law, Criminology and Police Science,* XLVIII (July–August, 1957), 149–63.

An analysis of scores made by ninth-grade students on the Minnesota Multiphasic Personality Inventory, with reference to personality patterns of the after-test delinquents as compared with non-delinquents.

Havighurst, Robert J. "Poor Reading and Delinquency May Go Hand in Hand," *Nation's Schools,* LXIV (November, 1959), 55–58.

Children who are deprived of affection, of a good model, of intellectual stimulation, may become poor readers and candidates for truancy and delinquency.

———, and Stiles, Lindley J. "National Policy for Alienated Youth, *Phi Delta Kappan,* XLII (April, 1961), 283–91.

Recommends a work-experience program for alienated youth. Proposes a three-stage program with a decrease in supervision at each stage. Program would be followed by community action to improve the social environment of these young people. Also asks for preventive measures in the elementary grades to decrease the enrollment in the work-experience group.

Herbert, W. L., and Jarvis, F. V. *Dealing with Delinquents.* New York: Emerson Books, 1962.

Concerned mainly with the treatment of delinquents and potential delinquents, especially in their own home environment. Also discusses school problems, female delinquents, and role of social workers.

Hersko, Marvin. "Group Psychotherapy with Delinquent Adolescent Girls," *American Journal of Orthopsychiatry,* XXXII (January, 1962), 169–75.

Recommends group psychotherapy as a promising method for modifying self-concepts and antisocial values. Discusses resistance to therapy, role of the therapist, content of the session, level of anxiety, acting out, transference, and countertransference.

Hess, Albert G. *The Young Adult Offender: A Review of Current Practices and Programmes in Prevention and Treatment.* New York: United Nations, 1965.

A largely descriptive summary of information received from many countries, with some analysis of the information within the framework of current theories and knowledge. Prepared and written by the Assistant Director of the Information Center on Crime and Delinquency NCCD.

Hoover, John Edgar. "Juvenile Delinquency: An Unconquered Frontier," *Educational Forum,* XX (November, 1955), 45–49.

The lack of proper home guidance is stressed as a crucial factor in aberrant behavior. Considers that the teacher is in a unique position to help many of the children in difficulty.

Howard, F. M. "If Institutional Treatment Is To Succeed," *Children,* III (September, 1956), 187–91.

Enumerates major remedies needed if children placed in institutions are to be helped.

Hunt, Elizabeth V. "Foster Care for Delinquent Girls," *Children,* IX (September–October, 1962), 183–88.

Describes the outcomes of a foster-home placement. Discusses role of foster parents, social worker, and values gained from placement in carefully selected and carefully supervised foster homes.

"Improving Learning Conditions for Delinquent and Predelinquent Adolescents: Symposium," *California Journal of Secondary Education,* XXXV (March, 1960), 175–202.

Eight action programs described by school and community workers.

International Bibliography on Crime and Delinquency, Vol. 2, No. 3 (May, 1965). Bethesda, Maryland: U. S. Department of Health, Education, and Welfare, Public Health Service, 698, Publication No. 1315.

Prepared under contract by the National Clearinghouse for Mental Health Information, every article is indexed according to a key word system by title, author, and subject; including journals, reports, unpublished material, books, and pamphlets, with a special bibliography on crime and delinquency.

International Bibliography on Crime and Delinquency, Vol. 3, No. 1 (June, 1965). Bethesda, Maryland: U. S. Department of Health, Education, and Welfare, Public Health Service Publication No. 1324, 158.

Gives abstracts of publications; a summary of current projects in the field; a list of the journals cited; and an index.

Isaacs, William. "Juvenile Delinquency: Perspective for Teachers," *High Points,* XL (June, 1958), 18–33.

Contrasts the approach of a "police school" with that of a "sociopsychiatric school."

Jackson, Stanley E. "The Juvenile Decency Corps: An Answer to Delinquency," *Educational Leadership,* XXI (May, 1964).

Describes a community effort in the District of Columbia that emphasizes character formation and service to others as its major goals.

Jaffe, Lester D., and Polansky, Norman. "Verbal Inaccessibility in Young Adolescents Showing Delinquent Trends," *Journal of Health and Human Behavior,* III (Summer, 1962), 105–11.

Study of the child's readiness to express his most important attitudes and feelings directly in verbal communication. Suggests that boys who have delinquent tendencies tend to be relatively inaccessible verbally.

————. "Delinquency Proneness and Family Anomie," *Journal of Criminal Law, Criminology and Police Science,* LIV (June, 1963), 146–54.

Found a high correlation between a pattern of three variables in the anomic family and susceptibility to delinquency.

"Juvenile Delinquency: A Symposium," *Religious Education,* L (March, 1955), 83–102.

Presents four articles by different authorities on the nature of the delinquency problem, the church's opportunity, the operation of a neighborhood center, and an experiment using lay women with a strong religious orientation.

"Juvenile Delinquency: Concrete Understanding and Practical Solutions," *Nervous Child,* XI (October, 1955), 5–59.

Eleven authors discuss various aspects of the delinquency problem.

Juvenile Delinquency: Hearings before Senate Subcommittee, 83d. Congress, 2nd. Session Pursuant to S. Res. 89, 1954–55. Washington: Government Printing Office, 1955.

A series of official documents on different aspects of the delinquency problem gathered from different sections of the country. Statements, testimony, and exhibits presented before the Senate Subcommittee to Investigate Juvenile Delinquency are reported on the following topics: television programs, delinquency in California, delinquency among Indians, youth employment, Miami hearings, report from the Committee on Rules and Administration to Accompany Senate Resolution 62, plural marriages, obscene and pornographic materials, and motion pictures.

Juvenile Delinquency Prevention in the United States. Washington, D. C.: Children's Bureau, U. S. Department of Health, Education, and Welfare, 1965.

Prepared by the Division of Juvenile Delinquency Service of the Children's Bureau for the Third United Nations Congress on the Prevention of Crime and Treatment of Offenders held at Stockholm, Sweden, on August 9–18, 1965.

"Juvenile Delinquency: Theory and Practice," *Education*, LXXXI (March, 1961), 386–440.

A symposium on delinquency conducted at Boston University; authors are engaged in action programs. Symposium is followed by a series of articles by several specialists.

Kahn, Alfred J. "The Policy Vacuum and Delinquency," *Federal Probation*, XXIV (September, 1960), 32–34.

Stresses need for formulation of sound community policy by agencies concerned with delinquency. Also emphasizes the need for planning and co-ordinating community services. Points out how bigness, specialization, and bureaucratic reform complicate the task of helping the delinquent.

Kelley, Jerry L. "The School and Unmarried Mothers," *Children*, X (March–April, 1963), 60–64.

Indicates what schools can do to provide continuing education for unmarried mothers. Poses questions for prevention as well as rehabilitation.

Kenny, John P., and Pursuit, Dan G. *Police Work with Juveniles*. Springfield, Illinois: Charles C. Thomas, Publisher (327 East Lawrence Avenue), 1954.

A comprehensive textbook describing the organization and administration of a juvenile-control division in a police department, police relations with other community groups, and individualization of the police approach to juveniles.

Khleif, B. B. "Teachers as Predictors of Juvenile Delinquency and Psychiatric Disturbance," *Social Problems*, XI (Winter, 1964), 270–82.

Reports results of an attempt to identify children whose disturbed behavior eventually leads them into legal or psychiatric difficulties. Based on data from the school cumulative record of the pupil's first five years of school life.

Kinch, John W. "Continuities in the Study of Delinquent Types," *Journal of Criminal Law, Criminology, and Police Science*, LIII (September, 1962), 323–28.

Analyzes the nature of previous typology analyses of juvenile delinquents. Points out the need for a synthesis of typological theory.

Kodman, Frank, Jr., and Others. "Some Implications of Hearing Defective Juvenile Delinquents," *Exceptional Children*, XXV (October, 1958), 54–56+.

A sample of juvenile delinquents showed a higher incidence of hearing loss than a sample of public school children.

Kosofsky, Sidney. "Directive Therapy with Female Juvenile Delinquents," *Journal of Clinical Psychology,* XI (October, 1955), 357–61.

Gives the results of an experiment in the case of directive therapy over a one-year period with a segregated group of the most overtly maladjusted girls at the New Jersey State Home for Girls. Reports successful outcomes in most cases.

Kvaraceus, William C. "Alienated Youth Here and Abroad," *Phi Delta Kappan,* XLV (November, 1963), 87–91.

Indicates the need to find a function for youth in today's society. Points to promising approaches in various countries, including the USA.

———. *The Community and the Delinquent.* New York: Harcourt, Brace and World, Inc., 1954.

Outlines a community-wide program for study and control of juvenile delinquency. Indicates what various agencies can do to identify the delinquent and predelinquent at an early date, to study and diagnose their needs, and to administer treatment, using all community resources.

———. "The Counselor's Role in Combating Juvenile Delinquency," *Personnel and Guidance Journal,* XXXVI (October, 1957), 99–104.

Describes seven functions of the school counselor that help to prevent and control undesirable behavior.

———. "Delinquency International—Ambivalent Obsession," *NEA Journal,* LI (September, 1962), 22–24.

Contrasts attitude and approaches toward the delinquent in different countries. Concludes that it is not yet possible to make meaningful direct comparisons across national borders.

———. "Forecasting Delinquency: A Three-Year Experiment," *Exceptional Children,* XXVII (April, 1961), 429–35.

A report of an experiment to validate the Kvaraceus Delinquency Proneness Scale, Non-Verbal Form. Results throw light on the value of teacher ratings and testing procedures for the non-reader.

———. *Forecasting Juvenile Delinquency: Supplement to the Manual of Directions for KD Proneness Scale and Check List.* New York: Harcourt, Brace and World, Inc., 1956.

Reports reliability and validation studies on two prediction techniques.

———. "Helping the Socially Inadapted Pupil in the Large City Schools," *Exceptional Children,* XXVIII (April, 1962), 399–404.

Analyzes the role of the teacher as a person and as a professional worker in schools in crowded urban centers, where children and youth appear more likely to be inadapted socially.

————."If Your School and Community Want the Facts on Juvenile Delinquency," *Exceptional Children*, XXV (October, 1958), 57–66.

Discusses three levels of knowledge: theory, information on local situations, and case study. Selected and annotated bibliography.

———— (editor). *International Journal of Adult and Youth Education*, XV (January, 1963), 3–50.

The entire issue of six articles is devoted to adult concerns, involvement, and competencies in understanding and helping the delinquent.

————. "Introductory Report" and "General Report," *International Child Welfare Review*, XIX (No. 1, 1965), 7–42.

Reporting results of a survey by questionnaire of prevention programs in the field of juvenile delinquency and of the Eleventh Session of the Advisory Committee on Delinquent and Socially Maladjusted Children and Youth at Vaucresson.

————. *Juvenile Delinquency.* What Research Says to the Teacher, No. 15. Washington: Department of Classroom Teachers and American Educational Research Association, National Education Association, 1958.

Draws implications and offers suggestions on the broad base of existing research.

————. *Juvenile Delinquency: A Problem for the Modern World.* Paris: UNESCO, 1964.

Presents the delinquency story to laymen, parents, and students in the belief that every citizen and every parent and every youth must share in the task of prevention and rehabilitation.

————. "Mental Retardation and Norm Violation," *Journal of Education, 147* (October, 1964) 17–24.

Report on a three-year study supported through the Cooperative Research Program of the U. S. Office of Education, a study which raises several crucial questions regarding the relation between intelligence and norm violations.

————. "Prediction Studies of Delinquent Behavior," *Personnel and Guidance Journal*, XXXIV (November, 1955), 147–49.

Calls attention to the available instruments that purport to identify the predelinquent. Indicates the problems that must be faced in the validation of these instruments.

————. "Prediction of Maladjustive Behavior." *Proceedings of the 1958 Invitational Conference on Testing Problems*, pp. 26–34. Princeton, New Jersey: Educational Testing Service, 1959.

Outlines methodological requirements for constructing and validating prediction instruments. Evaluates status of available tools and techniques.

————. "Preventing and Treating Juvenile Delinquency: Some Basic Approaches," *School Review,* LXIII (December, 1955), 477–79.

An over-all statement indicating the need to uncover the predelinquent early, the need for child-study and diagnostic facilities, and the requirements for co-operative treatment.

————. "The School as a Catalyst in Precipitating Delinquency," *Elementary School Journal,* LIX (January, 1959), 211–14.

Indicates how the "good" school can automatically trigger norm-violating behavior.

————. "Teachers' Check List for Identifying Potential Delinquents," *Journal of Education,* XVII (February, 1955), 21–22.

Lists eighteen factors that can be used by teachers to spot the child most vulnerable, susceptible, or exposed to the development of delinquent behavior.

————. "What Kind of Help for the Delinquent?" *NEA Journal,* XLVIII (February, 1959), 12–15.

Tells how several school systems have approached the problem of delinquency.

————. "What's the Score on Juvenile Delinquency?" *National Parent-Teacher,* LV (November, 1960), 4–7.

Describes attitudes toward juvenile delinquency held in many communities. Presents guides to community action for prevention and control.

Lander, Bernard. *Towards an Understanding of Juvenile Delinquency: A Study of 8464 Cases of Juvenile Delinquency in Baltimore.* New York: Columbia University Press, 1954.

An extensive analysis of a variety of data available on a census tract as related to the study of differential juvenile-delinquency rates.

Leibrecht, Walter. "The Challenge of Juvenile Delinquency," *Phi Delta Kappan,* XXXIX (January, 1958), 162–67.

Cites the absence of true authority and responsibility as a basic cause of juvenile delinquency; finds both schools and church weakened in their present program.

Lentz, William. "Rural Urban Differentials and Juvenile Delinquency," *Journal of Criminal Law, Criminology and Police Science,* XLVII (September–October, 1956), 331–39.

Reports some significant differences between 130 rural boys and 290 urban boys committed to a state school for delinquents.

Lively, Edwin L., and Others. "Self Concept as a Predictor of Juvenile Delinquency," *American Journal of Orthopsychiatry*, XXXII (January, 1962), 159–68.

Made a cross-sectional assessment of children twelve to fifteen years of age. Data analyzed by sex, race, and type of neighborhood. Children all lived in the same city. Authors report stable average scores for various age groups. Results indicate differences in ability to direct self. Twelve-year-olds seemed to show greatest promise for effective results in prevention.

Lohman, Joseph D. "A Sociologist-Sheriff Speaks Out about Juvenile Delinquency," *Phi Delta Kappan*, XXXIX (February, 1958), 206–14.

A diagnosis of the problem of delinquency with a plea for control of negative feelings toward the delinquent. Calls for a national program involving close co-operation of police with schools.

Lourie, Reginald Spencer. "Delinquency Prevention—A Health Worker's Job, Too." *Children*, II (September–October, 1955), 168–72.

States that 80 per cent of children's problems are not deep-seated and can be solved through the help of a competent health worker, thus preventing more serious personality distortions.

Ludwig, Frederick J. *Youth and the Law*. New York: Foundation Press, 1955.

A valuable sourcebook of laws pertaining to juveniles. Stresses the need for a unified court for older juvenile delinquents (ages 16–21) and points to the fallacy of forcing parents to assume responsibility for the delinquent acts of their children.

Massimo, Joseph L., and Shore, Milton F. "The Effectiveness of a Comprehensive, Vocationally Oriented Psychotherapeutic Program for Adolescent Delinquent Boys," *American Journal of Orthopsychiatry*, XXXIII (July, 1963), 634–42.

Describes how a single practitioner using job placement, remedial education, and intensive psychotherapy in a concrete and individualized manner brought about significant improvement in learning, personality structure, and overt behavior of delinquents.

———. "Job-Focused Treatment for Antisocial Youth," *Children*, XI (July–August, 1964), 143–46.

A mental health clinic experiment involving comprehensive, vocationally oriented psychotherapy. Purpose: to reach and treat antisocial youth who are out of school.

McCann, Richard. "The Self-image and Delinquency: Some Implications for Religion," *Federal Probation*, XX (September, 1956), 14–23.

A seminar of twenty theological students concludes that a boy's heroes often provide clues to understanding the delinquent's problems.

————. *Delinquency: Sickness or Sin*. New York: Harper & Row, Publishers, 1957.

A churchman discusses delinquency with the focus on self-concept and ways the clergy can help the young offender.

McCord, William, and McCord, Joan. *Psychopathology and Juvenile Delinquency*. New York: Grune & Stratton, 1956.

A comprehensive review of the related thinking and research, with a brief evaluation of milieu therapy at Wiltwyck School for Boys.

McDavid, John W., and McCandless, Boyd R. "Psychological Theory, Research, and Juvenile Delinquency," *Journal of Criminal Law, Criminology, and Police Science*, LIII (March, 1962), 1–14.

Considers the contributions, failures, and prospects of psychology. Points to paths of study that offer the greatest promise for the accumulation of reliable scientific evidence on the etiology of delinquency.

Michaels, Joseph J. *Disorders of Character*. Springfield, Illinois: Charles C. Thomas, Publisher, 1955.

A bio-psycho-social interpretation of clinical data, attesting to an intimate relation between persistent enuresis and personality malintegration, as seen particularly in the delinquent and psychopathic personality.

Miller, Walter B. "The Impact of a 'Total-Community' Delinquency Control Project," *Social Problems*, X (Fall, 1962), 168–91.

Describes and evaluates action programs directed to the community, the family, and the gang in one large city.

Monihan, Thomas P. "The Trend in Broken Homes among Delinquent Children," *Marriage and Family Living*, XIX (November, 1957), 362–65.

Analyzes home situations of delinquents in Philadelphia. Finds a persistently high number of broken homes but questions the belief in any overriding importance of the socially broken home as against the orphaned home.

Moore, Milburne M. *Juvenile Delinquency: Research, Theory and Comment*. Washington: Association for Supervision and Curriculum Development, 1958.

Reviews various research-oriented theories and draws suggestions for school workers.

Mulligan, R. A. "Theory and Juvenile Delinquency," *Journal of Educational Sociology*, XXXIII (May, 1960), 365–72.

Points out that the individual delinquent is a product of the same processes that produce non-delinquents. Holds that a theory of juvenile delinquency should explain all social behavior.

Myerhoff, Howard L., and Myerhoff, Barbara G. "Field Observations of Middle-Class Gangs," *Social Forces*, XLII (March, 1964), 328–36.

Describes experiences of a participant-observer who spent two weeks with several groups of middle-class deviant youth. Used concepts on prevention. Compares characteristics of lower- and middle-class groups.

National Education Association Juvenile Delinquency Project. *Delinquent Behavior: Culture and the Individual*, Washington: National Education Association, 1959.

An interdisciplinary approach to the meaning and causes of norm-violating behavior. Suggested as a working base for school and community practices for prevention and control.

National Education Association Juvenile Delinquency Project. *Delinquent Behavior: Principles and Practices*, Washington: National Education Association, 1959.

Presents guidelines for school action based on an integrated theory of delinquency. Many illustrations of school programs aimed to help the norm-violating student.

Nelson, Joy. "The Girls at the End of the Viaduct," *Federal Probation*, XXV (September, 1961), 55–58.

A Cincinnati youth worker tells of her experiences with a group of thirty girls in a slum area.

Neumeyer, Martin H. "International Trends in Juvenile Delinquency," *Sociology and Social Research*, XLI (November–December, 1956), 93–99.

Scans recent UNESCO publications and reports some common denominators and divergent trends in juvenile delinquency.

Newman, Ruth G. "The 'Acting-out' Boy," *Exceptional Children*, XXII (February, 1956), 186–90.

Preliminary report of a National Institute of Mental Health school program for an overt and expressive boy. Tentative guiding principles are drawn concerning the learning problems of the boy himself, program-planning, and teacher relationships.

New York City Youth Board. *Delinquency Predictions: A Progress Report, 1952–1956*. New York: Research Department of New York City Youth Board, July, 1957.

A preliminary report of a before-and-after prediction study based on the Glueck Table of Social Factors.

New York City Youth Board. *Reaching the Fighting Gang*. New York: New York City Youth Board, 1960.

A detailed account and appraisal of eight years of experience in working with the more than one hundred gang groups in New York City. Provides insights and working principles. Dynamic case material.

Nolan, Esther Grace, and Others. "Symposium: Secondary Schools and Juvenile Delinquency," *California Journal of Secondary Education,* XXX (December, 1955), 473–507.

Six professional workers representing the schools, courts, youth authority, and community co-ordinating councils make practical suggestions as to what might be done by the schools in working with other agencies to help its delinquents.

Novick, Abraham G. "Integrating the Delinquent and His Community," *Federal Probation,* XX (June, 1956), 38–43.

Stresses the need to reach children and families early by improving over-all co-ordination and methods of communication, especially with the general public and decision-making bodies.

Nye, F. Ivan. *Family Relationships and Delinquent Behavior.* New York: John Wiley & Sons, Inc., 1958.

Tests and significance of relations between family attitudes and delinquent behavior.

————. "The Rejected Parent and Delinquency," *Marriage and Family Living,* XVIII (November, 1956), 291–300.

Presents data suggesting that the concept of rejection of the parent by the adolescent be added to family theory.

————, and Others. "Socioeconomic Status and Delinquent Behavior," *American Journal of Sociology,* LXIII (January, 1958), 381–89.

Checks hypothesis that there is no significant difference in the amount of delinquent behavior of boys and girls in different socioeconomic strata. Slight differences that were found favored the low-status group as often as the high-status group.

Orlov, Victor. "Juvenile Delinquency in the U.S.S.R.," *International Journal of Adult and Youth Education,* XV (April, 1963), 59–64.

Reports the reduction and the eradication of juvenile delinquency through public participation, youth organizations, and local and state administrative bodies. In 1959 only 3.3 per cent of all persons convicted of crime were reported to be minors under eighteen.

"Our Restless Youth: What Are Our Next Steps?" *High Points,* LXII (February, 1960), 17–24.

Representatives of the school, of youth committees, of police, and of labor discuss what should be done about delinquency in New York City.

Owen, John E. "How Delinquent Are Our Juveniles?" *Educational Forum,* XXI (January, 1957), 203–6.

An overview of the number and types of juvenile delinquents in the United States, what is and can be done for them, and an attempt to list and discuss possible causes for their delinquency.

Papanek, Ernst. "Re-education and Treatment of Juvenile Delinquents," *American Journal of Psychotherapy*, XII (April, 1958), 269–96.

Considers cultural factors in delinquency; discusses punishment and therapy with special reference to milieu therapy as illustrated in Wiltwyck School for Boys.

Peck, Harris B., and Bellsmith, Virginia. *Treatment of the Delinquent Adolescent: Group and Individual Therapy with Parent and Child.* New York: Family Service Association of America, 1954.

Using case studies, the writer discusses various aspects of the delinquency problem and presents treatment practices and processes that seem especially promising.

Perlman, I. Richard. *Juvenile Court Statistics, 1956.* Statistical Series, No. 47. Washington: Children's Bureau, U.S. Department of Health, Education, and Welfare, 1958.

Reports statistics on the number of children's cases handled by juvenile courts; notes that 2.2 per cent of all children aged ten to seventeen were involved in delinquency cases in 1956.

————. "Reporting Juvenile Delinquency," *National Probation and Parole Association Journal*, III (June, 1957), 242–49.

Considers the adequacy of present methods for reporting at the national, state, and local levels and makes recommendations for improvement of present practices.

Peterson, Donald R., and Others. "Personality and Background Factors in Juvenile Delinquency as Inferred from Questionnaire Responses," *Journal of Consulting Psychology*, XXIII (October, 1959), 395–99.

Factor analysis revealed five characteristics that differentiate delinquents from non-delinquents. Findings revealed three personality dimensions (psychopathic behavior, impulse anti-social behavior, and incompetence) and two background factors (family dissension and difficulty in school).

————, Quay, Herbert C., and Tiffany, Theodore L. "Personality Factors Related to Juvenile Delinquency," *Child Development*, XXXII (June, 1961), 355–72.

Results of a factor analysis of four delinquency questionnaires to isolate personality factors related to delinquent behavior.

Piper, Bertha J., and LeGrow, Dorothy. "Tutoring for Behavioral Delinquents," *American Journal of Occupational Therapy*, X (July–August, 1956), 147–49.

Argues for scholastic instruction in addition to the usual prescribed therapeutic occupations.

Pleune, F. Gordon. "Effects of State Training School Programs on Juvenile Delinquents," *Federal Probation*, XXI (March, 1957), 24–32.
Asserts that training schools are not meeting needs of most delinquents and that the "true" delinquent may be further damaged by training-school programs. Points up obstacles and needed steps for improvement.

Polier, Justine Wise. "The Back-to-the-Woodshed Trend," *Child Study*, XXXI (Summer, 1954), 12–17.
Comment on the revival of the authoritarian approach to many child problems, including delinquency, as a measure of today's retreat from democratic ideals and scientific knowledge.

"Psychiatry and Treatment of Delinquency," *Chronicle of the World Health Organization*, XX (October, 1958), 329–34.
Report of a seminar on the role of psychiatry; emphasis on recent trends and advances.

Quay, Herbert C. "The Delinquent," *Behavioral Research on Exceptional Children*, pp. 318–56. Edited by Samuel A. Kirk and Bluma B. Weiner. Washington, D.C.: Council for Exceptional Children, National Education Association, 1963.
A comprehensive and critical review of research on the delinquent.

————. "Dimensions of Personality in Delinquent Boys as Inferred from the Factor Analysis of Case History Data," *Child Development*, XXV (June, 1964), 479–84.
A sample of 115 institutionalized male delinquents were rated on 29 traits of behavior. The analysis yields four orthogonal factors reinforcing earlier research studies.

————, and Peterson, D. R. "Personality Factors in the Study of Juvenile Delinquency," *Exceptional Children*, XXVI (May, 1960), 472–76.
Differentiates the delinquent. Identifies two dimensions of personality along which delinquency may be seen to vary.

————, and Peterson, Donald R. "A Brief Scale for Juvenile Delinquency," *Journal of Clinical Psychology*, XIV (April, 1958), 139–42.
A forty-item scale used to classify delinquents in an experimental study.

Reckless, Walter C., Dinitz, Simon, and Murray, Ellen. "Self Concept as an Insulator against Delinquency," *American Sociological Review*, XXI (December, 1956), 744–46.
Reports a study of self-images of sixth-grade boys in one city and identifies certain components that enable young boys to withstand delinquent behavior.

————. "Teacher Nominations and Evaluations of "Good" Boys in High Delinquency Areas," *Elementary School Journal*, LXII (January, 1957), 221–23.
Data indicate that teachers are competent in judging the delinquency potential of their pupils.

Redl, Fritz. "Our Troubles with Defiant Youth," *Children*, II (January–February, 1955), 5–9.

States that adults, confused by youthful behavior, display collective antagonism toward teen-agers as a group whenever questionable behavior is involved. Describes causes and degrees of defiance and classifies the "defiant ego" as delinquency. Feels that more research on early identification of behavior disorders and more education of the public are necessary.

————. "Research Needs in the Delinquency Field," *Children*, IV (January–February, 1957), 15–19.

Stresses the importance of practice-geared research and suggests some research projects.

Re-Educating Confined Delinquents: Selected materials related to experimental and training projects at the Federal Correctional Institution, Englewood, Colorado, 1961 to 1964. Washington, D. C.: Bureau of Prisons, U. S. Department of Justice, July, 1965.

Includes a chapter describing a three-year pilot project at Englewood, followed by several valuable chapters on re-education of delinquents aimed at their learning to be adequate adults and contrasting such self-development with the stagnation and institutionalization that results from the usual correctional experience.

Reiff, Robert, and Riessman, Frank. *The Indigenous Nonprofessional: A Strategy of Change in Community Action and Community Mental Health Programs.* Report No. 3, National Institute of Labor Education Mental Health Program, November, 1964, Mimeographed.

Discusses why and how the lower socioeconomic groups and particularly the poor can and should participate in community mental health and anti-poverty programs.

Reports of the Committee on the Judiciary of the Subcommittee to Investigate Juvenile Delinquency, Pursuant to S.Res. 173 (84th Congress, 2d. Session), Relative to the Investigation of Juvenile Delinquency in the United States. Washington: Government Printing Office, 1956.

A continuing series of reports concerning juvenile delinquency among the Indians, television and juvenile delinquency, motion pictures and juvenile delinquency, and juvenile delinquency in Alaska and in Providence (Rhode Island).

"Report of the Superintendent's Committee on Delinquency in the Secondary Schools," *High Points in the Work of the High Schools of New York City*, XXXVI (April, 1954), 5–40.

Presents the recommendations of a special committee of principals in academic and vocational high schools on the delinquency problem.

Resnick, Joseph. "Juvenile Delinquent: An Explanation," *Educational Administration and Supervision*, XLI (April, 1955), 218–23.

Indicates six ways in which the school can help the delinquent and pre-delinquent make a better adjustment.

Rhodes, William C. "Curriculum and Disordered Behavior," *Exceptional Children*, XXX (October, 1963), 61–66.

Concerned with the philosophical basis and the guidelines of curriculums to stabilize new and ordered behaviors.

Rice, Roger E., and Adams, Stuart. *The Correctional Cost of Serviced and Unserviced Juvenile Gangs:* an evaluation of a detached worker program. Los Angeles, California: Los Angeles County Probation Department Research Office, Report No. 23, 1965.

Compares the success of work with juvenile gangs on a basis of correctional costs per capita, before and after the program of street-corner work, and considers some of the reasons for success or lack of it. Appendices show an area analysis and posting and tabulating instructions for comparing correctional costs.

Riley, Ralph. "Who Is a Juvenile Delinquent?" *Federal Probation*, XXII (June, 1958), 20–25.

Discusses the difficulties in attempts to find a workable statutory definition of delinquency.

Roberts, Charles Lenz. "Ninth Graders Tackle Juvenile Delinquency," *Clearing House*, XXXI (April, 1957), 463–65.

Tells how a teacher and students explored possible causes of juvenile delinquency and sought to understand the psychology of delinquent behavior.

Robinson, S. M. *Juvenile Delinquency*. New York: Holt, Rinehart & Winston, 1960.

Analyzes various theories of delinquency. Discusses treatment and rehabilitation in institutions and agencies faced with the responsibility of helping young people in trouble.

Rosenfield, Eva. "Social Research and Social Action in Prevention of Juvenile Delinquency," *Social Problems*, IV (October, 1956), 138–48.

Discusses methodological reasons for deficiencies in our knowledge of how to prevent delinquency.

Roucek, Joseph S. (editor). *Juvenile Delinquency*. New York: Philosophical Library, 1958.

Fourteen papers on a variety of topics related to delinquency: definitions, search for causes, evaluation of attempts at solution, and international trends.

Rubin, Sol. *Crime and Juvenile Delinquency*. New York: Oceana Publications, 1959.

A lawyer discusses current legislation on the delinquent and his parents. Legislation discussed against a background of psychosocial theory.

Schaff, Adam. "Social and Psychological Aspects of the Maladjustment of Young People," *International Journal of Adult and Youth Education*, XIII, Nos. 1–2 (1961), 49–55.

A brief examination of the symptoms of delinquency, as expressed in countries throughout the world. Purpose of inquiry: to throw light on the need for specific preventative and remedial measures appropriate to the individual case.

"School's Role in Preventing and Combating Juvenile Delinquency," *School Executive*, LXXV (September, 1955), 73–85.

A series of articles presenting the points of view of a superintendent of schools, a state education official, a principal, a visiting teacher, a parent, and a psychologist.

Schreiber, Daniel. "Juvenile Delinquency and the School Dropout Problem," *Federal Probation*, XXVII (September, 1963), 15–19.

Distinguishes between the dropout problem and delinquency. Shows how they are related to each other. Looks beyond these two problems to basic issues of disadvantaged and alienated youth.

————, Kaplan, Bernard A., and Strom, Robert D. *Dropout Studies: Design and Conduct*, Project: School Dropouts, Washington, D. C., National Education Association, 1965.

A guidance tool aimed to provide a reliable annual index against which renewal or extended guidance efforts might be reviewed.

Scott, Edward M. "Investigation of Juvenile Profiles on the Szondi Test," *Journal of Clinical Psychology*, XI (January, 1955), 46–50.

Presents the results of the Szondi Test administered to twelve hundred adolescents, analyzed according to sex, delinquency, and type of school attended. Reports a significant difference in several areas between delinquents and nondelinquents.

Scudder, Kenyon J., and Beam, Kenneth S. *The Twenty Billion Dollar Challenge: A National Program for Delinquency Prevention*. New York: G. P. Putnam's Sons, 1961.

Offers a program for the prevention of social delinquency. Program stresses professional and community co-operation in changing social conditions that contribute to delinquency.

Selvidge, Jean. "The Police Juvenile Bureau's Job," *National Probation and Parole Association Journal*, III (January, 1957), 39–47.

Describes the work of the policewoman or the juvenile officer who works with girls. Tells the story of a runaway girl.

Short, James F. "The Sociocultural Context of Delinquency," *Crime and Delinquency*, VI (October, 1960), 365–75.

A critical survey of current theories that view delinquent behavior in terms of status and subcultural determinants.

Silver, Albert W. "Delinquency, Juvenile Courts and Chronic Unemployment," *Mental Hygiene*, XLVII (October, 1963), 583–90.

Describes a typical delinquent. Relates his behavioral problems to displacement and material deprivation of parents and their children in a technologically complex and freely competitive society.

Slack, Charles W. "Experimenter-Subject Psychotherapy: A New Method of Introducing Intensive Office Treatment in Unreachable Cases," *Mental Hygiene*, LXIV (April, 1960), 238–56.

Describes the use of a new approach to counseling hard-core delinquents who were paid to visit a therapeutic center.

Stark, Heman. "California Revives Town Meeting Idea to Combat Delinquency," *Federal Probation*, XX (September, 1956), 59–62.

Describes how local communities aided by state departments undertook to study delinquency and to implement adaptations to prevent or control undesirable behavior.

Stullken, Edward H. "Thirty Years' Work with Problem Children," *Federal Probation*, XXVI (September, 1962), 14–23.

Offers basic principles for dealing with delinquent and disturbed children. Principles based on first-hand knowledge.

————. "What Can the Home and the School Do about the Juvenile Delinquency Problem?" *Bulletin of the National Association of Secondary-School Principals*, XXXVIII (April, 1954), 181–83.

Defines principles that will aid the school in making its optimum contribution in preventing and controlling delinquency.

Sutherland, Robert L. "Delinquency and Mental Health," *Federal Probation*, XXI (March, 1957), 20–23.

Explains the relationship between mental health and behavior. Stresses the prevention of delinquency through the application of mental-health principles.

Thacker, E. H. "Roving Leaders Extend Our Reach," *Recreation*, LIII (April, 1960), 162–63.

Tells how detached workers seek out and serve young people who do not frequent public or private agencies.

Thompson, Charles H. (editor). *Juvenile Delinquency among Negroes in the United States.* Journal of Negro Education, Yearbook Number, Vol. XXVII, No. 3. Washington: Published for the Bureau of Educational Research, Howard University, by the Howard University Press, 1959. pp. 187–387.

Authorities consider the problems of delinquency as they relate to the Negro, his family, and his culture.

Travers, J. E. "Schools and Delinquency," *Education,* LXXX (February, 1960), 367–68.

Indicates that the school can function effectively in three areas of delinquency control: identification, treatment, and referral.

Trends in the Administration of Justice and Correctional Programs in the United States. Washington, D. C.: United States Bureau of Prisons, Department of Justice, 1965.

A report prepared by an editorial committee, with contributions from a number of professionals in the field of correction, for the Third United Nations Congress on the Prevention of Crime and Treatment of Offenders held at Stockholm, Sweden, on August 9–18, 1965.

Trent, Richard D. "Relationship of Anxiety to Popularity and Rejection among Institutionalized Delinquent Boys," *Child Development,* XXVIII (September, 1957), 379–84.

A study of sixty-three institutionalized delinquent boys representing two cottage groups indicated that popularity was positively related to rejection and that the more anxious boys were less popular.

U.S. Children's Bureau. *Juvenile Delinquency: Facts and Facets.* U.S. Department of Health, Education, and Welfare. Washington: Government Printing Office, 1960.

A series of sixteen pamphlets that summarize research and current thinking on prevention, control, causation of juvenile delinquency and the role and the responsibility of federal, state, and local government, police, courts, probation, and other responsible groups and agencies.

――――. *Report on the National Conference on Juvenile Delinquency.* Washington: Government Printing Office, 1954.

Summarizes the deliberations of a conference on juvenile delinquency which aimed to review past accomplishments, define the most urgent present needs, and formulate policies for the future.

――――. *Report to the Congress on Juvenile Delinquency.* U.S. Department of Health, Education, and Welfare. Washington: Government Printing Office, 1960.

A comprehensive report prepared in cooperation with the National Institute of Mental Health. Traces the history of the concept of juvenile delinquency and what is known about its causes. Also discusses prevention and control.

Van Egmond, Elmer. "Socialization Processes and Education," *Review of Educational Research,* XXXI (February, 1961), 80–90.

Reviews the literature on the socialization process. Includes research on cultural milieu, family relationships, delinquency causation, and the school as an agency of socialization.

Vedder, Clyde B. *Juvenile Offender: Perspective and Readings.* Garden City, New York: Doubleday & Co., 1954.

A compilation of readings culled from the periodical literature on many aspects of the delinquency problem.

Walker, Clare C. "A Positive Approach to Delinquency," *NEA Journal,* XLVII (October, 1958), 466–68.

Points out some of the roots of anti-social behavior of teen-agers. Cites need to capitalize on the capacities of young people.

Wallace, Helen M., Igel, Amelia, and Losty, Margaret A. "A Report on Foster Home Placement as a Resource for Handicapped Children," *Pediatrics,* XX (August, 1957), 358–61.

Discusses the need for foster homes and notes that some handicapped children in the New York City area are being retained in hospitals and convalescent homes for social rather than for medical reasons.

Washburn, Wilbur C. "The Effects of Sex Differences on Protective Attitudes in Delinquents and Nondelinquents," *Exceptional Children,* XXX (November, 1963), 111–17.

Explores patterns of protective attitudes in an effort to identify crucial differences in the dynamics underlying behavior of male as contrasted with female delinquents.

Wattenberg, William W. "Difference between Girl and Boy Repeaters," *Journal of Educational Psychology,* XLVII (March, 1956), 137–46.

Reports a distinctive quality of factors surrounding girls' delinquency based on study of significance of differences on a number of variables.

———. "Girl Repeaters," *National Probation and Parole Association Journal,* III (January, 1957), 48–53.

Searches out the feminine pattern of repeating juvenile misconduct as contrasted with the pattern of boy repeaters.

———. "Ten-Year-Old Boys in Trouble," *Child Development,* XXVIII (March, 1957), 43–46.

Compares data relating to 207 ten-year-old boys and 3,663 older boys interviewed on complaint by the Youth Bureau of the Detroit Police Department. Attempts to trace further the influence of developmental stages on delinquency.

———. "Factors Associated with Repeating among Preadolescent Delinquents," *Journal of Genetic Psychology,* LXXXIV (June, 1954), 189–95.

Compares records of 99 "repeaters" against 235 boys who had only one police contact. Repeating was highly associated with poor school work, low intellectual ability, membership in unruly gangs, and reputation for mischief.

Webb, Robert, and Webb, Muriel. *The Churches and Juvenile Delinquency.* New York: Association Press, 1957.

Points up the responsibility of the churches for juvenile delinquency, presents a brief summary of contemporary Christian thought on the subject, and suggests ways in which the church may help.

Weber, George H. "The Boy Scout Program as a Group Approach in Institutional Delinquency Treatment," *Federal Probation,* XIX (September, 1955), 47–54.

Presents a careful analysis of the values of the Boy Scout program, based on the author's experience with the scouting program at the Kansas Boys' Industrial School.

———. "The Organization of Camps for Delinquent Boys," *American Journal of Orthopsychiatry,* XXXII (October, 1962), 824–36.

Discusses theoretical considerations and operating principles. Includes four models.

Weeks, Herbert Ashley. "Study of the Treatment of Juvenile Delinquency in Ohio," *Educational Research Bulletin,* XXXIV (March, 1955), 57–62.

Reviews the type of research being carried on by the Bureau of Educational Research of Ohio State University in its evaluation of the state's services to the delinquent.

"White House Conference Recommendations Relating to Delinquency," *Federal Probation,* XXIV (September, 1960), 55–57.

Summarizes recommendations for federal, state, and local action. Deals with identification and diagnosis; correction and treatment; and research and reporting from the *Composite Report of Forum Findings.*

Willie, Charles V. "Anti-Social Behavior among Disadvantaged Youth: Some Observations on Prevention for Teachers," *Journal of Negro Education,* XXXIII (Spring, 1964), 176–81.

Discusses three ways of reducing societal rejection of youth and, thus, interrupting a process of alienation. The ways: instructing young people in the rules, values, customs of society; demonstrating to young people their individual rights, responsibilities, and obligations in a society; and receiving and accepting young people as significant human beings whose contributions are necessary for the society.

Witmer, Helen Leland. "Juvenile Delinquency and *Anomie,*" *Children,* II (September, 1955), 188–91.

Interprets the Lander research studies in Baltimore with special reference to economic factors and *anomie.* Stresses the need to reorganize the community so that parents and children will be given a clear sense of social direction and purpose.

———, and Kotinsky, Ruth (editors). *New Perspectives for Research on Juvenile Delinquency*. Washington: Children's Bureau, U.S. Department of Health, Education, and Welfare, 1956.

The report of a conference on the interrelation and relevance for delinquency of certain concepts from sociology and psychiatry.

Wolfgang, Marvin E., and Others. *The Sociology of Crime and Delinquency*. New York: John Wiley and Sons, Inc., 1962.

Collection of readings on the sociology of crime and delinquency. Selections cover contemporary research and theory.

Whiteman, Amran, "Governors on Juvenile Delinquency," *High Points*, XLIII (June, 1961), 23–31.

Summarizes the ideas of thirty-two governors on the causes and the prevention of delinquency.

Young, Florene M. "Responses of Juvenile Delinquents to the Thematic Apperception Test," *Journal of Genetic Psychology*, LXXXVIII (June, 1956), 251–59.

Describes the responses of thirty-four delinquent boys and thirty-four delinquent girls to sixteen cards from the Thematic Apperception Test.

Index